THE LAW
IS FOR ALL

Other Controversial Titles From New Falcon

THE LAW IS FOR ALL

An Extended Commentary On
THE BOOK OF THE LAW

By ALEISTER CROWLEY

Edited With An Introduction By
ISRAEL REGARDIE

1993
NEW FALCON PUBLICATIONS
PHOENIX, ARIZONA, U.S.A.

International Standard Book Number: 0-56184-005-X
Library of Congress Catalog Card Number: 83-81021

First Edition 1975
First Falcon Edition 1983
Second Printing 1985
Third Printing 1986
Fourth Printing 1988
Fifth Printing 1991
Sixth Printing 1993

New Falcon Publications
655 East Thunderbird
Phoenix, Arizona 85022 U.S.A.

TABLE OF CONTENTS

ILLUSTRATIONS

Acknowledgments

The publisher wishes to express deepest gratitude to Frater V.V.V. whose encouragement and financial support made the 1983 publication of this work possible.

To the memory of Aleister Crowley

THE COMMENT

Do what thou wilt shall be the whole of the Law.
The study of this Book is forbidden. It is wise to
destroy this copy after the first reading.

Whosoever disregards this does so at his own risk
and peril. These are most dire.

Those who discuss the contents of this Book are
to be shunned by all, as centres of pestilence.

All questions of the Law are to be decided only by
appeal to my writings, each for himself.

There is no law beyond Do what thou wilt.

Love is the law, love under will.

The priest of the princes,

Ankh-f-n-khonsu

A L

(LIBER LEGIS)

THE BOOK OF THE LAW

sub figura xxxi

as delivered by

93   —AIWASS—   418

to

Ankh-f-n-khonsu

**The Priest of the Princes
who is**

6 6 6

Introduction

Introduction

In the year 1920, Aleister Crowley established his Abbey of Thelema in the village of Cefalu in Sicily. There he wrote his commentary on *The Book of the Law.* It is in many ways the most important and powerful document he ever penned. For the first time, he recorded with some degree of completeness his basic attitudes toward sex and love. He had never attempted anything comparable before. Here and there, it is true, were some sporadic excursions into the subject, but any comprehensive delineation of the doctrine of his heart, as it were, somehow always got sidetracked despite his extensive literary output.

I

In the book *Magick without Tears* (St. Paul: Llewellyn Publications, 1971), he had made some significant but short remarks about the triad of sex, drugs and religion. His commentary is in reality a systematic elaboration on all three matters in addition to the topic of violence, which has only recently zoomed into the headlines throughout this country.

For example, so far as sex is concerned, Crowley rhapsodizes:

We of Thelema are not the slaves of Love. "Love under Will" is the Law. We refuse to regard Love as shameful and degrading, as a peril to body and soul. We refuse to accept it as the surrender of the divine to the animal; to us it is the means by which the animal may be made the Winged Sphinx which will bear man aloft to the House of the Gods.

Our current sexual attitudes, which he constantly attacked, are irrational. The Supreme Court of the United States has defined pornography in such a way that to write about sex and sexual acts is approved so long as the writing does not stimulate lascivious or sexual feelings. The writing must be kept subservient to the dictates of social significance and art—a fundamentally sex-negative outlook. Such a ruling is analogous to saying that it is legitimate for a writer to describe gourmet foods or fine cooking without stimulating the appetite or making one's mouth water, or that a writer may describe the beauty of the Greek isles and the clarity of sky and air, but only in such a way that no reader becomes imbued with the desire to travel there. None of this makes any sense. If a woman reads a fashion magazine describing new clothes without feeling moved to acquire a new wardrobe, then quite evidently the writing has failed to achieve an effect, and the magazine should go out of business.

A young contemporary writer, Mark Gerzon, wrote recently that the major characteristic of the young people's rebellion against the sexual values of adult society is perhaps the practically total rejection of tradition by many of his generation. He then adds that those of this generation are characterized by their psychological orientation, their need to be involved, and their awareness that the essence of life is human relations. The acceptance of current social values, he feels, leads to emotional isolation. So it is of little wonder that many young people react to socially patterned sexual frustration with such vehemence. Even marriage, which society offers as the answer to their problems, comes under criticism. Marriage, as it is now, seems hardly the answer.

Regarding the next topic, drugs, Crowley sermonizes in his commentary:

> Therefore they [the puritanical slaves] fly to drink and drugs as to an anesthetic in the surgical operation of introspection.
>
> The craving for these things is caused by the internal misery which their use reveals to the slave-souls. If you are really free, you can take cocaine as simply as salt-water taffy. There is no better rough test of a soul than its attitude to drugs. If a man is simple, fearless, eager, he is all right; he will not become a slave. If he is afraid, he is already a slave. Let the whole world take opium, hashish, and the rest; those who are liable to abuse them were better dead.

This may or may not be valid reasoning. Marijuana and perhaps lysergic acid (LSD) may be taken without threat of physical addiction. The reasoning is hardly valid when heroin and morphine are concerned. The facts are too evident in the social debacle of today. Crowley himself struggled for several years toward the end of his life to free himself from addiction to heroin—unsuccessfully. It had originally been prescribed for him in 1919 by a physician for the treatment of his bronchial asthma. Much in the preceding passage has to be dismissed as fine-sounding rhetoric, not fact, written during Crowley's own intoxication with heroin.

Again, compare this with some of Gerzon's thinking on the same topic. His book *The Whole World Is Watching* (New

York: Paperback Library, 1970) should be read as an adjunct to Crowley's commentary.

The current reaction to popular psychedelic drugs in the West suggests that the individual feels he was not aware of his life to the maximum before using these drugs. The cumulative effect of psychedelic exaltation is to feel more aware (i.e., more open and prone to perceive) of the beauty that is part of life. The common reaction is that the drug user realizes that, despite the luxury, the ease, and the convenience of modern culture, its members are missing much of the beauty and pleasure they could experience.

According to drug ideology, the inner, psychic world is made more sensitive, much like the senses. It is clear to the devotee that mental associations are liberated from the constraints imposed upon them by cultural patterns. Memories and feelings usually repressed are freed. The college generation uses drugs as tools for furthering self-analysis designed to eradicate the self-defeating engrams that have been left by mass society.

Religion, in the commentary, gets the following treatment by Crowley:

> There are to be no regular temples of Nuit and Hadit, for They are incommensurables and absolutes. Our religion, therefore, for the people, is the Cult of the Sun, who is our particular star of the Body of Nuit, from whom, in the strictest scientific sense, come this earth, a chilled spark of Him, and all our Light and Life. His vice-regent and representative in the animal kingdom is His cognate symbol the Phallus, representing Love and Liberty. Ra-Hoor-Khuit, like all true Gods, is therefore a Solar-Phallic deity. . . .
>
> All those acts which excite the divine in man are proper to the rite of invocation.

Religion, as understood by the vile Puritan, is the very opposite of all this. He—it—seems to wish to kill his—its—soul by forbidding every expression of it, and every practice which might awaken it to expression. To Hell with this Verbotenism!

In particular, let me exhort all men and all women, for they are Stars! Heed well this holy verse!

True Religion is intoxication, in a sense. We are told elsewhere to intoxicate the innermost, not the outermost; but I think that the word "wine" should be taken in its widest sense as meaning that which brings out the soul. Climate, soil and race change conditions; each man or woman must find and choose the fit intoxication. Thus hashish in one or other of its forms seems to suit the Moslem, to go with dry heat; opium is right for the Mongol; whiskey for the dour temperament and damp cold climate of the Scot. . . . Religious ecstasy is necessary to man's soul. Where this is attained by mystical practices, directly, as it should be, people need no substitute. . . .

He could have added that the clear vodka is ideal for the manic-depressive Russian in his icy cold climate, and that rum is appropriate for the Caribbean and the Polynesian areas.

That Crowley is writing directly for the young people of today is self-evident. The commentary is to be contrasted with Gerzon's criticism of religion as practiced in America today.

Religion in American society, Gerzon feels, has come to appear so hypocritical that young people feel they can gain more by turning to the religions of other cultures. The God presented to this generation by adult society is a shallow one. It is a God donated to the parents by their parents before them who had been raised in nineteenth-century fundamentalism. But the God this generation's parents were given in their childhood didn't fit in post-World War II American society. Most parents were unable to reject the religious beliefs of their childhood, but somehow could manage to adapt their social behavior to the secular, consumption-and-prestige oriented culture of the 1950's and 1960's. This generation saw and rejected the ambivalence of the religious values of adult society exemplified in their parents.

And so far as violence is concerned, Crowley vividly expresses his point of view thus:

> Fight! Fight like gentlemen, without malice, because fighting is the best game in the world, and love the second best! Don't slander your enemy, as the newspapers would have you do; just kill him, and then bury him with honour. Don't keep crying "Foul" like a fifth-rate pugilist. Don't boast! Don't squeal. If you're down, get up and hit him again! Fights of that sort make fast friends.

Would that Crowley had been able to fight in this way—instead of merely preaching it!

Throughout the second chapter of the commentary, and only occasionally in the third, is a recurrent theme, a chorus as it were, of "the Christians to the Lions." He is here expressing his thoroughgoing contempt for Christianity in all its forms, a contempt which had its origins in his early revolt against the excessive fundamentalism of the Plymouth Brethren, the religion of his parents. "My primary objection to Christianity," he writes here, "is 'gentle Jesus, meek and mild,' the pacifist, the conscientious objector, the Tolstoyan, the passive resister."

Every now and again, he begrudgingly strives to make an exception of the Catholics in Latin countries, feeling that they were essentially pagan in outlook, only to revoke it a few paragraphs later. All Protestants of every denomination come within the jurisdiction of his condemnation to the lions. The Jews also are condemned roundly, though in one paragraph he confines his condemnation to Jews living in America. Apparently, they are not bellicose enough to come up to his standards. He did not live long enough to see a handful of Israelis take on the surrounding Arab nations who numbered millions. Though *Liber Legis* does mildly castigate the Moslems, Crowley still retains his profound admiration for the so-called manliness of the Arab, his courage and ferocity. It may be that his homosexual experiences in the Sahara influenced profoundly his attitude toward them.

There is also some magnificent if wild humor in these pages. Whether it is intentional or inadvertent is hard to judge from the nature of the remarks. But his panagyric about Woman—which would in part please the current feminist movement, and horrify them at the same time—is so outrageously funny as well as rhetorical, that it should become a classic of the English language to be employed whenever the "fair sex" needs mentioning. The first of these reads:

> Hence, the pretence that a woman is "pure," modest, delicate, aesthetically beautiful and morally exalted, ethereal and unfleshly, though in fact they know her to be lascivious, shameless, coarse, ill-shapen, unscrupulous, nauseatingly bestial both physically and mentally. The advertisements of "dress-shields," perfumes, cosmetics, anti-sweat preparations, and "beauty treatments" reveal woman's nature as seen by the clear eyes of those who would lose money if they

misjudged her; and they are loathsomely revolting to read. Her mental and moral characteristics are those of the parrot and the monkey. Her physiology and pathology are hideously disgusting, a sickening slime of uncleanliness.

Her virgin life is a sick ape's, her sexual life a drunken sow's, her mother life all bulging filmy and sagging udders.

This is countered by:

Not only art thou Woman, sworn to a purpose not thine own; thou art thyself a star, and in thyself a purpose to thyself. Not only mother of men art thou, or whore to men; serf to their need of Life and Love, not sharing their Light and Liberty; nay, thou art Mother and Whore for thine own pleasure; the Word I say to Man I say to thee no less: Do what thou wilt shall be the whole of the Law! . . .

There is a Cry in an unknown tongue, it resounds through the Temple of the Universe; in its one Word is Death and Ecstasy, and the title of honour, o thou, to Thyself High Priestess, Prophetess, Empress, to Thyself the Goddess whose Name means Mother and Whore!

However—and this is the most important issue—anybody who hitherto had entertained any doubts or misconceptions as to what Aleister Crowley stood for concerning these topics and life itself, must now find here some absolute clarification. If for no other reason than the above, his commentary expounding his life philosophy represents a high-water mark in Crowley's literary and spiritual career.

It would be wise to remember that Crowley reached his majority in the *fin-de-siècle* when some very good minds as well as many dilettantes were attacking the establishment in Great Britain. There it was represented by Queen Victoria, whom many regarded as the staid and last bulwark of Christian morality and order.

There was as yet no psychoanalytic literature to reveal what volcanic force and fire burned in man's unconscious deeps. Freud had begun hesitantly and falteringly to write in 1895, and then only in German. It took many years for his explosive and shattering ideas to filter down through the different European languages, including English, and reach the intelligentsia.

By then, Sir Richard Burton had translated *The Arabian Nights*. It included some erudite footnotes together with a lengthy appendix mostly about the geography and distribution of homosexual practices. In addition, there were some few other enterprising and original souls represented by the *Yellow Book* and similar literary ventures.

There was, however, no clear delineation or final formulation of a general creed of sexual liberation, save for the idealistic writing of a very few writers. Even in the year 1904 when *The Book of the Law* came to be written down, Europe and America were still bound up in the heavy iron chains of Judeo-Christian morality. God was not dead—yet—though Nietzsche had tried his utmost to inter him. Nor had any great majority of that generation made any concerted move to scrap the existent moral and social systems. It is true that just prior to World War II there was a widespread pacifist movement. However, it ended almost wholly with the German invasion of Poland and the Japanese aerial assault on Pearl Harbor. That generation, however, was pacifist only, not having yet come to formulate any concept of a total rejection of *all* of society, including its roots and foundations.

It has only been in recent years, with the rise of this

current generation—white as well as black—the descendants of the Beat generation, that contemporary standards have been challenged successfully and are in danger of being overthrown. *The Sexual Revolution* and other timely and important books written by Wilhelm Reich in the 1930's and early 1940's, obviously have had a great deal to do with this challenge. In fact, he was a pioneer where this great social work is concerned, and is being widely read today.

Aldous Huxley perhaps leads off the contemporary parade with his little book, *Doors of Perception,* written after his mescaline experience. That book and that experience demonstrated to the world at large that fixed and conventional attitudes toward general living were arbitrary and could be transcended in a sensory and mind-expanding experience, initiated by certain drugs. Many others, it is true, had written of this long before Huxley's time and his book. De Quincey, Ludlow, Baudelaire, and many others had experimented with psychedelic drugs. (See *The Marijuana Papers,* edited by David Solomon; New York: Signet Books, 1966.) But none of these people seem to have made the considerable impact on the general public that Huxley achieved.

I am almost of the opinion that it was not until Leary, Alpert and Metzner overtly began to experiment with psychedelic drugs, thus earning their expulsion from Harvard University in the 1960's, that an insidiously quiet but overwhelmingly powerful movement was initiated, which would spread across not merely the United States but all over Europe and in fact the whole world. While we need not be in accord with the overfacile slogan, "Turn on, tune in, and drop out," nevertheless, Leary deserves great commendation for his heroic efforts to state the unpopular facts regarding the sacramental usage of drugs, regardless of what his motives may or may not have been.

More closely than anybody else, he seems to have approached the attitudes of Aleister Crowley almost exactly. I made some comparisons of these not too long ago in *Roll Away the Stone* (St. Paul, Minnesota: Llewellyn Publications, 1969). In fact, while reading Leary's interview with one of the editors of *Playboy* magazine some years ago, it seemed almost possible to hear the overtones of Crowley speaking a half-century previously. For it was in that interview that Leary expounded not only the possibility of the transcendental experience in the usage of marijuana, etc., but its tendency also to liberate sexual drives and feelings, which was the reason, so he felt, for the opposition by the establishment.

In this I am not to be construed as condoning the *indiscriminate* usage of drugs—certainly not those labeled "hard" narcotics. These are definitely not for young people to play with, nor adults either, for that matter. Intelligent familiarity with usage, purpose and pharmaco-dynamics of the psychedelic agents is still required for those old enough to use them seriously. Otherwise there may be an increasingly large harvest of psychotic breakdowns—heavy enough at this writing—due to spontaneous eruptions from an unconscious psyche whose thresholds have been recklessly opened up by ignorant tampering. The dangers are real enough, and need to be evaluated, and the psychological stability of the users estimated. With such knowledge and with proper (that is, trained or professional) supervision, experiments can be carried on with a view to determining how deeper self-knowledge and perception may be possible.

I do not deny that there have been many disasters due to the contemporary use of drugs. The doubters should visit any mental hospital. I am sure that there must be thousands of ill-advised users who have fallen heir to psychic disaster. There are bound to be many who, for one reason or another, have become victims of this rebellion. This is the price that unfortunately does have to be paid.

If marijuana and lysergic acid, with its attendant disasters, are the means of opening a whole new generation to the "cult of the occult," as Rollo May once termed it, then that really is a very small price to pay. I take the viewpoint of Crowley here. If some are overcome and die or are killed, then they are merely through for this incarnation and free to resume the struggle for freedom in the next life. One has to view man's progress not merely in the light of the here and now, which is important enough, but also *sub species eternitatis*.

> *Never the spirit was born,*
> *The spirit shall cease to be never.*
> *Never was time it was not,*
> *End and beginning are dreams.*
> *Birthless and deathless and changeless*
> *Remaineth the spirit for ever;*
> *Death hath not touched it at all,*
> *Dead though the house of it seems!*
> —Sir Edwin Arnold
> *The Song Celestial*

It is worthwhile to quote directly from *The Whole World Is Watching,* for the young author has something most important to add in this connection:

Marijuana was not invented in 1965. It is ancient. Even in America it has been used for decades in urban sub-cultures and in rural areas where it grows wild. The only thing that is new is the extent of alienation in white, middle-class, educated young people and their consequent openness to the values of pot-smoking.

Much of the recent severe criticism of marijuana is the result not of new and more accurate research but of the spread of its use into "respectable" society. . . .

Unaware of the nature of youth culture, most adults consider the popularity of marijuana as ephemeral as that of a new dance. "Oh, those kids!" an old lady exclaimed to me. "It's a new dance or a new singing group every few months. And now drugs too. The fads pass, but some of them are dangerous." This lady felt that drugs were something that just caught kids' fancies. Complacent adults sit back and wait for pot to go out like the hula hoop.

What is frightening is how poorly these adults read the signs of their own culture. Rather than being a passing breeze (or smoke fume), marijuana is an element of youth culture that has taken root in the soil of this generation's psychological alienation. The plant will not be uprooted unless the deep roots of discontent are recognized. Drug usage will not diminish as long as the alienation in youth culture grows.

Before leaving this topic of drugs, attention ought to be directed to some observations of Dr. Don Wilson who, for three years, served as a prison psychologist at Fort Leavenworth. He wrote the popular book, *My Six Convicts,* as a result of that experience, but some of his shrewd observations and conclusions seem to have been entirely overlooked during the past two decades. For example, he wrote: "The physical damage done by phenobarbital compounds is more insidious and extensive than that of the dangerous drugs under discussion." And so far as marijuana addiction is concerned, he wrote as long ago as 1952:

The upper- and middle-class users in medicine, business,

law, engineering, teaching and the theater use discretion, watch their health, show none of the symptoms of addiction, and are almost never detected or apprehended. Statements regarding this high-class user are based on individual observation, while researches made on masses are heavily weighted with people from the wrong side of the tracks who are maladjusted, maladroit and inadequate in the face of life and pressure.

It is in the nature of things that vast movements in one direction are followed by a movement in its direct opposite. In fact, we already see the beginning of what may be an extensive backlash against drug usage, the youth revolt, college demonstrations, and black violence. It may almost seem as if most of the modern progressive movements will be negated and replaced by the most conservative trends. It is also in the nature of things that the backlash will be succeeded by its opposite. In due time, however, what little progress was involved in these pendulum swings will become apparent. But this may not be clarified for some hundreds of years, at least until the new Aeon really gets under way. We are merely in the opening stages of this Age of Aquarius, and there is likely to be a great deal of instability until the essential characteristics of the Age assert themselves.

More and more evidence presents itself to indicate an ever-widening alienation between conventional society, i.e., the establishment, and the younger generation. The better the education of the latter, the wider seems the alienation. In other words, this generation does not fit into society as we know it. Their aims, ideals and standards bear little relation to those widely accepted. To be alienated, states Gerzon, certainly does not imply that one has to be sitting on the curb, barefoot, somewhere on Sunset Strip, with a beard on one's face, beads around the neck, and a joint hanging from the corner of the mouth. To be alienated means to be dissatisfied with the kind of personality and life experience that our culture recognizes and expects. The number of possibly alienated young people far exceeds the estimates behind which adult society hides from the truth.

It is for them, then, that Crowley wrote his commentary. They are the early representatives of the Aquarian Age, the aeon of the new crowned and conquering child Horus, the Lord of the New Aeon. They are the love children who are violent and militant and epicene—simultaneously. One of the commonest of current jokes relates to the difference between the two sexes becoming so flimsy as to render recognition at first sight almost impossible. A couple of youngsters go to a gynecologist. They both have long hair, smooth, girlish skin and faces, and wear fringed leather jackets and worn blue jeans. The doctor, not wishing to embarrass them by asking which one of the two was the girl in need of attention, asks instead, "Which of you has the menstrual cycle?" They both answer, perplexed, "Oh—we drive Hondas!"

One of Crowley's most frequently expressed ideas was that as the years progress into this new age, more and more people will come into incarnation with bisexual characteristics. They will be epicene. I never expected to see this statement corroborated as early as it has been.

For example, homosexuals who previously had kept themselves well concealed from public view are now emerging in full sight. I am thinking specifically of Los Angeles where a gay liberation group is overtly declaring itself, but this is the case elsewhere too. There have been several mass demonstrations, and announcements are regularly publicized naming their meetings for all to see and attend. Harassment from police authorities still exists but is diminishing, and in due course must cease altogether. It is more than likely that their numbers will grow considerably as others, who previously were cautious and frightened, come out of hiding. Current laws relative to homosexuality will have to be modified or repealed as they have already been in Great Britain.

Female homosexuals, lesbians, are also undergoing a similar metamorphosis. Practically the entire front page of one section of the *Sunday Times* in Los Angeles was recently given over to a frank discussion of lesbians and their characteristics and problems in modern society. What is particularly interesting in this connection is the developing insistence that the sexual deviate is not sick, or no more sick than the average heterosexual in our society. Those of us who retained a static psychoanalytic orientation relative to homosexuality, male or female, were all to prone to attribute homosexuality to basic dynamic factors and conflicts in childhood. This was my point of view expressed in *The Eye in the Triangle,* published by Llewellyn Publications in 1970 but begun around 1965. Less and less credibility is to be attached to this attitude today and I think the change is a healthy one.

"Ye are against the people, O my chosen." The common man is the advocate of commonness. A new name has recently been coined for this specimen of humanity. Roger Price has written a new book entitled *The Great Roob Revolution* (New York: Random House, 1970).

The author paints a picture of the Roobs—mass men, the *homo normalis* so contemptuously named by Reich—having come into their own as a dynamic social force. Since their numbers are overwhelming and they are enjoying affluence for the first time, they are attempting to impose still further their ideas and attitudes upon the total population. Mass taste rules the world.

If this is indeed the case, then evidently in these transitional stages of the New Aeon a great deal of public ferment and disorder is certain, at least in the early years. For *The Book of the Law,* as quoted above, is adamantly against the rule of mass man. We shall witness many disturbances in the years to come as their bad taste in social organization, religion and politics gradually increases and then diminishes.

The mid-fifties were characterized by theories and feelings that a revolution in social thinking was overdue. Apparently, however, no one could work up enough of a head of steam to get things moving. But the theoretical concepts were there. For example, I am thinking of one fine psychological writer in particular, the late Robert Lindner. He was the author of *Prescription for Rebellion* which *almost* made the mark, though I suspect the time was not yet ripe for the emergence of a movement to devise widespread change of patterns of thought and behavior. Attention needs to be redirected to it, however, because there are some saving principles enunciated there.

It was basic to his thinking that all Western society is "neurotic" since Western man lives only according to taboos, myths, legends—beliefs without foundation in fact. Yet the average psychiatrist, Lindner complained, tries to "adjust" his patients to placid acceptance of a maladjusted society. This procedure has caused many to condemn psychological practice as a "quack religion." And so it is, according to Lindner, whenever it offers the individual no more than resubmergence in mass man. If psychological science is sound, then in order to save Western man, our fundamental behavior and basic beliefs must be made to yield to the efforts of informed rebels. It has taken several years for the "informed rebels" to surface and make their influence felt.

As I understand it from frequent discussions with patients from the young hip generation, many of them turned on to the new sexual, social and political attitudes through their initial use of marijuana. However much some adults may be shocked and horrified by this revelation, it is more than clear than the psychedelic drugs have to take prime place as factors responsible for the overturning of contemporary moral, religious and social standards, for the transvaluation of values. This is the prelude to an eventual development of a radically new code of behavior and therefore of a radically new type of society, as indicated by *The Book of the Law.*

Who could have foreseen in 1904 that the world was about to take a radical turn in the direction of chaos and disaster? It seems that the rationalists then were absolutely convinced that more education, more commerce, more science, more of everything was on its way; and that these would initiate the golden age of peace, security and universal brotherhood.

For example, in *This Fabulous Century* (New York: Time-Life Books, 1970) were several statements typifying the above attitude. At the opening of the century, Mark Hanna of Ohio said, "Furnaces are glowing, spindles are singing their song. Happiness comes to us all with prosperity."

And the Rev. Newell Dwight Hillis of Brooklyn wrote, "Laws are becoming more just, rulers humane; music is becoming sweeter and books wiser."

Those of us who knew the League of Nations, and who believed in its present-day successor, the United Nations, had high hopes initially that here were the answers to many age-old problems and that nations would not go to war any more. They would lay down their armaments and turn them into pruning hooks and the lion would lie down with the lamb. How wrong we were! And how unaware of the fundamentally biological facts of human nature, as indicated in *African Genesis*, for instance. But *The Book of the Law* and Aleister Crowley correctly assessed the situation as no one else had. That is the miracle. And whatever criticism I or anyone else may level at Crowley, we have to come to terms with the total revolution predicted by that book as early as 1904. This is Crowley's justification. And this is the final warrant demanding that at least he be given a fair hearing.

In *Magick without Tears,* Crowley discussed his serial publication *The Equinox* and his motives for publishing it. One of his remarks is fascinating: "They [the Secret Chiefs of the Order] . . . were agreed on measures calculated to assure the survival of the Wisdom worth saving until the time, perhaps three hundred or six hundred years later, when a new current should revive the shattered thought of mankind."

In the last chapter of *The Eye in The Triangle,* I had interpreted one verse in *Liber Legis* to imply that a holocaust or a vast natural cataclysm was in the offing, to occur sometime during the 1980's, when Pluto moves into Scorpio. Whatever this event may turn out to be, it could hold up the wheels of progress for some considerable time, perhaps for as long as Crowley has predicted above.

Somewhere around 1990, there will be a great conjunction of planets in the heavens that augur very little good for anybody. Neptune, Uranus, Saturn, Mars, Mercury, Venus, the Sun and the Moon will be in conjunction in the sign of Capricorn, around January-February, 1990. At the same time, Jupiter will be in square aspect to the sign Libra. China is Libra-ruled according to the astrologers, and Africa is ruled by Capricorn. Just what the significance of the above conjunction is, most astrologers will not say; that would be sticking their necks out entirely too far. But if this conjunction and the previous predictions are tied together, perhaps some vague intimation may be obtained of what kind of Dark Age lies ahead.

It may also serve to explain what Crowley referred to as

"a new current ... [to] revive the shattered thought of mankind."

II

In order to render this most important volume as complete as possible, I have taken certain liberties which perhaps were not contemplated by Crowley in the writing of it. For example, I have included the Stele of Revealing primarily because there are so many references to it that the student approaching this matter for the first time may not understand what is referred to. Of course, he could consult either *The Equinox,* Vol. I, No. 10, or *The Equinox of the Gods* where this Stele is reproduced. But that would entail some inconvenience which can be obviated by simply reproducing it here.

Moreover, since the last chapter of *The Book of the Law* commands, "Paste the sheets from right to left and from top to bottom: then behold!," with the inference that there is a mystery concealed within the holograph manuscript, I have decided to conform to its dictates. I have, therefore, included Crowley's reproduction of the holograph pages conforming to the above, taken from *The Equinox,* Vol. I, No. 10, on the supposition that it will facilitate study of the original.

Again, though *The Book of the Law* is given *in toto* in the commentary, it is broken up into sections that are specifically commented upon. I have decided to reproduce the entire book itself as it was printed in *The Equinox*, Vol. I, No. 9, as a preliminary to the rest. This too may prove to be useful.

The distribution of Crowley's commentaries is interesting. He originally wrote a brief commentary which was published in *The Equinox,* Vol. I, No. 7. In his *Extenuation,* he reproduced the brief commentary to chapters two and three and labeled it the "old comment" to precede his later remarks, which he called the "new comment." Only in chapter one has he omitted the old comment, and his new remarks are reproduced without the adjective "new" in the heading. New students would need to consult the mentioned volume of *The Equinox* in order to read what the old comment to chapter one stated. Again, in order to obviate the necessity for consulting other books, I have taken the liberty of following Crowley's example in the last two chapters of this volume, by breaking up the old comment in *The Equinox* into its appropriate parts, labeling it as the "old comment," and following it immediately by what I have now called the "new comment." Nothing is changed in the wording of the text. It is simply an inclusion which I believe to be a logical necessity. It is one which renders easier the study of this book.

In presenting Crowley's *Extenuation* to the general public, I should mention that I have not dared to meddle with the text, except to standardize somewhat spelling, punctuation and capitalization. I have wanted to, I must admit. In many places I have thought it redundant, verbose and occasionally mystifying. In fact, some years ago my original impression was that it included some superb prose, a large number of "purple passages," and a vast amount of just plain rhetoric.

For example, a "purple passage" typical of many is the following:

> The supreme and absolute injunction, the crux of your knightly oath, is that you lay your lance in rest to the glory of your Lady, the Queen of the Stars, Nuit. Your knighthood depends on your refusal to fight in any lesser cause. This is what distinguishes you from the brigand and the bully. You give your life on her altar. You make yourself worthy of Her by your readiness to

fight at any time, in any place, with any weapon, and at any odds. For Her from Whom you came, of Whom you are, to Whom you go, your life is no more and no less than one continuous sacrament. You have no word but her praise, no thought but love of Her. You have only one cry, of inarticulate ecstasy, and intense spasm, possession of Her, and Death, to Her. You have no act but the priest's gesture that makes your body Hers. . . . ''

And as for rhetoric, there is a great deal of it, characterized by such sentences as:

Alas! it is I the Beast that roared that Word so loud, and wakened Beauty.

Your tricks, your drowsy drugs, your life, your hypnotic passes—they will not serve you.

Make up your minds to be free men, fearless as I, fit mates for women no less free and fearless!

For I, the Beast, am come; an end to the evils of old, to the duping and clubbing of abject and ailing animals, degraded to that shameful state to serve that shameful pleasure.

The essence of my Word is to declare Woman to be Herself, or, to and for, Herself; and I give this one irresistible Weapon, the expression of Herself and Her will through sex, to Her on precisely the same terms as to man.

Fortunately, good prose runs throughout the whole book. There is no special need to highlight any particular paragraph or passage. The reader can open the book at any page at random to find some splendid writing.

Regardless of my feelings in this matter, and no matter

how I personally may feel about *The Book of the Law* or Aleister Crowley, both should be permitted to speak for themselves.

The sole substantive editing that I have confined myself to, therefore, is merely to clarify the topic of several dates, using the common method rather than referring all events back to the date of *The Book of the Law*, in 1904. I have removed some of his Qabalistic renderings of both the Greek and Hebrew alphabets to an appendix. This makes for easier reading.

Incidentally, the text speaks of an appendix. In my copy of the *Extenuation*—whoever originally typed it out—there is no appendix at all. I have taken the liberty of using the last page in *The Equinox of the Gods,* which deals with the Hebrew and Greek gematria of several important names and words. I have corrected several errors there, rewritten it, and reproduced it here as the Appendix. I trust it will serve the purpose.

Finally, I have to call attention to Crowley's selection of a title for this book: *An Extenuation of the Book of the Law.* I feel this is a rather clumsy title which may have little to say to most readers. I have accordingly deleted it and substituted a phrase taken from the text itself, *The Book of the Law.* Admittedly this presumption may not convey much more—certainly not that it is a commentary at great length on the Law—but at least it is simpler and may intrigue the casual reader enough to demand that he open the book and glance at its contents.

How and why *The Book of the Law* came to be written has been amply described by Crowley himself both in *The Temple of Solomon the King,* a serial biography running through the various numbers of *The Equinox* (1909-1914), and in *The Equinox of the Gods,* published in 1936 by the O.T.O. in England. Since that time, Crowley's own autobiography—also written in the Cefalu period—has appeared (New York: Hill and Wang, 1970). Some of the details are amplified in this commentary to considerable advantage for all readers.

However, certain problems and questions still remain unanswered. I have, therefore taken the liberty of using a revised version of chapter fifteen of my own book *The Eye in The Triangle* to deal with some of these. In so doing I am not unmindful of the fact that Crowley, were he alive, would have wholly disapproved of my action. I am aware furthermore of what sometimes happens to those foolhardy souls who tamper with the writings of greater minds than their own. They go down to oblivion. Those who tampered, for example, with the text of Madame Blavatsky's monumental work, *The Secret Doctrine*, are well on their way toward being forgotten, while her book itself may well survive the deluge. I have to take the chance that some people today as well as in future generations may regard my writing as gross meddling and demand editions of this book without any of my editing or introductory comments. So be it.

III

In the month of August, 1903, Aleister Crowley was introduced to Rose Kelly, the sister of one of his very close friends, Gerald Kelly. This was the painter who later became a member and finally president of the Royal Academy, at which time his friendship with Crowley was terminated.

Crowley had come down from a Himalayan mountain-climbing expedition, dispirited over the failure of the venture. On the spur of the moment, the couple decided to elope and get married. It was a strange marriage; they had so little in common. For awhile they travelled—to Europe, Egypt and the Far East. During their protracted honeymoon in Ceylon in 1904, Crowley discovered that Rose was pregnant. Immediately all previous plans for going on to China were scrapped, and after some big-game hunting in Hambantota county of Ceylon, they decided to go back home to Boleskine in Scotland. However, on the way back from the East, it occurred to them to stop off in Cairo, there to rent a flat during the month of February. Scotland could be dismally cold and grey during the winter months, and Cairo would be warmer and brighter.

To have registered at a hotel as Mr. and Mrs. Aleister Crowley would never have done. It sounded far too prosaic. So, "having to choose a Persian name," he wrote in his *Confessions*:

I made it Chioa Khan (Hiwa Kahn) being the Hebrew for Beast. (Khan is one of the numerous honorifics common in Asia.) I had no conscious magical intention in doing so. (Let me here mention that I usually called my wife Ouarda, one of the many Arabic words for Rose.)

I was not for a moment deceived by my own pretext that I wanted to study Mohammedanism, and in particular the mysticism of the Fakir, the Darwesh, and the Sufi, from within, when I proposed to pass myself off in Egypt for a Persian prince with a beautiful English wife. I wanted to swagger about in a turban with a diamond aigrette and sweeping silk robes or a coat of cloth-of-gold, with a jeweled talwar by my side, and two gorgeous runners to clear the way for my carriage through the streets of Cairo. . . .

As to my study of Islam, I got a Sheikh to teach me Arabic and the practices of ablution, prayer and so on, so that at some future time I might pass for a Moslem among them. I had it in my mind to repeat Burton's journey to Mecca sooner or later. I learnt a number of chapters of the Qu'ran by heart. I never went to Mecca, it seemed rather *vieux jeu,* but my ability to fraternise fully with Mohammedans has proved of infinite use in many ways.

During this short stay in Cairo, in the early months of 1904, an incident occurred which Crowley insisted throughout the rest of his earthly days was the most important single event of his entire lifetime. Everything prior was merely preparatory. Anything subsequent, he considered to be destiny and fulfillment. It dominated his every activity, after an initial five-year period during which he was reluctant even to acknowledge the existence of the book then dictated. But after this period of time, culminating in *The Vision and the Voice* experience in North Africa, he became totally identified with it, for good or for ill. Crowley and the document containing the phrase, "Do what thou wilt," then became inseparable.

What occurred in early April, 1904, has been described by Crowley on several different occasions and in several different books. It is a long, complicated story with subtle ramifications, but it can be reduced to the following simple account.

Though he claimed to have given up all magical work, there is every evidence of some intense magical preoccupation in the several weeks prior to April 8. (This is described at some length in an unpublished diary now in the possession of Mr. Gerald Yorke, and which I hope one day in the near future will be published with other diary material.) As a result of this, his wife became restless, finally saying to her husband, "They are waiting for you!" After many excursions and discussions, she finally persuaded him to conform to her "hunch," though I imagine this was far from easy. He sat alone daily in the living room of their Cairo apartment. For one full hour on each of three successive days beginning on April 8, 1904, a voice dictated to him what was called *The Book of the Law,* often written as *Liber Al vel Legis.*

This document of three short chapters purports to have been dictated by a preterhuman intelligence named Aiwass. For many long years, Crowley claimed unequivocally that Aiwass was one of the Secret Chiefs of the Third Order of the A∴A∴, an intelligence so far beyond Crowley's as his was superior to that of a bushman. Some time later, he asserted that Aiwass was none other than his Holy Guardian Angel, his Higher Self. As a result, he pronounced, "I lay claim to be the sole authority competent to decide disputed points with regard to *The Book of the Law,* seeing that its author, Aiwaz, is none other than mine own Holy Guardian Angel, to Whose Knowledge and Conversation I have attained, so that I have exclusive access to Him. I have duly referred every difficulty to Him directly, and received his answer; my award is therefore absolute without appeal."

If Aiwass was his own Higher Self, then the inference can be none other than that Aleister Crowley was the author of the book, and that he was but the external mask for a variety of different hierarchical personalities including Aiwass. Thus, if we catalog the various magical pseudonyms that he used at different states of his magical career, we find:

Frater Perdurabo	0 = 0	is Aleister Crowley
Frater O.S.V.	6 = 5	is Aleister Crowley
Frater O.M.	7 = 4	is Aleister Crowley
V. V. V. V. V.	8 = 3	is Aleister Crowley
To Mega Therion	9 = 2	is Aleister Crowley

The personality known as Aleister Crowley was the

The Seal
of
V.V.V.V.V.
8° – 3°

The Seal
of
O.S.V.
6° – 5°

The Seal
of
D.D.S.
7° – 4°

A∴A∴

The Oath of a Probationer.

I, *Aleister Crowley*, being of sound mind and
body, on this *21st* day of *March* [An ⊙ ⊙ in
___ ° of ♈] do hereby resolve: in the Presence
of ʹΟΥ ΜΗ a neophyte of the A∴A∴
To prosecute the Great Work: which is, to obtain a scientific
knowledge of the nature and powers of my own being.

    May the A∴A∴ crown the work, lend me of Its wisdom
in the work, enable me to understand the work!

    Reverence, duty, sympathy, devotion, assiduity, trust do
I bring to the A∴A∴ and in one year from this date may I
be admitted to the knowledge and conversation of the A∴A∴!

Witness my hand *Aleister Crowley*

Motto *Perdurabo.*

The Seal
of
N.S.F.
5° – 6°

lowest rung of a hierarchical ladder, the outer shell of a God, even as we all are, the persona of a Star. "Every man and every woman is a Star."

Pertaining to his thesis, I have included a copy of the Oath of a Probationer recently forwarded to me by a member of the Order. While the A∴A∴ was not organized until well after the China episode in 1907, yet the Oath bears the date March, 1904, o.s. (old style). Clearly it has been backdated.

But what is important is that Crowley who had already adopted the motto "Perdurabo" as a Neophyte in the Golden Dawn, again employs the motto as a Probationer for the A∴A∴. He takes his Oath in the presence of OU MH, a 7=4 of the A∴A∴, that is, himself. (We are never informed who authorized the passage of Crowley from one grade to a higher after he had arrived at 5=6 in the Golden Dawn.) As indicated above Crowley is both Perdurabo and OU MH, and has several other magical mottoes besides. It is *not* wholly impossible that Aiwass is the highest rung of that hierarchical ladder. We need not indulge in the pseudo-scholarly lucubrations of Kenneth Grant's *The Magical Revival*, which flogs the weary horse that Aiwass was the name of an Akkadian or Sumerian deity.

In this connection, Grant should recall that Crowley laid claim "to be the sole authority competent to decide disputed points with regard to *The Book of the Law*, seeing that its author, Aiwaz, is none other than mine own Holy Guardian Angel. . . .My award is therefore absolute without appeal."

Crowley is, then, the author of *The Book of the Law*, even as he was the inspired author of *Liber LXV* and *Liber VII*, etc. I have discussed at length in *The Eye in the Triangle* how these two latter holy books reveal a dialogue between the component parts of Crowley. *Liber AL* also indicates a dialogue between Aiwass and the scribe, Aleister Crowley. It is my assumption that, basically, *Liber AL is similar in origin.*

Crowley's attitude, however, is totally different. He is willing to admit that in a sublime sense, he was the author of the two holy books mentioned above. But in no similar manner was he the author of *Liber Legis.* The latter, he avers, was dictated to him as objectively and audibly as if he were dictating this material to a secretary.

He has, in part, anticipated some of these criticisms and this type of argument. For example, in *The Equinox of the Gods,* he writes: "Of course I wrote them, ink on paper, in the material sense; but they are not MY words, unless Aiwaz be taken to be no more than my subconscious self, or some part of it."

I must interpolate at this juncture that this is in fact one kind of psychological interpretation that he had essayed himself during the Cefalu period. In a discussion with a disciple from Australia, Frater Progradior, he actually identified the Holy Guardian Angel with the unconscious: "In that case, my conscious self being ignorant of the Truth in the Book and hostile to most of the ethics and philosophy of the Book, Aiwaz is a severely suppressed part of me." Then he added a footnote to the above: "Such a theory would further imply that I am, unknown to myself, possessed of all sorts of preternatural knowledge and power. The Law of Parsimony of Thought (Sir W. Hamilton) appears in rebuttal."

It can safely be said that all current psychological theory would agree that any one person possesses all sorts of knowledge and power of which he is totally unconscious, Hamilton's law notwithstanding. Both Freudian and Jungian theory are on the side of such an assumption, through the complete spelling out of each theory would present somewhat different pictures.

That Aiwass might, in truth, be a dissociated or hitherto unrecognized facet of his psychic structure could be confirmed by the fact that, even to his death in 1947, Crowley is said to have found some parts of the book quite foreign, even repugnant, to himself. But this is not far from common experience. A person might awaken to mull over a long dream he has had to find it foreign, strange, disagreeable and quite unacceptable. And those impressions might remain uunaltered for the rest of his lifetime. The *Extenuation* overtly states that chapter three remained largely a mystery to him, even after years of study.

If a poem, or any work of art, is a geyser of the unconscious, as Crowley wrote in the preface to *The City of God,* then *Liber Legis* must represent an upwelling of powerful images and effects from his unconscious psyche. After the failure of the Kangchenjunga expedition, he wrote a letter to his brother-in-law, Gerald Kelly, asserting that he was fed up to the gills with almost everything he had so far accomplished. As a result, he now wanted something vehement and vigorous in his life, some murder or rape, or something equally dramatic and violent. Although written about a year *after* the dictation of *Liber Legis,* after the manuscript was lost and he had repudiated the book, the letter presents some sharp insights into what was troubling him. It depicts some of the raw conflicts and archetypal movements deep down in the unconscious levels of his psyche.

Though he had apparently repudiated the book, there is a fascinating reference in his 1906 diaries, written right after the China episode, which indicates that the book may have been very much in the foreground of his conscious mind and not at all forgotten, as he had claimed. The 1905 letter to Kelly does not mention *The Book of the Law,* it is true, but on April 30, 1906, some days after he had left Shanghai, he wrote in his diary: "It has struck me—in connection with reading Blake—that Aiwass, etc., 'Force and Fire' is the very thing I lack. My 'conscience' is really an obstacle and a delusion, being a survival of heredity and education."

This is a most illuminating admission. As a boy he had been shy and bashful, regardless of how these characteristics came to be developed. His early religious training would certainly have aided in the development of a rigid superego, or conscience. In the course of his subsequent revolt against Christianity, then, he must have yearned for qualities and traits of character diametrically opposed to those he was trying to slough off. In *The Book of the Law* the wish is fulfilled. Simply stated, this emergence from his unconscious psyche represented, among other things, a colossal wish-fulfillment. Or, should we wish to follow Jung, it represented an unconscious compensatory reaction to a top-heavy Christian attitude. Since it was unconscious, it was just as extreme as the conscious attitude had been, and no equilibrium could have been reached unless and until each had modified the other.

If he had really wanted "blasphemy, murder, rape, revolution, anything, bad or good, but strong," as he averred in that significant letter to Gerald Kelly, then all I can say is that he got them. For the book which he scribed contains all of that—and more!

Both the Kelly letter and the book itself express a dynamic response to all the frustration and bitterness of his life—a response of violence, contempt and anger on the one hand, yet with sublimity and majesty on the other. The book visibly embodies all the contradictions and internal conflicts of which he was capable and by which he was being torn. Though he categorically denies having had any conscious hand in its composition and creation—and this may be literally correct on the prosaic everyday waking level—nevertheless, if Aiwass is equated with his unconscious self, then the book nonetheless is his, and is his Law.

When discussing *The Book of the Law,* two main facts

need to be remembered. (The quotations which follow were originally written by Crowley and are extrapolated from *The Equinox of the Gods.*)

1. After the Ceylon illumination, Crowley more or less discontinued every type of occult practice.

From the moment of his marriage to Rose Kelly, or more accurately from the time of his Ceylon *dhyana* a couple of years earlier, he had tired of his mystical ambitions. "All that he had obtained, he abandoned. The intuitions of the Qabalah were cast behind him with a smile at his youthful folly; magic, if true, led nowhere."

We must recall that this conclusion related to his concepts of magic prior to the year 1903. It had absolutely no reference to his achievement of three years later following the Augoeides invocations in China, nor to his Samadhi in 1909.

"Yoga had become psychology. For the solution of his original problems of the universe he looked to metaphysics; he devoted his intellect to the cult of absolute reason." It took the drastic experience of walking across the lower borders of China to remedy this grievous situation, for there he was brought abjectly to his knees. Then he was forced to realize that reason *per se* is unable to solve the great problems of the universe. Below the Abyss, in the realm of the so-called practical, in the mundane areas of science, commerce and industry, it is a fine precision tool, but that is all.

"He took up once more with Kant, Hume, Spencer, Huxley, Tyndall, Maudsley, Mansel, Fichte, Schelling, Hegel and many another; while as for his life, was he not a man? He had a wife; he knew his duty to the race, and to his own ancient graft thereof. He was a traveller and a sportsman; very well, live it. So we find that from November 1901, he did no practices of any kind until the Spring Equinox of

1904, with the exception of a casual week in the summer of 1903, and an exhibition game of Magick in the King's Chamber of the Great Pyramid in November 1903. . . .We find him climbing mountains, skating, fishing, hunting big game, fulfilling the duties of a husband; we find him with the antipathy to all forms of spiritual thought and work which marks disappointment." Such was his point of view at the time, just prior to the dictation of *The Book of the Law.*

2. His wife Rose was not the least bit interested in his intellectual or spiritual pursuits.

However true this statement may be, one should keep in mind that what was true many years afterwards may also have obtained in 1904. Crowley felt constrained to use every device to further or develop any latent clairvoyant ability in whatever woman he lived with. His methods were none other than the liberal use of alcoholic libations and sexual activity pursued to the point of conscious exhaustion. Years later, Rose became a dipsomaniac, for which reason Crowley ostensibly divorced her.

"He had yet to learn that the story of Balaam and his prophetic ass might be literally true. For the great Message that came to him came, not through the mouth of any person with any pretensions to any knowledge of this or any other sort, but through an empty-headed woman of society."

Crowley has gone out of his way repeatedly to inform us that Rose was stupid. I presume he has done this, apart from lesser motives, to render all the more impressive her bout of psychic perception in Cairo. Furthermore, it is evident from his *Confessions* that he regarded *all* women as his intellectual inferiors and therefore stupid. Could it be that she really was not as dumb as he would have liked us to believe? Even if we assume this, however, it does not help very much where *The Book of the Law* is concerned.

When Rose began to insist that "they are waiting for

you," he may at first have attributed her wild rambling to a species of insanity he attributed to both menstruating and pregnant women. But when she began to use the cues and symbols in his own private magical cipher, of which theoretically she could have known nothing, he had to sit up and take notice.

It was possible, naturally, for Rose to have glanced through some of his notebooks where he was making tabulations and classifications of symbols and mythologies that one day would become *Liber 777*. Like most married women, she had perhaps learned to sit quietly while her husband used her as a sounding board for his own reflections. It is conceivable that she had heard him talk in the same way that he had written her brother after the ill-fated Himalayan venture. Crowley was never any good at keeping things to himself. In the Sahara in 1909, even the demon Choronzon when confronting Neuburg said that Crowley talked too much. During their married years, therefore, Rose must have heard him talk a lot about his attitudes toward life, magic and everything else.

But this is of no real help in understanding why, during a trip to the Boulak Museum in Cairo, she led him to an exhibition case bearing the number 666, which was meaningful to him. Or why she selected Horus of all the possible Egyptian Gods as the presiding genius of the events about to transpire. What is even more remarkable is that after the completion of the three days of dictation, it fell to Rose (who knew nothing of magick) to fill in a couple of blank spaces for words that Crowley had not heard aright!

Apparently Rose filled, temporarily, a mediumistic role in these psychic episodes of 1904, and Crowley heard "direct-voice" communications and experienced other similar psychic phenomena. Some of these he resented, so we are led to believe by his comments, which resulted in his putting aside the message and losing it for five years. A large series of questions remain unanswered to this day.

He did keep a diary or two during the opening phases of this cycle, but many entries were in cipher and are not altogether clear. His memory was unable later to decipher these entries, regardless of his every effort. Even so, several of the obscure entries consisting of a string of numbers and letters are meaningful in one or more ways, if we assume that when he wrote them he knew what he was doing. It was only after the passage of years that they became completely mysterious to him.

As the reader will notice when reading the end of the second chapter of *The Book of the Law,* there are a whole string of letters and numbers that, to date, are quite without meaning. "Aye! listen to the numbers & the words: 4 6 3 8 A B K 2 4 A L G M O R 3 Y X 24 89 R P S T O V A L." And tauntingly, it goes on to ask: "What meaneth this, O prophet? Thou knowest not; nor shalt thou know ever. There cometh one to follow thee; he shall expound it."

If the book states that he does not know the meaning of a dictated set of letters and numbers, in one sense the mystery is no stranger than a similar set of letters and numbers he had himself written long ago in his own diary and could not decipher. He had written both—both were mysterious to him.

With regard to the case in the Boulak Museum in Cairo to which Rose led him after he had carefully cross-examined her again and again, do note that the case bore the number 666. It contained the Stele of Revealing, as it has since come to be known.

It has played a prominent role in the life of Crowley after the dictation of the Book. It had an important message for him. He arranged for a copy of the original to be made for him, and it accompanied him wherever he went. Some of

his more enthusiastic disciples have either had copies
similarly made, or else have had the colored reproduction in
The Equinox mounted or framed. Some of the versified
translations of the Egyptian text of the Stele were inserted
into the body of *The Book of the Law* as directed,
apparently to save time. It comes in for considerable
discussion in the course of Crowley's commentary.

There are innumerable traces of the influence of the
Hermetic Order of the Golden Dawn throughout the entire
book. Merely the replacement of Osiris by Horus as Lord of
the Aeon has basic reference to the Ceremony of the
Equinox, when one set of officers was installed to replace the
retiring officiants. In the book are innumerable references to
the Qabalah and the Tarot—all stored in the contents of
Crowley's psyche, materials derived from the Order that
shaped his inner life. (See *The Eye in the Triangle* for
corroboration of this statement.) It was also on the basis of
one verse, "Abrogate are all rituals, all ordeals, all words and
signs," that he wrote to MacGregor Mathers informing him
that the Secret Chiefs had appointed him, Crowley, to be
head of the Order.

One of the most conspicuous aspects of *The Book of
the Law* is that its stand on almost every moral issue runs
counter to the accepted social one of today. Certainly it is in
direct opposition to the Judeo-Christian code that today
regulates our behavior. However, with the extraordinary
social changes in the air today—violent changes being
wrought in the streets, in foreign wars, and by the young
people on college campuses—and with the wholesale rejection
of previously accepted norms of conduct, it is not too much
to say that in the contemporary scene Crowley has a
multitude of allies and adherents.

Up to the time of the dictation of *Liber Legis*,
Crowley's emotional momentum had led him to challenge

and then to discard the basic moral attitudes of his parents and the type of Christianity they and their representatives had imparted to him. His life expressed an open revolt against them. There was never any secret or mystery about this. It represented the very core of his existence. It was stated a hundred times or more in everything he wrote and in everything he did. Under these circumstances it would be most surprising if his book, whether dictated by a preterhuman intelligence or composed by Crowley himself, did not take an identical stand. The miracle in his life would have been if it had agreed with all that he had been opposed to. But this particular miracle did not occur. With fervor, the book echoes Crowley's fundamental moral, religious and social attitudes without equivocation or doubt. Whether dictated or emerging from his unconscious psyche, it is his book.

When the dictation of *The Book of the Law* was completed on that fateful day in April, 1904, so was Crowley. There was much that he claimed was repugnant to him, particularly in the third chapter. He put the manuscript aside, and to all intents and purposes, lost it. But one coincidence after another occurred, until he could no longer believe they were mere coincidences. They formed a string of curious events, apparently connected by some prearranged inevitability which *forced* him into line, into taking up the burden of responsibility indicated by the book. Crowley was obliged to develop a theory that Aiwass, be he Angel or preterhuman intelligence or a member of the Third Order, or whatever, was able to influence the course of events in his life by subtle means, to bring him back to the way he must go. Aiwass was destiny.*

*It is worth noting that Crowley who, at the very least, knew how to use the English language, deliberately employed the phrase "preterhuman intelligence." He did not use the word "extraterrestrial," as some of the modern revisionist commentators propose. Had he meant "extraterrestrial" or implied any

Crowley was thus not only a man of the world, not only a distinguished literary man, not only a mystic of considerable attainment; but against his will, so it seems, he was transformed into a man with a message for the whole of mankind.

A great deal of this thesis has already been discussed in that final chapter of *The Eye in the Triangle,* and I do not wish to repeat it at length here, but simply refer the interested student to it. It merely complements what Crowley has to say in his commentary. It is a more prosaic view of what may be a more magical or romantic attitude toward the phenomenon of "dictation."

His commentary is certain to stir up controversy; this is to be expected and to be hoped for. It may, for some people, prepare them for the expansion of consciousness which, after all, is the major function of the Law and his commentary upon it.

One final word before closing. A certain Gilbert Highet some years ago wrote a book entitled *Talents and Geniuses* (New York: Meridian Books, 1959). According to the blurb on the back of that book, he was a radio commentator who had "captured a wide, literate audience during recent years." It also averred that "he here displays his varied interests, his wit, and his erudition in discussions of topics ranging from Bach to Zen Buddhism."

Highet offers an essay on Crowley which begins with a review of Somerset Maugham's *The Magician* in which the protagonist, Oliver Haddo, is modeled after Crowley. From this review, he concludes that Crowley was not a *fake* as some people had been led to believe, but a *failure.* In

theory relative to UFO's, it is quite certain he would have employed pertinent terms. Kenneth Grant and some other would-be successors have already commenced the insidious process of interpolating their own theories, and modifying Crowley's by emphasizing how wrong he was, to prove that the mantle of successorship has fallen on their shoulders. The inflation of the ego is a devastating process.

opposition to Christianity which is essentially sex-negative, Crowley had wished to establish a solar-phallic religion (a felicitous phrase borrowed from Jung's *Psychology of the Unconscious*). He had in mind a type of worship which would be rooted in man's deepest biological and spiritual needs. "When you have proved that God is merely a name for the sex instinct, it appears to me not far to the perception that the sex instinct is God." This is the essence of Crowley's viewpoint which is elaborated at great length in his commentary. Highet claims that this type of religion quite clearly has not succeeded in spreading to any extent; therefore, Crowley has failed in his aims.

Some years ago this would have appeared valid. Nevertheless, we have to remember that the early preaching of the Gospels was not a startling success for a considerable time. Actually, some scholars and critics wonder it it ever really succeeded in making anything but the most trivial impact on the everyday lives of most people. It took centuries of violence and bloodshed to convert the masses to Christianity.

Crowley has been dead less than three decades. Who can estimate how many hundreds of people have been influenced in one way or another? Thelema may have to wait awhile before it can show, better than Christianity, its capability for transforming our society. Yet the transvaluation of values documented in this introduction suggests that Crowley has succeeded beyond his wildest dreams. What he was writing about decades ago has already begun to arrive. The young generation presently active is his enthusiastic audience and his congregation. And he has been dead less than twenty-five years!

It really makes little difference in the long run whether *The Book of the Law* was dictated to him by a preterhuman intelligence named Aiwass or whether it stemmed from the creative deeps of Aleister Crowley. The book was written. And he became the mouthpiece for the *Zeitgeist*, accurately expressing the intrinsic nature of our time as no one else has done to date. Thus his failures and excesses and stupidities are simply the hallmark of his humanity. Was he not, by his own admission, the Beast, whose number is 666, which is the number of Man?

—Israel Regardie

Studio City, California
November, 1970.

LIBER LEGIS

The Book
of The Law

SVB FIGURA
CCXX
AS DELIVERED BY
XCIII=418
TO
DCLXVI

A∴ A∴

Publication in Class A

Imprimatur:

ㄱ ㄱ ㄱ

V.V.V.V.V.

N.   Fra. A∴ A∴

O.M.   7°=4°

D.D.S.   7°=4° Praemonstrator

O.S.V.   6°=5° Imperator

I.M.   5°=6° Cancellarius

Given at our College S.S. in the Mountain of
Abiegnus ☉ in ♎ An. IX

The Book
of The Law

1. Had! The manifestation of Nuit.

2. The unveiling of the company of heaven.

3. Every man and every woman is a star.

4. Every number is infinite; there is no difference.

5. Help me, o warrior lord of Thebes, in my unveiling before the Children of men!

6. Be thou Hadit, my secret centre, my heart & my tongue!

7. Behold! it is revealed by Aiwass the minister of Hoor-paar-kraat.

8. The Khabs is in the Khu, not the Khu in the Khabs.

9. Worship then the Khabs, and behold my light shed over you!

10. Let my servants be few & secret: they shall rule the many & the known.

11. These are fools that men adore; both their Gods & their men are fools.

12. Come forth, o children, under the stars, & take your fill of love!

13. I am above you and in you. My ecstasy is in yours. My joy is to see your joy.

14. Above, the gemmèd azure is
    The naked splendour of Nuit;
She bends in ecstasy to kiss
    The secret ardours of Hadit.
The wingèd globe, the starry blue,
Are mine, O Ankh-af-na-khonsu!

15. Now ye shall know that the chosen priest & apostle of infinite space is the prince-priest, the Beast; and in his woman called the Scarlet Woman is all power given. They shall gather my children into their fold: they shall bring the glory of the stars into the hearts of men.

16. For he is ever a sun, and she a moon. But to him is the winged secret flame, and to her the stooping starlight.

17. But ye are not so chosen.

18. Burn upon their brows, o splendrous serpent!

19. O azure-lidded woman, bend upon them!

20. The key of the rituals is in the secret word which I have given unto him.

21. With the God & the Adorer I am nothing: they do not see me. They are as upon the earth; I am Heaven, and there is no other God than me, and my lord Hadit.

22. Now, therefore, I am known to ye by my name Nuit, and to him by a secret name which I will give him when at last he knoweth me. Since I am Infinite Space, and the Infinite Stars thereof, do ye also thus. Bind nothing! Let there be no difference made among you between any one thing & any other thing; for thereby there cometh hurt.

23. But whoso availeth in this, let him be the chief of all!

24. I am Nuit, and my word is six and fifty.

25. Divide, add, multiply, and understand.

26. Then saith the prophet and slave of the beauteous one: Who am I, and what shall be the sign? So she answered

him, bending down, a lambent flame of blue, all-touching, all penetrant, her lovely hands upon the black earth, & her lithe body arched for love, and her soft feet not hurting the little flowers: Thou knowest! And the sign shall be my ecstasy, the consciousness of the continuity of existence, the omnipresence of my body.

27. Then the priest answered & said unto the Queen of Space, kissing her lovely brows, and the dew of her light bathing his whole body in a sweet-smelling perfume of sweat: O Nuit, continuous one of Heaven, let it be ever thus; that men speak not of Thee as One but as None; and let them speak not of thee at all, since thou art continuous!

28. None, breathed the light, faint & faery, of the stars, and two.

29. For I am divided for love's sake, for the chance of union.

30. This is the creation of the world, that the pain of division is as nothing, and the joy of dissolution all.

31. For these fools of men and their woes care not thou at all! They feel little; what is, is balanced by weak joys; but ye are my chosen ones.

32. Obey my prophet! follow out the ordeals of my knowledge! seek me only! Then the joys of my love will redeem ye from all pain. This is so; I swear it by the vault of my body; by my sacred heart and tongue; by all I can give, by all I desire of ye all.

33. Then the priest fell into a deep trance or swoon, & said unto the Queen of Heaven; Write unto us the ordeals; write unto us the rituals; write unto us the law!

34. But she said: the ordeals I write not: the rituals shall be half known and half concealed: the Law is for all.

35. This that thou writest is the threefold book of Law.

36. My scribe Ankh-af-na-khonsu, the priest of the princes, shall not in one letter change this book; but lest

there be folly, he shall comment thereupon by the wisdom of Ra-Hoor-Khu-it.

37. Also the mantras and spells; the obeah and the wanga; the work of the wand and the work of the sword; these he shall learn and teach;

38. He must teach; but he may make severe the ordeals.

39. The word of the Law is θελημα.

40. Who calls us Thelemites will do no wrong, if he look but close into the word. For there are therein Three Grades, the Hermit, and the Lover, and the man of Earth. Do what thou wilt shall be the whole of the Law.

41. The word of Sin is Restriction: O man! refuse not thy wife, if she will! O lover, if thou wilt, depart! There is no bond that can unite the divided but love: all else is a curse. Accursed! Accursed be it to the aeons! Hell.

42. Let it be that state of manyhood bound and loathing. So with thy all; thou hast no right but to do thy will.

43. Do that, and no other shall say nay.

44. For pure will, unassuaged of purpose, delivered from the lust of result, is every way perfect.

45. The Perfect and the Perfect are one Perfect and not two; nay, are none!

46. Nothing is a secret key of this law. Sixty-one the Jews call it; I call it eight, eighty, four hundred & eighteen.

47. But they have the half: unite by thine art so that all disappear.

48. My prophet is a fool with his one, one, one; are not they the Ox, and none by the Book?

49. Abrogate are all rituals, all ordeals, all words and signs. Ra-Hoor-Khuit hath taken his seat in the East at the Equinox of the Gods; and let Asar be with Isa, who also are one. But they are not of me. Let Asar be the adorant, Isa, the

sufferer; Hoor in his secret name and splendour is the Lord initiating.

50. There is a word to say about the Hierophantic task. Behold! there are three ordeals in one, and it may be given in three ways. The gross must pass through fire; let the fine be tried in intellect, and the lofty chosen ones in the highest; Thus ye have star & star, system & system; let not one know well the other!

51. There are four gates to one palace; the floor of that palace is of silver and gold; lapis lazuli & jasper are there; and all rare scents; jasmine & rose, and the emblems of death. Let him enter in turn or at once the four gates; let him stand on the floor of the palace. Will he not sink? Amn. Ho! warrior, if thy servant sink? But there are means and means. Be goodly therefore: dress ye all in fine apparel; eat rich foods and drink sweet wines and wines that foam! Also, take your fill and will of love as ye will, when, where and with whom ye will! But always unto me.

52. If this be not aright; if ye confound the space-marks, saying: They are one; or saying, They are many; if the ritual be not ever unto me: then expect the direful judgments of Ra Hoor Khuit!

53. This shall regenerate the world, the little world my sister, my heart & my tongue, unto whom I send this kiss. Also, o scribe and prophet, though thou be of the princes, it shall not assuage thee nor absolve thee. But ecstasy be thine and joy of earth: ever To me! To me!

54. Change not as much as the style of a letter; for behold! thou, o prophet, shalt not behold all these mysteries hidden therein.

55. The child of thy bowels, *he* shall behold them.

56. Expect him not from the East, nor from the West; for from no expected house cometh that child. Aum! All

words are sacred and all prophets true; save only that they understand a little; solve the first half of the equation, leave the second unattacked. But thou hast all in the clear light, and some, though not all, in the dark.

57. Invoke me under my stars! Love is the law, love under will. Nor let the fools mistake love; for there are love and love. There is the dove, and there is the serpent. Choose ye well! He, my prophet, hath chosen, knowing the law of the fortress, and the great mystery of the House of God.

All these old letters of my Book are aright; but ﬞ is not the Star. This also is secret: my prophet shall reveal it to the wise.

58. I give unimaginable joys on earth: certainty, not faith, while in life, upon death; peace unutterable, rest, ecstasy; nor do I demand aught in sacrifice.

59. My incense is of resinous woods & gums; and there is no blood therein: because of my hair the trees of Eternity.

60. My number is 11, as all their numbers who are of us. The Five Pointed Star, with a Circle in the Middle, & the circle is Red. My colour is black to the blind, but the blue & gold are seen of the seeing. Also I have a secret glory for them that love me.

61. But to love me is better than all things: if under the night-stars in the desert thou presently burnest mine incense before me, invoking me with a pure heart, and the Serpent flame therein, thou shalt come a little to lie in my bosom. For one kiss wilt thou then be willing to give all; but whoso gives one particle of dust shall lose all in that hour. Ye shall gather goods and store of women and spices; ye shall wear rich jewels; ye shall exceed the nations of the earth in splendour & pride; but always in the love of me, and so shall ye come to my joy. I charge you earnestly to come before me in a single robe, and covered with a rich head-dress. I love you! I yearn to you! Pale or purple, veiled or voluptuous, I

who am all pleasure and purple, and drunkenness of the innermost sense, desire you. Put on the wings, and arouse the coiled splendour within you: come unto me!

62. At all my meetings with you shall the priestess say—and her eyes shall burn with desire as she stands bare and rejoicing in my secret temple—To me! To me! calling forth the flame of the hearts of all in her love-chant.

63. Sing the rapturous love-song unto me! Burn to me perfumes! Wear to me jewels! Drink to me, for I love you! I love you!

64. I am the blue-lidded daughter of Sunset; I am the naked brilliance of the voluptuous night-sky.

65. To me! To me!

66. The Manifestation of Nuit is at an end.

1. Nu! the hiding of Hadit.

2. Come! all ye, and learn the secret that hath not yet been revealed. I, Hadit, am the complement of Nu, my bride. I am not extended, and Khabs is the name of my House.

3. In the sphere I am everywhere the centre, as she, the circumference, is nowhere found.

4. Yet she shall be known & I never.

5. Behold! the rituals of the old time are black. Let the evil ones be cast away; let the good ones be purged by the prophet! Then shall this Knowledge go aright.

6. I am the flame that burns in every heart of man, and in the core of every star. I am Life, and the giver of Life, yet therefore is the knowledge of me the knowledge of death.

7. I am the Magician and the Exorcist. I am the axle of the wheel, and the cube in the circle. "Come unto me" is a foolish word; for it is I that go.

8. Who worshipped Heru-pa-kraath have worshipped

me; ill, for I am the worshipper.

9. Remember all ye that existence is pure joy; that all the sorrows are but as shadows; they pass & are done; but there is that which remains.

10. O prophet! thou hast ill will to learn this writing.

11. I see thee hate the hand & the pen; but I am stronger.

12. Because of me in Thee which thou knewest not.

13. for why? Because thou wast the knower, and me.

14. Now let there be a veiling of this shrine: now let the light devour men and eat them up with blindness!

15. For I am perfect, being Not; and my number is nine by the fools; but with the just I am eight, and one in eight: Which is vital, for I am none indeed. The Empress and the King are not of me; for there is a further secret.

16. I am The Empress & the Hierophant. Thus eleven, as my bride is eleven.

17. Hear me, ye people of sighing!
   The sorrows of pain and regret
   Are left to the dead and the dying,
   The folk that not know me as yet.

18. These are dead, these fellows; they feel not. We are not for the poor and sad: the lords of the earth are our kinsfolk.

19. Is a God to live in a dog? No! but the highest are of us. They shall rejoice, our chosen: who sorroweth is not of us.

20. Beauty and strength, leaping laughter and delicious languor, force and fire, are of us.

21. We have nothing with the outcast and the unfit: let them die in their misery. For they feel not. Compassion is the vice of kings: stamp down the wretched & the weak: this is

the law of the strong: this is our law and the joy of the world. Think not, o king, upon that lie: That Thou Must Die: verily thou shalt not die, but live. Now let it be understood: If the body of the King dissolve, he shall remain in pure ecstasy for ever. Nuit! Hadit! Ra-Hoor-Khuit! The Sun, Strength & Sight, Light; these are for the servants of the Star & the Snake.

22. I am the Snake that giveth Knowledge & Delight and bright glory, and stir the hearts of men with drunkenness. To worship me take wine and strange drugs whereof I will tell my prophet, & be drunk thereof! They shall not harm ye at all. It is a lie, this folly against self. The exposure of innocence is a lie. Be strong, o man! lust, enjoy all things of sense and rapture: fear not that any God shall deny thee for this.

23. I am alone: there is no God where I am.

24. Behold! these be grave mysteries; for there are also of my friends who be hermits. Now think not to find them in the forest or on the mountain; but in beds of purple, caressed by magnificent beasts of women with large limbs, and fire and light in their eyes, and masses of flaming hair about them; there shall ye find them. Ye shall see them at rule, at victorious armies, at all the joy; and there shall be in them a joy a million times greater than this. Beware lest any force another, King against King! Love one another with burning hearts; on the low men trample in the fierce lust of your pride, in the day of your wrath.

25. Ye are against the people, O my chosen!

26. I am the secret Serpent coiled about to spring: in my coiling there is joy. If I lift up my head, I and my Nuit are one. If I droop down mine head, and shoot forth venom, then is rapture of the earth, and I and the earth are one.

27. There is great danger in me; for who doth not understand these runes shall make a great miss. He shall fall

down into the pit called Because, and there he shall perish with the dogs of Reason.

28. Now a curse upon Because and his kin!

29. May Because be accursèd for ever!

30. If Will stops and cries Why, invoking Because, then Will stops & does nought.

31. If Power asks why, then is Power weakness.

32. Also reason is a lie; for there is a factor infinite & unknown; & all their words are skew-wise.

33. Enough of Because! Be he damned for a dog!

34. But ye, o my people, rise up & awake!

35. Let the rituals be rightly performed with joy & beauty!

36. There are rituals of the elements and feasts of the times.

37. A feast for the first night of the Prophet and his Bride!

38. A feast for the three days of the writing of the Book of the Law.

39. A feast for Tahuti and the child of the Prophet—secret, O Prophet!

40. A feast for the Supreme Ritual, and a feast for the Equinox of the Gods.

41. A feast for fire and a feast for water; a feast for life and a greater feast for death!

42. A feast every day in your hearts in the joy of my rapture!

43. A feast every night unto Nu, and the pleasure of uttermost delight!

44. Aye! feast! rejoice! there is no dread hereafter. There is the dissolution, and eternal ecstasy in the kisses of Nu.

45. There is death for the dogs.

46. Dost thou fail? Art thou sorry? Is fear in thine heart?

47. Where I am these are not.

48. Pity not the fallen! I never knew them. I am not for them. I console not: I hate the consoled & the consoler.

49. I am unique & conqueror. I am not of the slaves that perish. Be they damned & dead! Amen. (This is of the 4: there is a fifth who is invisible, & therein am I as a babe in an egg.)

50. Blue am I and gold in the light of my bride: but the red gleam is in my eyes; & my spangles are purple & green.

51. Purple beyond purple: it is the light higher than eyesight.

52. There is a veil: that veil is black. It is the veil of the modest woman; it is the veil of sorrow, & the pall of death: this is none of me. Tear down that lying spectre of the centuries: veil not your vices in virtuous words: these vices are my service; ye do well, & I will reward you here and hereafter.

53. Fear not, o prophet, when these words are said, thou shalt not be sorry. Thou art emphatically my chosen; and blessed are the eyes that thou shalt look upon with gladness. But I will hide thee in a mask of sorrow: they that see thee shall fear thou art fallen: but I lift thee up.

54. Nor shall they who cry aloud their folly that thou meanest nought avail; thou shall reveal it: thou availest: they are the slaves of because: They are not of me. The stops as thou wilt; the letters? change them not in style or value!

55. Thou shalt obtain the order & value of the English Alphabet; thou shalt find new symbols to attribute them unto.

56. Begone! ye mockers; even though ye laugh in my honour ye shall laugh not long: then when ye are sad

know that I have forsaken you.

57. He that is righteous shall be righteous still; he that is filthy shall be filthy still.

58. Yea! deem not of change: ye shall be as ye are, & not other. Therefore the kings of the earth shall be Kings for ever: the slaves shall serve. There is none that shall be cast down or lifted up: all is ever as it was. Yet there are masked ones my servants: it may be that yonder beggar is a King. A King may choose his garment as he will: there is no certain test: but a beggar cannot hide his poverty.

59. Beware therefore! Love all, lest perchance is a King concealed! Say you so? Fool! If he be a King, thou canst not hurt him.

60. Therefore strike hard & low, and to hell with them, master!

61. There is a light before thine eyes, o prophet, a light undesired, most desirable.

62. I am uplifted in thine heart; and the kisses of the stars rain hard upon thy body.

63. Thou art exhaust in the voluptuous fullness of the inspiration; the expiration is sweeter than death, more rapid and laughterful than a caress of Hell's own worm.

64. Oh! thou art overcome: we are upon thee; our delight is all over thee: hail! hail: prophet of Nu! prophet of Had! prophet of Ra-Hoor-Khu! Now rejoice! now come in our splendour & rapture! Come in our passionate peace, & write sweet words for the Kings!

65. I am the Master: thou art the Holy Chosen One.

66. Write, & find ecstasy in writing! Work, & be our bed in working! Thrill with the joy of life & death! Ah! thy death shall be lovely: whoso seeth it shall be glad. Thy death shall be the seal of the promise of our agelong love. Come! lift up thine heart & rejoice! We are one; we are none.

67. Hold! Hold! Bear up in thy rapture; fall not in swoon of the excellent kisses!

68. Harder! Hold up thyself! Lift thine head! breathe not so deep—die!*

69. Ah! Ah! What do I feel? Is the word exhausted?

70. There is help & hope in other spells. Wisdom says: be strong! Then canst thou bear more joy. Be not animal; refine thy rapture! If thou drink, drink by the eight and ninety rules of art: if thou love, exceed by delicacy; and if thou do aught joyous, let there be subtlety therein!

71. But exceed! exceed!

72. Strive ever to more! and if thou art truly mine—and doubt it not, an if thou art ever joyous!—death is the crown of all.

73. Ah! Ah! Death! Death! thou shalt long for death. Death is forbidden, o man, unto thee.

74. The length of thy longing shall be the strength of its glory. He that lives long & desires death much is ever the King among the Kings.

75. Aye! listen to the numbers & the words:

76. 4 6 3 8 A B K 2 4 A L G M O R 3 Y X 24 89 R P S T O V A L. What meaneth this, o prophet? Thou knowest not; nor shalt thou know ever. There cometh one to follow thee: he shall expound it. But remember, o chosen one, to be me; to follow the love of Nu in the star-lit heaven; to look forth upon men, to tell them this glad word.

77. O be thou proud and mighty among men!

78. Lift up thyself! for there is none like unto thee among men or among Gods! lift up thyself, o my prophet, thy stature shall surpass the stars. They shall worship thy name, foursquare, mystic, wonderful, the number of the

*"Harden," not "Harder," as the manuscript indicates. The memory of DCLXVI says, though with diffidence, that the former is correct.

man; and the name of thy house 418.

79. The end of the hiding of Hadit; and blessing & worship to the prophet of the lovely Star!

1. Abrahadabra; the reward of Ra Hoor Khut.

2. There is division hither homeward; there is a word not known. Spelling is defunct; all is not aught. Beware! Hold! Raise the spell of Ra-Hoor-Khuit!

3. Now let it be first understood that I am a god of War and of Vengeance. I shall deal hardly with them.

4. Choose ye an island!

5. Fortify it!

6. Dung it about with enginery of war!

7. I will give you a war-engine.

8. With it ye shall smite the peoples; and none shall stand before you.

9. Lurk! Withdraw! Upon them! this is the Law of the Battle of Conquest: thus shall my worship be about my secret house.

10. Get the stélé of revealing itself; set it in thy secret temple—and that temple is already aright disposed—& it shall be your Kiblah for ever. It shall not fade, but miraculous colour shall come back to it day after day. Close it in locked glass for a proof to the world.

11. This shall be your only proof. I forbid argument. Conquer! That is enough. I will make easy to you the abstruction from the ill-ordered house in the Victorious City. Thou shalt thyself convey it with worship, o prophet, though thou likest it not. Thou shalt have danger & trouble. Ra-Hoor-Khu is with thee. Worship me with fire & blood; worship me with swords & with spears. Let the woman be girt with a sword before me: let blood flow to my name.

Trample down the Heathen; be upon them, o warrior, I will give you of their flesh to eat!

12. Sacrifice cattle, little and big: after a child.

13. But not now.

14. Ye shall see that hour, o blessèd Beast, and thou the Scarlet Concubine of his desire!

15. Ye shall be sad thereof.

16. Deem not too eagerly to catch the promises; fear not to undergo the curses. Ye, even ye, know not this meaning all.

17. Fear not at all; fear neither men, nor Fates, nor gods, nor anything. Money fear not, nor laughter of the folk folly, nor any other power in heaven or upon the earth or under the earth. Nu is your refuge as Hadit your light; and I am the strength, force, vigour, of your arms.

18. Mercy let be off: damn them who pity! Kill and torture; spare not; be upon them!

19. That stélé they shall call the Abomination of Desolation; count well its name, & it shall be to you as 718.

20. Why? Because of the fall of Because, that he is not there again.

21. Set up my image in the East: thou shalt buy thee an image which I will show thee, especial, not unlike the one thou knowest. And it shall be suddenly easy for thee to do this.

22. The other images group around me to support me: let all be worshipped, for they shall cluster to exalt me. I am the visible object of worship; the others are secret; for the Beast & his Bride are they: and for the winners of the Ordeal x. What is this? Thou shalt know.

23. For perfume mix meal & honey & thick leavings of red wine: then oil of Abramelin and olive oil, and afterward soften & smooth down with rich fresh blood.

24. The best blood is of the moon, monthly: then the

fresh blood of a child, or dropping from the host of heaven: then of enemies; then of the priest or of the worshippers: last of some beast, no matter what.

25. This burn: of this make cakes & eat unto me. This hath also another use; let it be laid before me, and kept thick with perfumes of your orison: it shall become full of beetles as it were and creeping things sacred unto me.

26. These slay, naming your enemies; & they shall fall before you.

27. Also these shall breed lust & power of lust in you at the eating thereof.

28. Also ye shall be strong in war.

29. Moreover, be they long kept, it is better; for they swell with my force. All before me.

30. My altar is of open brass work: burn thereon in silver or gold!

31. There cometh a rich man from the West who shall pour his gold upon thee.

32. From gold forge steel!

33. Be ready to fly or to smite!

34. But your holy place shall be untouched throughout the centuries: though with fire and sword it be burnt down & shattered, yet an invisible house there standeth, and shall stand until the fall of the Great Equinox; when Hrumachis shall arise and the double-wanded one assume my throne and place. Another prophet shall arise, and bring fresh fever from the skies; another woman shall awake the lust & the worship of the Snake; another soul of God and beast shall mingle in the globèd priest; another sacrifice shall stain The tomb; another king shall reign; and blessing no longer be poured To the Hawk-headed mystical Lord!

35. The half of the word of Heru-ra-ha, called Hoor-pa-kraat and Ra-Hoor-Khut.

36. Then said the prophet unto the God:

37. I adore thee in the song—

I am the Lord of Thebes, and I
    The inspired forth-speaker of Mentu;
For me unveils the veilèd sky,
    The self-slain Ankh-af-na-khonsu
Whose words are truth. I invoke, I greet
    Thy presence, O Ra-Hoor-Khuit!

Unity uttermost showed!
    I adore the might of Thy breath,
Supreme and terrible God,
    Who makest the gods and death
To tremble before Thee:—
    I, I adore thee!

Appear on the throne of Ra!
    Open the ways of the Khu!
Lighten the ways of the Ka!
    The ways of the Khabs run through
To stir me or still me!
    Aum! let it fill me!

38. So that thy light is in me; & its red flame is as a
sword in my hand to push thy order. There is a secret door
that I shall make to establish thy way in all the quarters,
(these are the adorations, as thou hast written), as it is said:

The light is mine; its rays consume
    Me: I have made a secret door
Into the House of Ra and Tum,
    Of Khephra and of Ahathoor.
I am thy Theban, O Mentu,
    The prophet Ankh-af-na-khonsu!

By Bes-na-Maut my breast I beat;
   By wise Ta-Nech I weave my spell.
Show thy star-splendour, O Nuit!
   Bid me within thine House to dwell,
O wingèd snake of light, Hadit!
   Abide with me, Ra-Hoor-Khuit!

39. All this and a book to say how thou didst come hither and a reproduction of this ink and paper for ever—for in it is the word secret & not only in the English—and thy comment upon this the Book of the Law shall be printed beautifully in red ink and black upon beautiful paper made by hand; and to each man and woman that thou meetest, were it but to dine or to drink at them, it is the Law to give. Then they shall chance to abide in this bliss or no; it is no odds. Do this quickly!

40. But the work of the comment? That is easy; and Hadit burning in thy heart shall make swift and secure thy pen.

41. Establish at thy Kaaba a clerk-house: all must be done well and with business way.

42. The ordeals thou shalt oversee thyself, save only the blind ones. Refuse none, but thou shalt know & destroy the traitors. I am Ra-Hoor-Khuit; and I am powerful to protect my servant. Success is thy proof: argue not; convert not; talk not overmuch! Them that seek to entrap thee, to overthrow thee, them attack without pity or quarter; & destroy them utterly. Swift as a trodden serpent turn and strike! Be thou yet deadlier than he! Drag down their souls to awful torment: laugh at their fear: spit upon them!

43. Let the Scarlet Woman beware! If pity and compassion and tenderness visit her heart; if she leave my work to toy with old sweetnesses; than shall my vengeance be known. I will slay me her child: I will alienate her heart: I

will cast her out from men: as a shrinking and despised harlot shall she crawl through dusk wet streets, and die cold and an-hungered.

44. But let her raise herself in pride! Let her follow me in my way! Let her work the work of wickedness! Let her kill her heart! Let her be loud and adulterous! Let her be covered with jewels, and rich garments, and let her be shameless before all men!

45. Then will I lift her to pinnacles of power: then will I breed from her a child mightier than all the kings of the earth. I will fill her with joy: with my force shall she see & strike at the worship of Nu: she shall achieve Hadit.

46. I am the warrior Lord of the Forties: the Eighties cower before me, & are abased. I will bring you to victory & joy: I will be at your arms in battle & ye shall delight to slay. Success is your proof; courage is your armour; go on, go on, in my strength; & ye shall turn not back for any!

47. This book shall be translated into all tongues: but always with the original in the writing of the Beast; for in the chance shape of the letters and their position to one another: in these are mysteries that no Beast shall divine. Let him not seek to try: but one cometh after him, whence I say not, who shall discover the Key of it all. Then this line drawn is a key: then this circle squared in its failure is a key also. And Abrahadabra. It shall be his child & that strangely. Let him not seek after this; for thereby alone can he fall from it.

48. Now this mystery of the letters is done, and I want to go on to the holier place.

49. I am in a secret fourfold word, the blasphemy against all gods of men.

50. Curse them! Curse them! Curse them!

51.With my Hawk's head I peck at the eyes of Jesus as he hangs upon the cross.

52. I flap my wings in the face of Mohammed & blind him.

53. With my claws I tear out the flesh of the Indian and the Buddhist, Mongol and Din.

54. Bahlasti! Ompehda! I spit on your crapulous creeds.

55. Let Mary inviolate be torn upon wheels: for her sake let all chaste women be utterly despised among you!

56. Also for beauty's sake and love's!

57. Despise also all cowards; professional soldiers who dare not fight, but play: all fools despise!

58. But the keen and the proud, the royal and the lofty; ye are brothers!

59. As brothers fight ye!

60. There is no law beyond Do what thou wilt.

61. There is an end of the word of the God enthroned in Ra's seat, lightening the girders of the soul.

62. To Me do ye reverence! to me come ye through tribulation of ordeal, which is bliss.

63. The fool readeth this Book of the Law, and its comment; & he understandeth it not.

64. Let him come through the first ordeal, & it will be to him as silver.

65. Through the second, gold.

66. Through the third, stones of precious water.

67. Through the fourth, ultimate sparks of the intimate fire.

68. Yet to all it shall seem beautiful. Its enemies who say not so, are mere liars.

69. There is success.

70. I am the Hawk-Headed Lord of Silence & of Strength; my nemyss shrouds the night-blue sky.

71. Hail! ye twin warriors about the pillars of the world! for your time is nigh at hand.

72. I am the Lord of the Double Wand of Power; the wand of the Force of Coph Nia—but my left hand is empty, for I have crushed an Universe; & nought remains.

73. Paste the sheets from right to left and from top to bottom: then behold!

74. There is a splendour in my name hidden and glorious, as the sun of midnight is ever the son.

75. The ending of the words is the Word Abrahadabra.

The Book of the Law is Written
and Concealed.

Aum. Ha.

COMMENTARY
ON

The Book
of The Law

BY
ALEISTER CROWLEY
666

Part One

Part One

COMMENT

In the first edition this book is called L. L is the sacred letter in the Holy Twelve-fold Table which forms the triangle that stabilizes the universe. See *Liber 418*. L is the letter of Libra, Balance, and "Justice" in the Tarot. This title should probably be Al, "El," as the "L" was heard of the voice of Aiwaz, not seen. Al is the true name of the Book, for these letters and their number, 31, form the Master Key to its Mysteries.

In order that the ethical and philosophical comment should be "understood of the common people," without interruption, I have decided to transfer to an appendix all considerations drawn from the numerical system of cipher which is interspersed with the more straightforward matter of this book. In that appendix will be found an account of the character of this cipher, called "Qabalah," and the mysteries thus indicated; because of the impracticability of communicating them in verbal form, and of the necessity of proving to the student that the author of the book is possessed of knowledge beyond any yet acquired by man.

1. Had! The manifestation of Nuit.

OLD COMMENT

1. Compare II, 1, the complement of this verse.

In Nu is Had concealed; by Had is Nu manifested.

Nu being 56 and Had 9, their conjunction results in 65, Adonai, the Holy Guardian Angel.

See the Sepher Sephiroth and "the Wake-World" in "Konx Om Pax" for further details on 65.

Note, however, the sixty-five pages of the MS. of *Liber Legis.*

Or counting NV 56 HAD 10, we get 66, which is Σ (1-11).

Had is further the center of the key word *Abrahadabra.*

NEW COMMENT

The theogony of our Law is entirely scientific. Nuit is matter, Hadit is motion, in their full physical sense.* They are the Tao and Teh of Chinese philosophy; or, to put it very simply, the noun and verb in grammar. Our central truth—beyond other philosophies—is that these two infinities cannot exist apart. This extensive subject must be studied in our other writings, notably *Berashith,* my own Magical Diaries, especially those of 1919, 1920, and 1921, and *The Book of Wisdom or Folly.* See also *The Soldier and the Hunchback.* Further information concerning Nuit and Hadit

---

*The proton and the electron, in a metaphysical sense, suggest close analogies.

is given in the course of this book; but I must here mention that the Brother mentioned in connection with the "Wizard Amalantrah," etc. (Samuel bar Aiwaz), identifies them with Anu and Adad, the supreme mother and father deities of the Sumerians. Taken in connection with the Aiwaz identification, this is very striking indeed.

It is also to be considered that Nu is connected with the north, while Had is Sad, Set, Satan, Sat (equals "being" in Sanskrit), the south. He is then the sun, one point concentrating space, as also is any other star. The word Abrahadabra is from Abrasax, Father Sun, which adds to 365. For the north-south antithesis see Fabre d'Olivet's *Hermeneutic Interpretation of the Origin of the Social State in Man.* Note "sax" also as a rock, or stone, whence the symbol of the Cubical Stone, the Mountain Abiegnus, and so forth. Nu is also reflected in Naus, ship, etc., and that whole symbolism of hollow space which is familiar to all.* There is also a question of identifying Nu with On, Noah, Oannes, Jona, John, Dianus, Diana, and so on. But these identifications are all partial only, different facets of the Diamond Truth. We may neglect all these questions, and remain in the simplicity of this Her own Book.

---

2. The unveiling of the company of heaven.

OLD COMMENT
2. This book is a new revelation, or unveiling of the holy ones.

*In "Berashith" all qualities soever are considered as so many dimensions. I see no reason, nineteen years later, for receding from this view.

NEW COMMENT

This explains the general theme of this revelation: gives the dramatis personae, so to speak.

It is cosmographically, the conception of the two ultimate ideas: space and that which occupies space.

It will, however, appear later that these two ideas may be resolved into one, that of matter; with space, its "condition" or "form," included therein. This leaves the idea of "motion" for Hadit, whose interplay with Nuit makes the universe.

Time should perhaps be considered as a particular kind or dimension of space.

Further, this verse is to be taken with the next. The "company of heaven" is mankind, and its "unveiling" is the assertion of the independent godhead of every man and every woman!

Further, as Khabs (see v.8) is "star," there is a further meaning; this Book is to reveal the Secret Self of a man, i.e., to initiate him.

3. Every man and every woman is a star.

OLD COMMENT

3. This should not be understood in the spiritualistic sense. It means that in each person is the sublime starry nature, a consciousness to be attained by the prescribed methods.

(Yet it may mean some real connection between a given person and a given star. Why not? Still, this is not in my knowledge. See *Liber 418.*)

NEW COMMENT

This thesis is fully treated in *The Book of Wisdom or Folly*. Its main statement is that each human being is an element of the cosmos, self-determined and supreme, co-equal with all other gods.

From this the Law "do what thou wilt" follows logically. One star influences another by attraction, of course, but these are incidents of self-predestined orbits. There is, however, a mystery of the planets, revolving about a star of whom they are parts; but I shall not discuss it fully here.

Man is the middle kingdom. The great kingdom is heaven, with each star as an unit; the little kingdom is the molecule, with each electron as an unit. (The ratio of these three is regularly geometrical, each being 10^{22} times greater in size than its neighbor.)

See *The Book of the Great Auk*[*] for the demonstration that each "star" is the center of the universe to itself, and that a "star" simple, original, absolute, can add to its omnipotence, omniscience and omnipresence without ceasing to be itself; that its one way to do this is to gain experience, and that therefore it enters into combinations in which its true nature is for awhile disguised, even from itself. Analogously, an atom of carbon may pass through myriad Proteus-phases, appearing in chalk, chloroform, sugar, sap, brain and blood, not recognizable as "itself," the black amorphous solid, but recoverable as such, unchanged by its adventures.

This theory is the only one which explains why the Absolute limited itself and why It does not recognize Itself during its cycle of incarnation. It disposes of "evil" and the origin of evil; without denying reality to "evil," or insulting our daily observation and our common sense.

[*]A diary written in the American period, 1914-19, not yet published—I.R.

I here quote (with one or two elucidatory insertions) the original note originally made by me on this subject:

All elements must at one time have been separate—that would be the case with great heat. Now when atoms get to the sun, we get that immense, extreme heat, and all the elements are themselves again. Imagine that each atom of each element possesses the memory of all his adventures in combination. By the way, that atom, fortified with that memory, would not be the same atom; yet it is, because it has gained nothing from anywhere except this memory. Therefore, by the lapse of time and by virtue of memory, a thing (although originally an infinite perfection) could become something more than itself; and thus a real development is possible. One can then see a reason for any element deciding to go through this series of incarnations (God, that was a magnificent conception!) because so, and only so, can he go; and he suffers the lapse of memory of his own reality of perfection which he has during these incarnations, because he knows he will come through unchanged.

Therefore you have an infinite number of gods, individual and equal though diverse, each one supreme and utterly indestructible. This is also the only explanation of how a being could create a world in which war, evil, etc., exist. Evil is only an appearance because, like "good," it cannot affect the substance itself, but only multiply its combinations. This is something the same as mystic monism, but the objection to that theory is that God has to create things which are all parts of himself, so that their interplay is false. If we presuppose many elements, their interplay is natural. It is no objection to this theory to ask who made the elements—the elements are at least there, and God, when you look for him, is not there. Theism is *obscurum per obscurius.* A male star is built up from the center outwards, a female star from the circumference inwards. This is what is meant when we say that woman has no soul. It explains fully the difference between the sexes.

—May 14, 1919; 6:30 P. M.

4. Every number is infinite; there is no difference.

OLD COMMENT

4. The limited is a mere mask; the illimitable is the only truth.

NEW COMMENT

This is a great and holy mystery. Although each star has its own number, each number is equal and supreme. Every man and every woman is not only a part of God, but the Ultimate God. "The center is everywhere and the circumference nowhere." The old definition of God takes new meaning for us. Each one of us is the One God. This can only be understood by the initiate; one must acquire certain high states of consciousness to appreciate it.

I have tried to put it simply in the note to the last verse. I may add that in the trance called by me the "Star-Sponge"—see note to v. 59—this apprehension of the universe is seen as an astral vision. It began as "nothingness with sparkles" in 1916 E. V. by Lake Pasquaney in New Hampshire, U.S.A., and developed into fullness on various subsequent occasions. Each "star" is connected directly with

every other star, and the space being without limit (Ain
Soph, the Body of Nuit), any one star is as much the center
as any other. Each man instinctively feels that he is the
center of the cosmos, and philosophers have jeered at his
presumption. But it was he that was precisely right. The
yokel is no more "petty" than the king, nor the earth than
the sun. Each simple elemental self is supreme, Very God of
Very God. Ay, in this Book is Truth almost insufferably
splendid, for man has veiled himself too long from his own
glory: he fears the abyss, the ageless Absolute. But Truth
shall make him free!

*5. Help me, o warrior lord of Thebes, in my unveiling
before the Children of men!*

OLD COMMENT

5. Nu, to unveil herself, needs a mortal intermediary, in
the first instance.

It is to be supposed that Ankh-f-n-khonsu, the warrior
lord of Thebes, priest of Men Tu, is in some subtle manner
identical with either Aiwass or the Beast.

NEW COMMENT

Here Nuit appeals, simply and directly, recognizing the
separate function of each star of her body. Though all is One,
each part of that One has its own special work, each star its
particular orbit.

In addressing me as warrior lord of Thebes, it appears as
if She perceived a certain continuity or identity of myself
with Ankh-f-n-khonsu, whose Stele is the link with antiquity

of this revelation. See *The Equinox*, Vol. 1, No. 7, pp. 363-400a, for the account of this event.

The unveiling is the proclamation of the truth previously explained, that the Body of Nuit occupies infinite space, so that every star thereof is whole in itself, an independent and absolute unit. They differ as carbon and calcium differ, but each is a simple "immortal" substance, or at least a form of some simpler substance. Each soul is thus absolute, and "good" or "evil" are merely terms descriptive of relations between destructible combinations. Thus quinine is "good" for a malarial patient, but "evil" for the germ of the disease. Heat is "bad" for ice cream and "good" for coffee. The indivisible essence of things, their "souls," are indifferent to all conditions whatsoever, for none can in any way affect them.

---

6. *Be thou Hadit, my secret center, my heart & my tongue!*

7. *Behold! it is revealed by Aiwass the minister of Hoor-paar-Kraat.*

OLD COMMENT

6. The recipient of this knowledge is to identify himself with Hadit, and thus fully express the thoughts of her heart in her very language.

7. Aiwass—see Introduction. He is 78, Mezla the "influence" from the Highest Crown, and the number of cards in the Tarot, Rota, the all-embracing Wheel.

Hoor-paar-kraat. See II, 8.

Aiwass is called the minister of Hoor-paar-kraat, the

God of Silence; for his word is the Speech in the Silence.

NEW COMMENT

Aiwass is the name given by Ouarda the Seer as that of the intelligence communicating. See note to title.

Hoor-paar-Kraat, or Harpocrates, the "Babe in the Egg of Blue," is not merely the God of Silence in a conventional sense. He represents the Higher Self, the Holy Guardian Angel. The connection is with the symbolism of the dwarf in mythology. He contains everything in himself, but is unmanifested. See II, 8.

He is the first letter of the alphabet, Aleph, whose number is one, and his card in the Tarot is the Fool, numbered zero. Aleph is attributed to the element (in the old classification of things) of Air.

Now as "one," or Aleph, he represents the male principle, the first cause, and the free breath of life, the sound of the vowel "A" being made with the open throat and mouth.

As zero he represents the female principle, the fertile mother (an old name for the card is Mat, from the Italian "matto," fool, but earlier also from Maut, the Egyptian Vulture-Mother-Goddess); fertile, for the "Egg of Blue" is the uterus, and in the macrocosm the Body of Nuit, and it contains the unborn babe, helpless yet protected and nourished against the crocodiles and tigers shown on the card, just as the womb is sealed during gestation. He sits on a lotus, the yoni, which floats on the "Nile," the amniotic fluid.

In his absolute innocence and ignorance he is "the Fool"; he is the "Savior," being the Son who shall trample on the crocodiles and tigers, and avenge his father Osiris. Thus we see him as the "Great Fool" of Celtic legend, the "Pure Fool" of Act I of *Parsifal,* and, generally speaking, the insane person whose words have always been taken for oracles.

But to be "Savior" he must be born and grow to manhood; thus Parsifal acquires the Sacred Lance, emblem of virility. He usually wears the "coat of many colors" like Joseph the "dreamer"; so he is also now the Green Man of spring festivals. But his "folly" is now not innocence but inspiration of wine; he drinks from the Graal, offered to him by the Priestess.

So we see him fully armed as Bacchus Diphues, male and female in one, bearing the Thyrsus-rod, and a cluster of grapes or a wineskin, while a tiger leaps up by his side. This form is suggested in the Tarot card, where "the Fool" is shown with a long wand and carrying a sack; his coat is motley. Tigers and crocodiles follow him, thus linking this image with that of Harpocrates.

Almost identical symbols are those of the secret God of the Templars, the bisexual Baphomet, and of Zeus Arrhenothelus, equally bisexual, the Father-Mother of All in One Person. (He is shown in this full form in the Tarot Trump XV, "The Devil.") Now Zeus being the Lord of Air, we are reminded that Aleph is the letter of Air.

As Air we find the "Wandering Fool" pure wanton breath, yet creative. Wind was supposed of old to impregnate the vulture, which therefore was chosen to symbolize the Mother-Goddess.

He is the wandering knight or prince of fairy tales who marries the king's daughter. This legend is derived from certain customs among exogamic tribes, for which see *The Golden Bough.*

Thus Europa, Semele and others claimed that Zeus—Air*—had enjoyed them in the form of a beast, bird, or

---

*Zeus obtained Air for his kingdom in the partition with Hades, who took Fire, and Poseidon, who took Water. Shu is the Egyptian God of the Firmament. There is great difficulty here, etymologically. Zeus is connected with Iao, Abrasax, and the dental sibilant gods of the Great Mysteries, with the south and Hadit,

what not; while later Mary attributed her condition to the agency of a spirit—spiritus, breath, or air—in the shape of a dove.

But the "small person" of Hindu mysticism, the dwarf insane yet crafty of many legends in many lands, is also this same "Holy Ghost," or Silent Self of a man, or his Holy Guardian Angel.

He is almost the "unconscious" of Freud, unknown, unaccountable, the silent spirit, blowing "whither it listeth, but thou canst not tell whence it cometh or whither it goeth." It commands with absolute authority when it appears at all, despite conscious reason and judgment.

Aiwass is then, as this v. 7 states, the "minister" of this Hoor-paar-Kraat, that is of the Savior of the World in the larger sense, and of my own "Silent Self" in the lesser. A "minister" is one who performs a service, in this case evidently that of revealing; He was the intelligible medium between the Babe God—the New Aeon about to be born—and myself. This *Book of the Law* is the Voice of his Mother, His Father, and Himself. But on His appearing, He assumes the active form twin to Harpocrates, that of Ra-Hoor-Khuit. The Concealed Child becomes the Conquering Child, the armed Horus avenging his father Osiris. So also our own Silent Self, helpless and witless, hidden within us, will spring forth, and if we have craft to loose him to the light, spring lustily forward with his cry of battle, the word of our True Will.

This is the Task of the Adept, to have achieved the

Adad, Set, Saturn, Adonai, Attis, Adonis; he is even the "Jesus," slain with the lance, whose blood is collected in a cup. Yet he is also to be identified with the opposite party of the north and Nuit, with the "John" slain with the sword, whose flesh is placed upon a disk, in the Lesser Mysteries, baptizing with Water as "Jesus" with Fire, with On, Oannes, Noah, and the like.

It seems as if this great division, which has wrought such appalling havoc upon earth, were originally no more than a distinction adopted for convenience. It is indeed the task of this book to reduce theology to the interplay of the dyad Nuit and Hadit, these being themselves conceived as complementary, as two equivalent to naught, "divided for love's sake, for the chance of union."

knowledge and conversation of his Holy Guardian Angel, to become aware of his nature and his purpose, fulfilling them.

Why is Aiwass thus spelled, when Aiwaz is the natural transliteration of אױאז = 78? Perhaps because he was not content with identifying himself with Thelema, Agape, etc., by the number 93, but wished to express his nature by six letters (six being the number of the Sun, the God-man, etc.) whose value in Greek should be: A=1, I=10, F=6, A=1, S=200, S=200: total 418, the number of Abrahadabra, the magical formula for the New Aeon! Note that "I" and "V" are the letters of the Father and the Son, also of the Virgin and the Bull (see *Liber 418*), protected on either side by the letter of Air, and followed by the letter of Fire twice over.

---

8. The Khabs is in the Khu, not the Khu in the Khabs.

OLD COMMENT

8. Here begins the text.

Khabs is the secret Light or L.V.X.; the Khu is the magical entity of a man.

I find later (Sun in Virgo, 1911) that Khabs means star. In which case cf. v.3.

The doctrine here taught is that that Light is the innermost, essential man. *Intra* (not *Extra*) *Nobis Regnum Dei.*

NEW COMMENT

We are not to regard ourselves as base beings, without whose sphere is Light or "God." Our minds and bodies are veils of the Light within. The uninitiate is a "dark star," and the Great Work for him is to make his veils transparent by "purifying" them. This "purification" is really "simplification"; it is not that the veil is dirty, but that the complexity of its folds make it opaque. The Great Work therefore consists principally in the solution of complexes. Everything in itself is perfect, but when things are muddled, they become "evil." (This will be understood better in the light of "The Hermit of Esopus Island," q.v.) The doctrine is evidently of supreme importance, from its position as the first "revelation" of Aiwass.

This "star" or "inmost light" is the original, individual, eternal essence. The Khu is the magical garment which it weaves for itself, a "form" for its being beyond form, by use of which it can experience through self-consciousness, as explained in the note to verses 2 and 3. This Khu is the first veil, far subtler than mind or body, and truer; for its symbolic shape depends on the nature of its star.

Why are we told that the Khabs is in the Khu, not the Khu in the Khabs? Did we then suppose the converse? I think that we are warned against the idea of a Pleroma, a flame of which we are sparks, and to which we return when we "attain." That would indeed be to make the whole curse of separate existence ridiculous, a senseless and inexcusable folly. It would throw us back on the dilemma of Manicheeism. The idea of incarnations "perfecting" a thing originally perfect by definition is imbecile. The only sane solution is given previously: to suppose that the Perfect enjoys experience of (apparent) imperfection. (There are deeper resolutions of this problem appropriate to the highest grades of initiation; but the above should suffice the average intelligence.)

9. Worship then the Khabs, and behold my light shed over you!

OLD COMMENT

That Khabs is declared to be the light of Nu. It being worshiped in the center, the light also fills the circumference, so that all is light.

NEW COMMENT

We are to pay attention to this inmost light; then comes the answering light of infinite space. Note that the light of space is what men call darkness; its nature is utterly incomprehensible to our uninitiated minds. It is the "veils" mentioned previously in this comment that obstruct the relation between Nuit and Hadit.

We are not to worship the Khu, to fall in love with our magical image. To do this—we have all done it—is to forget our truth. If we adore form, it becomes opaque to being and may soon prove false to itself. The Khu in each of us includes the cosmos as he knows it. To me, even another Khabs is only part of my Khu. Our own Khabs is our one sole truth.

10. Let my servants be few & secret; they shall rule the many & the known.

OLD COMMENT

10. This is the rule of Thelema, that its Adepts shall be invisible rulers.

This, it may be remarked, has always been the case.

NEW COMMENT

The nature of magical power is quite incomprehensible to the vulgar. The prophet Ezekiel besieging a tile in order to destroy Jerusalem, and the adventure of Hosea with Gomer, seem as absurd to the "practical" man as do the researches of any other scientific man until the Sunday newspapers have furnished him with a plausible explanation which explains nothing. (*Book 4, Part III,* must be read in this connection.)

"My servants"; not those of the Lord of the Aeon. "The Law is for all"; there can be no secrecy about that. The verse refers to specially chosen "servants"; perhaps those who, worshiping the Khabs, have beheld her light shed over them. Such persons indeed consummate the marriage of Nuit and Hadit in themselves; in that case they are aware of certain ways to power.

There is also a mystical sense in this verse. We are to organize our minds thoroughly, appointing few and secret chiefs, serving Nuit, to discipline the varied departments of the conscious thought.

11. These are fools that men adore; both their Gods & their men are fools.

12. Come forth, o children, under the stars, & take your fill of love!

OLD COMMENT

11. "The many and the known," both among Gods and men, are revered; this is folly.

12. The key of the worship of Nu. The uniting of consciousness with infinite space by the exercise of love, pastoral or pagan love. But *vide infra.*

NEW COMMENT

The whole doctrine of "love" is discussed in *Liber Aleph (The Book of Wisdom or Folly)* and should be studied therein. But note further how this verse agrees with the comment above, how every star is to come forth from its veils, that it may revel with the whole world of stars. This is again a call to unite, or "love," thus formulating the equation $1+(-1)=0$*, which is the general magical formula in our cosmos.

"Come forth"—from what are you hiding? "Under the stars," that is openly. Also, let love be "under" or "unto" the Body of Nuit. But above all, be open! What is this shame? Is love hideous, that men should cover him with lies? Is love so sacred that others must not intrude? Nay, "under the stars," at night, what eye but theirs may see? Or, if one see, should not your worship wake the cloisters of his soul to echo sanctity for that so lovely a deed and gracious you have done?

---

13. I am above you and in you. My ecstasy is in yours. My joy is to see your joy.

14. Above the gemmèd azure is
        The naked splendour of Nuit.
    She bends in ecstasy to kiss
        The secret ardours of Hadit.
    The wingèd globe, the starry blue
        Are mine, O Ankh-f-na-khonsu!

15. Now ye shall know that the chosen priest & apostle of infinite space is the prince-priest, the Beast; and in his

*The Hon. Bertrand Russell might prefer to write this: $1+(-1)=0$. For Initiates of the IX° of O.T.O. it could be expressed: $\Phi K = T = 0$, and Φ and K are both positive integers.

woman called the Scarlet Woman is all power given. They shall gather my children into their fold; they shall bring the glory of the stars into the hearts of men.

16. For he is ever a sun, and she a moon. But to him is the winged secret flame, and to her the stooping starlight.

17. But ye are not so chosen.

18. Burn upon their brows, o splendrous serpent!

19. O azure-lidded woman, bend upon them!

20. The key to the rituals is in the secret word which I have given unto him.

21. With the God & the Adorer I am nothing; they do not see me. They are as upon the earth; I am Heaven, and there is no other God than me and my lord Hadit.

22. Now, therefore, I am known to ye by my name Nuit, and to him by a secret name which I will give him when at last he knoweth me. Since I am Infinite Space, and the Infinite Stars thereof, do ye also thus. Bind nothing! Let there be no difference made among you between any one thing and any other thing! For thereby there cometh hurt.

23. But whoso availeth in this, let him be the chief of all.

24. I am Nuit, and my word is six and fifty.

25. Divide, add, multiply, and understand.

26. Then saith the prophet and slave of the beauteous one: Who am I, and what shall be the sign? So she answered him bending down, a lambent flame of blue, all-touching, all-penetrant, her lovely hands upon the black earth, & her lithe body arched for love, and her soft feet not hurting the little flowers: Thou knowest! And the sign shall be my ecstasy, the consciousness of the continuity of existence, the omnipresence of my body.

27. Then the priest answered & said unto the Queen of Space, kissing her lovely brows, and the dew of her light bathing his whole body in a sweet smelling perfume of sweat;

O Nuit, continuous one of Heaven, let it be ever thus: that men speak not of Thee as One but as None; and let them speak not of thee at all, since thou art continuous!

28. None breathed the light, faint and faery, of the stars, and two.

29. For I am divided for love's sake, for the chance of union.

30. This is the creation of the world, that the pain of division is as nothing, and the joy of dissolution all.

31. For these fools of men and their woes care not thou at all! They feel little; what is, is balanced by weak joys; but ye are my chosen ones.

OLD COMMENT

13. This doctrine implies some mystic bond which I imagine is only to be understood by experience; this human ecstasy and that divine ecstasy interact.

A similar doctrine is to be found in the *Bhagavad Gita*.

14. This verse is a direct translation of the first section of the stele. It conceals a certain secret ritual, of the highest rank, connected with the two previous verses.

15. The authority of the Beast rests upon this verse; but it is to be taken in conjunction with certain later verses which I shall leave to the research of students to interpret. I am inclined, however, to believe that "the Beast" and "the Scarlet Woman" do not denote persons, but are titles of office, that of the Hierophant and High Priestess (ו and λ), else it would be difficult to understand the next verse.

16. In II, 16, we find that Had is to be taken as 11(see II, 16, comment). Then Hadit=421, Nuit=466.

421-3 (the moon)=418. 466+200 (the sun)=666.

These are the two great numbers of the Qabalistic

system that enabled me to interpret the signs leading to this revelation.

The winged secret flame is Hadit; the stooping starlight is Nuit; these are their true natures, and their functions in the supreme ritual referred to above.

17. "Ye" refers to the other worshipers of Nuit, who must seek out their own election.

18. The serpent is the symbol of divinity and royalty. It is also a symbol of Hadit, invoked upon them.

19. Nuit herself will overshadow them.

20. This word is perhaps Abrahadabra, the sacred word of 11 letters.

21. Refers to the actual picture on the stele. Nuit is a conception immeasurably beyond all men have ever thought of the Divine. Thus she is not the mere star-goddess, but a far higher thing, dimly veiled by that unutterable glory.

This knowledge is only to be attained by Adepts; the outer cannot reach to it.

22. A promise—not yet fulfilled. [Since Sun in Saggittarius, An. V., fulfilled.] A charge to destroy the faculty discriminating between illusions.

23. The chief, then, is he who has destroyed this sense of duality.

24. Nu ٦٦ =6+50=56.

25. Dividing 6/50=0.12.

0 the circumference, Nuit.

. the center, Hadit.

1 the Unity proceeding, Ra-Hoor-Khuit.

2 = the Coptic H, whose shape closely resembles the Arabic figure 2, the Breath of Life, inspired and expired. Human consciousness. Thoth.

Adding 50+6=56, Nu, and concentrating 5+6=11, Abrahadabra, etc.

Multiplying 50x6=300, ש and Ruach Elohim, the holy spirit.

I am inclined to believe that there is a further mystery concealed in this verse; possibly those of 418 and 666 again.

26. The prophet demanding a sign of his mission, it is promised: a Samadhi upon the Infinite.

This promise was later fulfilled—see "The Temple of Solomon the King," which proposes to deal with the matter in its due season.

27-31. Here is a profound philosophical dogma, in a sense possibly an explanation and illumination of the propositions in *Berashith*.

The dyad (or universe) is created with little pain in order to make the bliss of dissolution possible. Thus the pain of life may be atoned for by the bliss of death.

This delight is, however, only for the chosen servants of Nu. Outsiders may be looked on much as the Cartesians looked on animals.

NEW COMMENT

All this talk about "suffering humanity" is principally drivel based on the error of transferring one's own psychology to one's neighbor. The Golden Rule is silly. If Lord Alfred Douglas (for example) did to others what he would like them to do to him, many would resent his action.

The development of the Adept is by expansion—out of Nuit—in all directions equally. The small man has little experience, little capacity for either pain or pleasure. The bourgeois is a clod. I know better (at least) than to suppose that to torture him is either beneficial or amusing to myself.

This thesis concerning compassion is of the most palmary importance in the ethics of Thelema. It is necessary that we stop, once for all, this ignorant meddling with other people's business. Each individual must be left free to follow his own path! America is peculiarly insane on these points. Her people are desperately anxious to make the Cingalese wear furs and the Tibetans vote, and the whole world chew gum, utterly dense to the fact that most other nations, especially the French and British, regard "American institutions" as the lowest savagery, and forgetful or ignorant of the circumstance that the original brand of American freedom—which really was freedom—contained the precept to leave other people severely alone, and thus assured the possibility of expansion of his own lines to every man.

---

32. Obey my prophet! follow out the ordeals of my knowledge! seek me only! Then the joys of my love will redeem ye from all pain. This is so; I swear it by the vault of my body; by my sacred heart and tongue; by all I can give, by all I desire of ye all.

OLD COMMENT

32. The rule and purpose of the Order: the promise of Nuit to her chosen.

NEW COMMENT

It is proper to obey the Beast, because His Law is pure freedom, and He will give no command which is other than a right interpretation of this freedom. But it is necessary for the development of freedom itself to have an organization; and every organization must have a highly centralized control. This is especially necessary in time of war, as even the so-called democratic nations have been taught by experience, since they would not learn from Germany. Now this age is preeminently a "time of war," most of all now, when it is our work to overthrow the slave-gods.

The injunction "seek me only" is emphasized with an

oath, and a special promise is made in connection with it. By seeking lesser ideals one makes distinctions, thereby affirming implicitly the very duality from which one is seeking to escape. Note also that "me" may imply the Greek MH, "not." The word "only" might be taken as having (in Greek) the number 156, that of the secret name Babalon or Nuit. There are presumably further hidden meanings in the keyword "all."

---

33. Then the priest fell into a deep trance or swoon, and said unto the Queen of Heaven: Write unto us the ordeals; write unto us the rituals; write unto us the law!

OLD COMMENT
33. The prophet then demanded instruction: ordeals, rituals, law.

NEW COMMENT
Law, in the common sense of the word, should be a formulation of the customs of a people, as Euclid's propositions are the formulation of geometrical facts. But modern knavery conceived the idea of artificial law, as if one should try to square the circle by tyranny. Legislators try to force the people to change their customs, so that the "businessmen" whose greed they are bribed to serve may increase their profits.

"Law," in Greek, is NOMOK from NEMO and means strictly "anything assigned, that which one has in use or possession"; hence "custom, usage," and also "a musical strain." The literal equivalence of NEMO and the Latin *Nemo* is suggestive. In Hebrew, "law" is ThORA and equivalent to words meaning "the Gate of the Kingdom" and "the Book of Wisdom."

---

34. But she said: the ordeals I write not; the rituals shall be half known and half concealed: the Law is for all.

OLD COMMENT

34. The first demand is refused, or, it may be, is to be communicated by another means than writing.

(It has since been communicated.)

The second is partially granted; or, if fully granted, is not to be made wholly public.

The third is granted unconditionally.

NEW COMMENT

The ordeals are at present carried out unknown to the candidate by the secret magick power of the Beast. Those who are accepted by Him for initiation testify that these ordeals are frequently independent of His conscious care. They are not, like the traditional ordeals, formal, or identical for all; the candidate finds himself in circumstances which afford a real test of conduct, and compel him to discover his own nature, to become aware of himself by bringing his secret motives to the surface.

Some of the rituals have been made accessible; that is, the magical formulae have been published. See "The Rites of Eleusis," "Energized Enthusiasm," *Magick in Theory and Practice,* etc.

Note the reference to "not" and "all." Also the word "known" contains the root ΓΝ, "to beget," "to know"; while "concealed" indicates the other half of the human mystery.

35. This that thou writest is the threefold book of Law.

36. My scribe Ankh-af-na-khonsu, the priest of the princes, shall not in one letter change this book; but lest there be folly, he shall comment thereon by the wisdom of Ra-Hoor-Khu-it.

37. Also the mantras and spells; the obeah and the wanga; the work of the wand and the work of the sword; these he shall learn and teach.

OLD COMMENT

35. Definition of this book.

36. The first strict charge not to tamper with a single letter of this book.

The comment is to be written "by the wisdom of Ra-Hoor-Khu-it," i.e., by open, not by initiated wisdom.

37. An entirely new system of magic is to be learned and taught, as is now being done.

NEW COMMENT

Each star is unique, and each orbit apart; indeed, that is the cornerstone of my teaching, to have no standard goals or standard ways, no orthodoxies and no codes. The stars are not herded and penned and shorn and made into mutton like so many voters! I decline to bellwether, who am born a lion! I will not be a collie, who am quicker to bite than to bark. I refuse the office of shepherd, who bear not a crook but a club.

Wise in your generation, ye sheep, are ye to scamper away bleating when your ears catch my roar on the wind! Are ye not tended and fed and protected—until word come from the stockyard?

The lion's life for me! Let me live free, and die fighting!

Now one more point about the obeah and the wanga,

the deed and the word of magick. Magick is the art of causing change in existing phenomena. This definition includes raising the dead, bewitching cattle, making rain, acquiring goods, fascinating judges, and all the rest of the program. Good: but it also includes every act whatsoever? Yes; I meant it to do so. It is not possible to utter word or do deed without producing the exact effect proper and necessary thereto. Thus magick is the art of life itself.

Magick is the management of all we say and do, so that the effect is to change that part of our environment which dissatisfies us, until it does so no longer. We "remold it nearer to the heart's desire."

Magick ceremonies proper are merely organized and concentrated attempts to impose our will on certain parts of the cosmos. They are only particular cases of the general law.

But all we say and do, however casually, adds up to more, far more, than our most strenuous operations. "Take care of the pence, and the pounds will take care of themselves." Your daily drippings fill a bigger bucket than your geysers of magical effort. The "ninety and nine that safely lay in the shelter of the fold" have no organized will at all; and their character, built of their words and deeds, is only a garbage heap.

Remember also, that unless you know what your True Will is, you may be devoting the most laudable energies to destroying yourself. Remember that every word and deed is a witness to thought, that therefore your mind must be perfectly organized, its sole duty to interpret circumstances in terms of the will so that speech and action may be rightly directed to express the will appropriately to the occasion. Remember that every word and deed which is not a definite expression of your will counts against it, indifference worse than hostility. Your enemy is at least interested in you: you may make him your friend as you never can do with a neutral. Remember that magick is the art of life, therefore of causing change in accordance with will; therefore its law is "love under will," and its every movement is an act of love.

Remember that every act of "love under will" is lawful as such; but that when any act is not directed unto Nuit, who is here the inevitable result of the whole work, that act is waste, and breeds conflict within you, so that "the kingdom of God which is within you" is torn by civil war.

To the beginner I would offer this program:

- Furnish your mind as completely as possible with the knowledge of how to inspect and control it.
- Train your body to obey your mind, and not to distract its attention.
- Control your mind to devote itself wholly to discover your True Will.
- Explore the course of that will till you reach its source, your Silent Self.
- Unite the conscious will with the True Will, and the conscious ego with the Silent Self. You must be utterly ruthless in discarding any atom of consciousness which is hostile or neutral.
- Let this work freely from within, but heed not your environment, lest you make difference between one thing and another. Whatever it be, it is to be made one with you by love.

38. He must teach; but he may make severe the ordeals.
39. The word of the Law is Θελημα.
40. Who calls us Thelemites will do no wrong, if he look but close into the word. For there are therein Three Grades, the Hermit, and the Lover, and the Man of Earth. Do what

thou wilt shall be the whole of the Law.

41. The word of Sin is Restriction. O man, refuse not thy wife, if she will! O lover, if thou wilt, depart! There is no bond that can unite the divided but love: all else is a curse. Accursed! Accursed be it to the aeons! Hell.

OLD COMMENT

38. The usual charge in a work of this kind.

Every man has a right to attain; but it is equally the duty of the Adept to see that he duly earns his reward, and to test and train his capacity and strength.

39. Compare Rabelais. Also it may be translated, "Let will and action be in harmony."

But Θελημα also means will in the higher sense of magical one-pointedness, and in the sense used by Schopenhauer and Fichte.

There is also most probably a very lofty secret interpretation. I would suggest:

The	the essential את, Azoth, etc.=Θε.
Word	Chokmah, Thoth, the Logos, the Second Emanation.
of	the Partitive, Binah the Great Mother.
the	Chesed, the paternal power, reflection of the "The" above.
Law	Geburah, the stern restriction.
is	Tiphereth, visible existence, the balanced harmony of the worlds.
Θελημα	The idea embracing all this sentence in a word.

Or:

Θ The	= ע the Lion, "Thou shalt unite all these

symbols into the form of a Lion."

ε Word = ה the letter of Breath, the Logos.

λ of = ל ♎ the Equilibrium.

η the = ח 418, Abrahadabra.

μ Law = מ the Hanged Man, or Redeemer.

a is = א the 0 (zero, Nuit, which is Existence).

Θελημα the sum of all.

40. Θε, the Hermit, י invisible, yet illuminating. The A∴A∴

λη, the Lover, ו visible as is the lightning flash. The College of Adepts.

μa, the Man of Earth, פ the Blasted Tower. The 3 Keys add up to 31=לא Not and אל God. Thus is the whole of Θελημα equivalent to Nuit, the all-embracing.

See the Tarot Trumps for further study of these grades.

Θε=14, the Pentagram, rule of spirit over ordered matter. Strength and authority (ט and ה) and secretly 1+4=5, the Hierophant ו V. Also: ♌♈, the Lion and the Ram. Cf. Isaiah. It is a "millennial" state.

λη=38, the key word Abrahadabra, 418, divided by the number of its letters, 11. Justice or Balance and the Charioteer or Mastery. A state of progress; the church militant.

μa=41, the Inverted Pentagram, matter dominating spirit. The Hanged Man and the Fool. The condition of those who are not Adepts.

"Do what thou wilt" need not only be interpreted as license or even as liberty. It may, for example, be taken to mean, Do what thou (Ateh) wilt; and Ateh is 406=תאו=T, the sign of the cross. The passage might then be read as a charge to self-sacrifice or equilibrium.

I only put forward this suggestion to exhibit the

profundity of thought required to deal even with so plain a passage.

All the meanings are true, if only the interpreter be illuminated; but if not, they are all false, even as he is false.

NEW COMMENT

The first paragraph [first sentence of v. 41] is a general statement or definition of sin or error. Any thing whatsoever that binds the will, hinders it, or diverts it, is sin. That is, sin is the appearance of the dyad. Sin is impurity.*

The remainder of the paragraph takes a particular case as an example. There shall be no property in human flesh. The sex instinct is one of the most deeply seated expressions of the will; and it must not be restricted, either negatively by preventing its free function, or positively by insisting on its false function.

What is more brutal than to stunt natural growth or deform it? What is more absurd than to seek to interpret this holy instinct as a gross animal act, to separate it from the spiritual enthusiasm without which it is so stupid as not even to be satisfactory to the persons concerned?

The sexual act is a sacrament of will. To profane it is the great offense. All true expression of it is lawful; all suppression or distortion is contrary to the law of liberty. To use legal or financial constraint to compel either abstention or submission, is entirely horrible, unnatural and absurd. Physical constraint, up to a cerain point, is not so seriously

---

*One cannot say that it was "sin" for Naught to restrict itself within the form of Two; on the contrary. But sin is to resist the operation of the reversion to Naught. "The wages of sin is death"; for life is a continual harmonious and natural change. See *Liber 418* and *Liber Aleph.*

Sin (see *Skeat's Ety. Dict.*) is connected with the root "es," to be. This throws a new light on the passage. Sin is restriction, that is, it is "being" as opposed to "becoming." The fundamental idea of wrong is the static as opposed to the dynamic conception of the universe. This explanation is not only in harmony with the general teaching of *The Book of the Law,* but shows how profoundly the author understands Himself.

wrong; for it has its roots in the original sex-conflict which
we see in animals, and has often the effect of exciting love in
its highest and noblest shape. Some of the most passionate
and permanent attachments have begun with rape. Rome was
actually founded thereon. Similarly, murder of a faithless
partner is ethically excusable, in a certain sense; for there
may be some stars whose nature is extreme violence. The
collision of galaxies in a magnificent spectacle, after all. But
there is nothing inspiring in a visit to one's lawyer. Of course
this is merely my personal view; a star who happened to be a
lawyer might see things otherwise! Yet nature's unspeakable
variety, though it admits cruelty and selfishness, offers us no
examples of the puritan and the prig!

However, to the mind of law there is an order of going;
and a machine is more beautiful, save to the small boy, when
it works than when it smashes. Now the machine of
matter-motion is an explosive machine, with pyrotechnic
effects; but these are only incidentals.

Laws against adultery are based upon the idea that
woman is a chattel, so that to make love to a married woman
is to deprive the husband of her services. It is the frankest
and most crass statement of a slave-situation. To us, every
woman is a star. She has therefore an absolute right to travel
in her own orbit. There is no reason why she should not be
the ideal hausfrau, if that chance to be her will. But society
has no right to insist upon that standard. It was, for practical
reasons, almost necessary to set up such taboos in small
communities, savage tribes, where the wife was nothing but a
general servant, where the safety of the people depended
upon a high birth rate. But today woman is economically
independent, and becomes more so every year. The result is
that she instantly asserts her right to have as many or as few
men or babies as she wants or can get; and she defies the
world to interfere with her. More power to her—elbow!

The war has seen this emancipation flower in four years. Primitive people, the Australian troops, for example, are saying that they will not marry English girls, because English girls like a dozen men a week. Well, who wants them to marry? Russia has already formally abrogated marriage. Germany and France have tried to "save their faces" in a thoroughly Chinese manner, by "marrying" pregnant spinsters to dead soldiers!

England has been too deeply hypocritical, of course, to do more than "hush things up"; and is pretending "business as usual," though every pulpit is aquake with the clamor of bat-eyed bishops, squeaking of the awful immorality of everybody but themselves and their choristers. Englishwomen over thirty have the vote; when the young 'uns get it, goodbye to the old marriage system.

America has made marriage a farce by the multiplication and confusion of the divorce laws. A friend of mine who had divorced her husband was actually, three years later, sued by him for divorce!

But America never waits for laws; her people go ahead. The emancipated, self-supporting American woman already acts exactly like the "bachelor boy." Sometimes she loses her head, and stumbles into marriage, and stubs her toe. She will soon get tired of the folly. She will perceive how imbecile it is to hamstring herself in order to please her parents, or to legitimatize her children, or to silence her neighbors.

She will take the men she wants as simply as she buys a newspaper; and if she doesn't like the editorials, or the comics, it's only two cents gone, and she can get another.

Blind asses! who pretend that women are naturally chaste! The Easterners know better; all the restrictions of the harem, of public opinion, and so on are based upon the recognition of the fact that woman is only chaste when there is nobody around. She will snatch the babe from its cradle, or drag the dog from its kennel, to prove the old saying: *Natura abhorret a vacuo.* For she is the image of the soul of nature, the Great Mother, the Great Whore.

It is to be well noted that the great women of history have exercised unbounded freedom in love. Sappho, Semiramis, Messalina, Cleopatra, Ta Chhi, Pasiphae, Clytemnestra, Helen of Troy, and in more recent times Joan of Arc (by Shakespeare's account), Catherine II of Russia, Queen Elizabeth I of England, George Sand. Against these we can only put Emily Bronte, whose sex suppression was due to her environment, and so burst out in the incredible violence of her art, and the regular religious mystics, Saint Catherine, Saint Theresa, and so on, the facts of whose sex lives have been carefully camouflaged in the interests of the slave-gods. But, even on that showing, the sex life was intense, for the writings of such women are overloaded with sexual expression, passionate and perverted, even to morbidity and to actual hallucination.

Sex is the main expression of the nature of a person; great natures are sexually strong; and the health of any person will depend on the freedom of that function.

(See *Liber CI,* "de Lege Libellum," Cap. IV, in *The Equinox,* Vol. 3, No. 1.)

---

42. Let it be that state of manyhood bound and loathing. So with thy all; thou hast no right but to do thy will.

OLD COMMENT

41-42. Interference with the will of another is the great sin, for it predicates the existence of another. In this duality sorrow consists. I think that possibly the higher meaning is still attributed to *will*.

NEW COMMENT

"Manyhood bound and loathing." An organized state is a free association for the common weal. My personal will to cross the Atlantic, for example, is made effective by cooperation with others on agreed terms. But the forced association of slaves is another thing.

A man who is not doing his will is like a man with cancer, an independent growth in him, yet one from which he cannot get free. The idea of self-sacrifice is a moral cancer in exactly this sense.

Similarly, one may say that not to do one's will is evidence of mental or moral insanity. When "duty points one way, and inclination the other," it is proof that you are not one, but two. You have not centralized your control. This dichotomy is the beginning of conflict, which may result in a Jekyll-Hyde effect. Stevenson suggests that man may be discovered to be a "mere polity" of many individuals. The sages knew it long since. But the name of this polity is Choronzon, mob rule, unless every individual is absolutely disciplined to serve his own, and the common, purpose without friction.

It is of course better to expel or destroy an irreconcilable. "If thine eye offend thee, cut it out." The error in the interpretation of this doctrine has been that it has not been taken as it stands. It has been read: If thine eye offend some artificial standard of crustean morality, the ethics of the herd-men. One would have thought that a mere glance at nature would have sufficed to disclose her scheme of individuality made possible by order.

43. Do that, and no other shall say nay.

OLD COMMENT

43. *No other* shall say *nay* may mean: No-other (=Nuit) shall pronounce the word no, uniting the aspirant with Herself by denying and so destroying that which he is.

NEW COMMENT

The general meaning of this verse is that so great is the power of asserting one's right that it will not long be disputed. For by doing so one appeals to the Law. In practice it is found that people who are ready to fight for their rights are respected, and let alone. The slave-spirit invites oppression.

44. For pure will, unassuaged of purpose, delivered from the lust of result, is every way perfect.

OLD COMMENT

44. Recommends "non-attachment." Students will understand how in meditation the mind which attaches itself to hope of success is just as bound as if it were to attach itself to some base material idea. It is a bond; and the aim is freedom.

I recommend serious study of the word *unassuaged* which appears not very intelligible.

NEW COMMENT

This verse is best interpreted by defining "pure will" as the true expression of the nature, the proper or inherent motion of the matter concerned. It is unnatural to aim at any goal. The student is referred to the *Tao Teh King*. To *Liber LXV*, Cap. II, v. 24. This becomes particularly important in high grades. One is not to do Yoga, etc., in order to get Samadhi, like a schoolboy or a shopkeeper; but for its own sake, like an artist.

"Unassuaged" means "its edge taken off by" or "dulled by." The pure student does not think of the result of the examination.

---

45. The Perfect and the Perfect are one Perfect and not two; nay, are none!

46. Nothing is a secret key of this law. Sixty-one the Jews call it; I call it eight, eighty, four hundred & eighteen.

47. But they have the half: unite by thine art so that all disappear.

48. My prophet is a fool with his one, one, one; are not they the Ox and none by the Book?

49. Abrogate are all rituals, all ordeals, all words and signs. Ra-Hoor-Khuit hath taken his seat in the East at the Equinox of the Gods; and let Asar be with Isa, who also are one. But they are not of me. Let Asar be the adorant, Isa, the sufferer; Hoor in his secret name and splendor is the Lord initiating.

OLD COMMENT

45. Perhaps means that adding perfection to perfection results in the unity and ultimately the negativity.

But I think there is much more than this.

46. 61= א י ן. But the True Nothing of Nuit is 8, 80, 418. Now 8 is ח, which spelled fully, חית, is 418. And 418 is

Abrahadabra, the word of Ra-Hoor-Khuit. Now 80 is פ, the letter of Ra-Hoor-Khuit. [Qy. this.]

47. Let us, however add the Jewish half 61.

8+80+418=506. Cf. Verses 24, 25.

506+61=567=27x21=   ?

But writing 506 qabalistically backwards we get

605, and 605+61=666.

666=6x111, and 111=א=O in Taro. 666=1+2+ . . . +36, the sum of the numbers in the Magic Square of Sol.

666=the Number of the Beast

Or, taking the keys of 8, 80, 418, we get vii., xvi., vii., adding to 30.

30+61=91= אמן, Amen.

This may unite Nuit with Amoun the negative and concealed. Yet to my mind she is the greater conception, that of which Amoun is but a reflection.

48. See above for 111.

"My prophet is a fool," i.e. my prophet has the highest of all grades, since the Fool is א.

I note later (1909, Sun in Aquarius) that v. 48 means that all disappears when 61+8, 80, 418 are reduced to 1. And this may indicate some practical mystic method of annihilation. I am sure (Sun in Libra, 1911) that this is by no means the perfect solution of these marvellous verses.

49. Declares a new system of magic and initiation.

Asar—Isa—is not the Candidate, not the Hierophant.

Hoor—see Cap. III.—is the Initiator.

NEW COMMENT

This verse declares that the old formula of magick—the Osiris; Adonis; Jesus; Marsyas; Dionysus; Attis; etc. formula of the dying god—is no longer efficacious. It rested on the ignorant belief that the Sun died every day, and every year, and that its resurrection was a miracle.

The Formula of the New Aeon recognizes Horus, the child crowned and conquering, as God. We are all members of the Body of God, the Sun; and about our system is the ocean of space. This formula is then to be based upon these facts. Our "evil," "darkness," "illusion," whatever one chooses to call it, is simply a phenomenon of accidental and temporary separateness. If you are "walking in darkness," do not try to make the sun rise by self-sacrifice, but wait in confidence for the dawn, and enjoy the pleasures of the night meanwhile.

The general allusion is to the Equinox Ritual of the Golden Dawn, where the officer representing Horus of the previous six months took the place of the retiring Hierophant, who had represented Osiris.

Isa is the legendary "Jesus," for which Canidian concoction the prescription is to be found in my book bearing that title *Liber DCCCLXXXVIII*.

50. *There is a word to say about the Hierophantic task. Behold! there are three ordeals in one, and it may be given in three ways. The gross must pass through fire; let the fine be tried in intellect, and the lofty chosen ones in the highest. Thus ye have star & star, system & system; let not one know well the other!*

51. *There are four gates to one palace; the floor of that palace is of silver and gold; lapis lazuli & jasper are there; and all rare scents; jasmine and rose, and the emblems of death. Let him enter in turn or at once the four gates; let him stand on the floor of the palace. Will he not sink? Amn. Ho! warrior, if thy servant sink? But there are means and means. Be goodly therefore: dress ye all in fine apparel: eat rich food and drink sweet wines and wines that foam! Also take your*

fill and will of love as ye will, when, where and with whom ye will. But always unto me.

OLD COMMENT

50. Our system of initiation is to be triune.

For the outer, tests of labour, pain, etc.

For the inner, intellectual tests.

For the elect of the A∴A∴, spiritual tests.

Further, the Order is not to hold lodges, but to have a chain system.

51. The candidate will be brought through his ordeals in diverse ways.

The Order is to be of freemen and nobles.

NEW COMMENT

The first section of this verse is connected with the second only by the word "therefore." It appears to describe an initiation, or perhaps the Initiation, in general terms. I would suggest that the palace is the "holy house" or universe of the initiate of the New Law. The four gates are perhaps Light, Life, Love, Liberty—see *De Lege Libellum*. Lapis Lazuli is a symbol of Nuit, Jasper of Hadit. The rare scents are possibly various ecstasies or Samadhis. Jasmine and Rose are hieroglyphs of the two main sacraments, while the emblems of death may refer to certain secrets of a well known exoteric school of initiation whose members, with the rarest exceptions, do not know what it is all about.

The question then arises as to whether the initiate is able to stand firmly in this place of exaltation. It seems to me as if this refers to the ascetic life, commonly considered as an essential condition of participation in these mysteries. The answer is that "there are means and means," implying that no one rule is essential. This is in harmony with our general interpretation of the Law; it has as many rules as there are individuals.

This word "therefore" is easy to understand. We are to enjoy life thoroughly in an absolutely normal way, exactly as all the free and great have always done. The only point to remember is that one is a "member of the Body of God," a star in the Body of Nuit. This being sure, we are urged to the fullest expansion of our several natures, with special attention to those pleasures which not only express the soul, but aid it to reach the higher developments of that expression.

The act of love is to the bourgeois (as the "Christian" is called nowadays) a gross animal gesture which shames his boasted humanity. The appetite drags him at its hoofs; it tires him, disgusts him, diseases him, makes him ridiculous even in his own eyes. It is the source of nearly all his neuroses.

Against this monster he has devised two protections. Firstly, he pretends that it is a fairy prince disguised, and hangs it with the rags and tinsel of romance, sentiment, and religion. He calls it love, denies its strength and truth and worships this wax figure of him with all sorts of amiable lyrics and leers.

Secondly, he is so certain, despite all this theatrical wardrobe-work, that it is a devouring monster, that he resents with insane ferocity the existence of people who laugh at his fears, and tell him that the monster he fears is in reality not a fire-breathing worm, but a spirited horse well trained to the task of the bridle. They tell him not to be a gibbering coward, but to learn to ride. Knowing well how abject he is, the kindly manhood of the advice is, to him, the bitterest insult he can imagine, and he calls on the mob to stone the blasphemer. He is therefore particularly anxious to keep intact the bogey he so dreads; the demonstration that love is a general passion, pure in itself, and the redeemer of all of them that put their trust in Him, is to tear open the raw ulcer of his soul.

We of Thelema are not the slaves of love. "Love under will" is the Law. We refuse to regard love as shameful and degrading, as a peril to body and soul. We refuse to accept it as the surrender of the divine to the animal; to us it is the means by which the animal may be made the winged sphinx which shall bear man aloft to the house of the Gods.

We are then particularly careful to deny that the object of love is the gross physiological object which happens to be nature's excuse for it. Generation is a sacrament of the physical rite, by which we create ourselves anew in our own image, weave in a new flesh-tapestry the romance of our own soul's history. But also love is a sacrament of transsubstantiation whereby we initiate our own souls; it is the wine of intoxication as well as the bread of nourishment. "Nor is he for priest designed/Who partakes only in one kind."

We therefore heartily cherish those forms of love in which no question of generation arises; we use the stimulation effects of physical enthusiasm to inspire us morally and spiritually. Experience teaches that passions thus employed do serve to refine and to exalt the whole being of man or woman. Nuit indicates the sole condition: "But always unto me."

The epicure is not a monster of gluttony, nor the amateur of Beethoven a "degenerate" from the "normal" man whose only music is the tom-tom. So also the poisons which shook the bourgeois are not indulgences, but purifications; the brute whose furtive lust demands that he be drunk and in darkness that he may surrender to his shame, and that he lie about it with idiot mumblings ever after, is hardly the best judge even of Phryne. How much less should he venture to criticize such men and women whose imaginations are so free from grossness that the element of attraction which serves to electrify their magnetic coil is independent of physical form? To us the essence of love is that it is a sacrament unto Nuit, a gate of grace and a road of righteousness to Her high palace, the abode of peerless purity whose lamps are the stars.

"As ye will." It should be abundantly clear from the foregoing remarks that each individual has an absolute and indefeasible right to use his sexual vehicle in accordance with its own proper character, and that he is responsible only to himself. But he should not injure himself and his right aforesaid; acts invasive of another individual's equal rights are implicitly self-aggressions. A thief can hardly complain on theoretical grounds if he is himself robbed. Such acts as rape, and the assault or seduction of infants, may therefore be justly regarded as offenses against the law of liberty, and repressed in the interests of that law.

It is also excluded from "as ye will" to compromise the liberty of another person indirectly, as by taking advantage of the ignorance or good faith of another person to expose that person to the constraint of sickness, poverty, social detriment, or childbearing, unless with the well informed and uninfluenced free will of that person.

One must, moreover, avoid doing another injury by deforming his nature; for instance, to flog children at or near puberty may distort the sensitive nascent sexual character, and impress it with the stamp of masochism. Again, homosexual practices between boys may in certain cases actually rob them of their virility, psychically or even physically.

Trying to frighten adolescents about sex by the bogeys of hell, disease, and insanity, may warp the moral nature permanently, and produce hypochondria or other mental maladies, with perversions of the enervated and thwarted instinct.

Repression of the natural satisfaction may result in addition to secret and dangerous vices which destroy their victim because they are artificial and unnatural aberrations. Such moral cripples resemble those manufactured by beggars by compressing one part of the body so that it is compensated by a monstrous exaggeration in another part.

But on the other hand we have no right to interfere with any type of manifestation of the sexual impulse on a priori grounds. We must recognize that the lesbian leanings of idle and voluptuous women whose refinement finds the grossness of the average male repugnant, are as inexpungably entrenched in righteousness as the parallel pleasures of the English aristocracy and clergy whose aesthetics find women disgusting, and whose self-respect demands that love should transcend animal impulse, excite intellectual intimacy, and inspire spirituality by directing it towards an object whose attainment cannot inflict the degradation of domesticity, and the bestiality of gestation.

Every one should discover, by experience of every kind, the extent and intention of his own sexual universe. He must be taught that all roads are equally royal, and that the only question for him is "Which road is mine?" All details are equally likely to be of the essence of his personal plan, all equally "right" in themselves, his own choice of the one as correct as, and independent of his neighbor's preference for the other.

He must not be ashamed or afraid of being homosexual if he happens to be so at heart; he must not attempt to violate his own true nature because of public opinion, or medieval morality, or religious prejudice would wish he were otherwise. The oyster stays shut in his shell for all Darwin may say about his "low stage of evolution," or Puritans about priapic character, or idealists about his unfitness for civic government.

The advocates of homosexuality—*Primus inter pares,*

John Addington Symonds!—hammer away like Hercules at the spiritual, social, moral, and intellectual advantages of cultivating the caresses of a comrade who combines Apollo with Achilles and Antinous at the expense of escaping from a Chimera with Circe's head, Cleopatra's body, and Cressida's character.

Why can't they let one alone? I agree to agree; I only stipulate to be allowed to be inconsistent. I will confess their creed, so long as I may play the part of Peter until the cock crow thrice.

They urge more strenuously still the claims of homosexuality to heal the hurts and horrors of humanity, almost the "complete cohort." On this point I concur that they argue indisputably, with sober sense to support and stress of suffering to spur them. They prove with Euler's exactness and Hinton's passion that heterosexuality entrains an infinity of ills: jealousies, abortions, diseases, infanticides, frauds, intrigues, quarrels, poverty, prostitution, persecution, idleness, self-indulgence, social stress, overpopulation, sex-antagonism. They show with Poincare's precision that Jesus and Paul struck at the heart of hell when they proclaimed marriage a scourge, and offer the testimony of John and Timothy to support the plea of Plato on behalf of pederastic passion. Out of the court there slunk Mark Antony, his toga to his face, one of the legion of lost souls that woman had withered; behind him groped blind Samson, disinherited Adam, feeling his way along the table where they had piled countless papyri writ with the woes of kings and sages woman-wrecked, and many a map of towns and temples torn and trampled beneath the feet of love, their ashes smoldering still, and smoky with song to witness how Astarte's breath had kindled and consumed them. Extinguished empires owned that their doom was the device of Venus, her vengeance on virility.

By Paul sat Buddha smiling, Ananda's arm about his neck, while Mohammed paced the floor impatiently between two warrior comrades, his belt bearing an iron key, a whip, and a sword, wherewith to limit women's liberty, their love, their life, lest to his loss they lure him.

The Beast is there also, aloof, attentive. He will not weigh the evidence in the balances of any kind of advantage. He will not admit any standard as adequate to assess the Absolute. To him, the pettiest personal whimsy outweighs all wisdom, all philosophy, all private profit and all public prudence. The sexual obol of the meanest is stamped with the signature of his own sovereign soul, lawful and current coin no less than the gold talent of his neighbor. The derelict moon has the same right to drift round earth as Regulus to blaze in the heart of the lion.

Collision is the only crime in the cosmos.

The Beast refuses, therefore, to assent to any argument as to the propriety of any fashion of formulating the soul in symbols of sex. A canon is no less deadly in love than in art or literature; its acceptance stifles style, and its enforcement extinguishes sincerity.

It is better for a person of heterosexual nature to suffer every possible calamity as the indirect environment-evoked result of his doing his True Will in that respect than to enjoy health, wealth and happiness by means either of suppressing sex altogether, or debauching it to the services of Sodom or Gomorrah.

Equally it is better for the androgyne, the urning, or their feminine counterparts to endure blackmailers, private and public, the terrors of police persecution, the disgust, contempt and loathing of the vulgar, and the self-torture of suspecting the peculiarity to be a symptom of a degenerate nature, than to wrong the soul by damning it to the hell of abstinence, or by defiling it with the abhorred embraces of antipathetic arms.

Every star must calculate its own orbit. All is will, and yet all is necessity. To swerve is ultimately impossible; to seek to swerve is to suffer.

The Beast 666 ordains by His authority that every man, every woman, and every intermediately sexed individual, shall be absolutely free to interpret and communicate self by means of any sexual practices whatsoever, whether direct or indirect, rational or symbolic, physiologically, legally, ethically, or religiously approved or no, provided only that all parties to any act are fully aware of all the implications and responsibilities thereof, and heartily agree thereto.

Moreover, the Beast 666 adviseth that all children shall be accustomed from infancy to witness every type of sexual act, as also the process of birth, lest falsehood fog, and mystery stupefy, their minds, whose error else might thwart and misdirect the growth of their subconscious system of soul-symbolism.

"When, where, and with whom ye will."

The phrase "with whom" has been practically covered by the comment "as ye will." One need no more than distinguish that the earlier phrase permits all manner of acts, the latter all possible partners. There would have been no furies for Oedipus, no disaster for Othello, Romeo, Pericles of Tyre, Laon and Cythna, if it were only agreed to let sleeping dogs lie, and mind one's own business. In real life, we have seen in our own times Oscar Wilde, Sir Charles Dilke, Parness, Canon Aitken and countless others, many of them engaged in first-rate work for the world, all wasted, because the mob must make believe to be "moral." This phrase abolishes the eleventh commandment, "Not to be found out," by authorizing incest, adultery, and pederasty, which every one now practices with humiliating precautions, which perpetuate the schoolboy's enjoyment of an escapade, and make shame, slyness, cowardice and hypocrisy the conditions of success in life.

It is also the fact that the tendency of any individual to sexual irregularity is emphasized by the preoccupation with the subject which follows its factitious importance in modern society.

It is to be observed that politeness has forbidden any direct reference to the subject of sex to secure no happier result than to allow Sigmund Freud and others to prove that our every thought, speech, and gesture, conscious or unconscious, is an indirect reference!

Unless one wants to wreck the neighborhood, it is best to explode one's gunpowder in an unconfined space.

There are very few cases of "perverted hunger-instinct" in moderately healthy communities. War restrictions on food created dishonest devices to procure dainties, and artificial attempts to appease the ache of appetite by chemical counterfeits.

The south-sea islanders, pagan, amoral and naked, are temperate lovers, free from hysterical "crimes of passion," sex obsessions, and puritan persecution-mania; perversion is practically unknown, and monogamy is the general custom.

Even the civilized psychopaths of cities, forced into every kind of excess by the omnipresence or erotic suggestions and the contact of crazed crowds seething with suppressed sexuality, are not wholly past physical aid.

They are no sooner released from the persistent pressure by escaping to some place where the inhabitants treat the reproductive and the respiratory organs as equally innocent than they begin insensibly to forget their "fixed idea" forced on them by the foghorn of morality, so that their perversions perish, just as a coiled spring straightens itself when the external compulsion is removed. They revert to their natural sexual characters, which only in rare cases are other than simple, pure, and refined. More, sex itself ceases to play principal boy in the pantomime of life. Other interests resume their proper proportions.

We may now inquire why the Book is at pains to admit as to love "when" and "where" we will. Few people, surely, have been seriously worried about restrictions of time and place. One can only think of lovers who live with fearsome families or in inhospitable lodgings, on a rainy night, buffeted from one police-bullied hotel to another.

Perhaps this permission is intended to indicate the propriety of performing the sexual act without shame or fear, not waiting for darkness or seeking secrecy, but by daylight in public places, as serenely as if it were a natural incident in a morning stroll.

Custom would soon surfeit curiosity, and copulation would attract less attention than a new fashion in frocks. For the existing interest in sexual matters is chiefly because, common as the act is, it is closely concealed. Nobody is excited by seeing others eat. A "naughty" book is as dull as a volume of sermons; only genius can vitalize either.

Beyond this, once love is taken for granted, the morbid fascination of its mystery will vanish. The pander, the prostitute, the parasite will find their occupation gone. Disease will go straight to the doctor instead of to the quack, as it does; the altars of Mrs. Grundy run red with the blood of her faithful! The ignorance or carelessness of a raw youth will no longer hound him to hell. A blighted career or a ruined constitution will no more be the penalty of a moment's exuberance. Above all, the world will begin to appreciate the true nature of the sexual process, its physical insignificance as one among many parts of the body, its transcendent importance as the vehicle of the True Will and the first of the sheaths of the self.

Hitherto our sexual taboos have kept far ahead of

Gilbert and Sullivan. We have made love the lackey to property, as who should pay his rent by sneezing. We have swaddled it in politeness, as who should warn God off the grass. We have muddled it up with morality, as who should frown at the Himalayas on the one hand, and on the other, regulate his behavior by that of an ant-heap.

The Law of Thelema is here!

(It appears pertinent to add that the above ethical theories have stood the test of practice. Experiment shows that complete removal—in the most radical manner—of all the usual restrictions on conduct results, after a brief period of uneasiness of various kinds, in the subject's dropping entirely into the background; the parties concerned became natural, and led what would conventionally be called "strictly moral" lives without even knowing that they were doing so.)

As a postscript, let me contrast with the above theories two actual cases of marriage as it is in England.

No. 1. Mr. W., a solicitor and gentleman farmer of considerable wealth: a Plymouth Brother. Called, in Southsea, Hants., where he practised: "the honest lawyer." Every time that his wife gave birth to a child, or miscarried, she lay for weeks—often months—between life and death, with perityphlitis or peritonitis set up by difficulties of parturition. Yet this man, knowing this well, had gone on and on remorselessly. When I knew him he had eighteen children living, and two more were born during that period. It was evidently his view that he had an absolute right to impregnate his wife, and that it was her business whether she lived or died. During all those years, she was never permitted so much as a month's good health. This Mr. W. was a most kindly and genial man, devoted to her and his family, genuinely pious and tenderhearted. But it never occurred to him to refrain from exercising the right which he possessed to endanger her life every year. (He suffered intensely with anxiety for his wife's health.)

No. 2. Mr. H. a very skillful engraver and die-singer, a man of refined tastes and delicate feelings, sensitive beyond the common run, even of men in a far higher station of life and with a much better education. Since childhood he had suffered continually from an incurable form of psoriasis. This kept him in a state of almost constant irritation, spoiled his sleep, and made him lament that he was "a leper." In fact, the scales of the eruption were so plentiful that his sheets had to be cleaned every morning with a dustpan and brush! He could only obtain relief (before trying to sleep) by being rubbed with oil of wintergreen, which filled his whole house with a loathsome stench. One would have thought that the first wish of a man thus afflicted would be to sleep alone, that it would be utterly repugnant and revolting to him to sleep with another person, for his own sake, apart from any consideration for her. But his wife, herself an invalid—a huge, obese, greasy woman (of middle age when I knew the family), suffering from rheumatoid arthritis, tubercular trouble in the arms, etc.—was his wife: she must be immediately available should Mr. H. want to exercise his conjugal right. (In this case, too, Mrs. H. was likely to die if impregnated.) The extraordinary feature is that so extremely sensitive and refined a man could be so disgustingly callous on such a matter. Even vulgar people fear to appear physically repulsive to the person whom they love. It seems as if the fact of marriage destroys every natural characteristic, and has a set of rules of its own diametrically opposed in spirit and letter to those which govern love. I confidently appeal to impartial observers to say whether the ideals of the Book are not cleaner, more wholesome, more human, and more truly moral than those of marriage as it is.

52. If this be not aright; if ye confound the space-marks, saying: They are one: or saying,they are many; if the ritual be not ever unto me; then expect the direful judgments of Ra Hoor Khuit!

OLD COMMENT

52. But distinctions must not be made before Nuit, either intellectually, morally, or personally.

Metaphysics, too, is intellectual bondage; avoid it!

Otherwise one falls back to the Law of Hoor from the perfect emancipation of Nuit. This is a great mystery, only to be understood by those who have fully attained Nuit and Her secret Initiation.

NEW COMMENT

It is not true to say either that we are separate stars, or one star. Each star is individual, yet each is bound to the others by law. This freedom under law is one of the most difficult yet important doctrines of this Book. So too the ritual—our lives—must be unto Nuit; for She is the Ultimate to which we tend, the asymptote of our curve. Failure in this onepointedness sets up the illusion of duality, which leads to excision and destruction.

"Direful" because Ra Hoor Khuit is a "god of war and of vengeance"; see Cap. III.

The doctrine of the previous verses, which appears not merely to allow sexual liberty in the ordinary sense, but even to advocate it in a sense which is calculated to shock the most abandoned libertine, can do no less than startle and alarm the magician, and that only the more so as he is familiar with the theory and practice of his art. "What is this, in the name of Adonai?" I hear him exclaim: "Is it not the immemorial and unchallenged tradition that the exorcist who would apply himself to the most elementary operations of our art is bound to prepare himself by a course of chastity? Is it not notorious that virginity is by its own virtue one of the most powerful means, and one of the most essential conditions, of all magical works? This is no question of technical formula such as may, with propriety, be modulated in the event of an Equinox of the Gods. It is one of those eternal truths of nature which persist, no matter what the environment, in respect of place or period."

To these remarks I can but smile my most genial assent. The only objection that I can take to them is to point out that the connotation of the word "chastity" may have been misunderstood from a scientific point of view, just as modern science has modified our conception of the relations of the earth and the sun without presuming to alter one jot or tittle of the observed facts of nature. So we may assert that modern discoveries in physiology have rendered obsolete the Osirian conceptions of the sexual process which interpreted chastity as physical abstinence, small regard being paid to the mental and moral concomitants of the refusal to act, still less to the physical indications. The root of the error lies in the dogma of original sin, as a result of which pollution was actually excused as being in the nature of involuntary offense, just as if one were to assert that a sleepwalker who has fallen over a precipice were any less dead than Empedocles or Sappho.

The doctrine of Thelema resolves the whole question in conformity with the facts observed by science and the proprieties prescribed by magick. It must be obvious to the most embryonic tyro in alchemy that if there be any material substance whatsoever endowed with magical properties, one must class, *primus inter pares,* that vehicle of essential humanity which is the first matter of that Great Work wherein our race shares the divine prerogative of creating man in its own image, male and female. It is evidently of minor importance whether the will to create be consciously formulated. Lot in his drunkenness served the turn of his two daughters, no less than Jupiter, who prolonged the night to forty-eight hours in order to give himself time to beget Hercules.

Man is in actual possession of this supreme talisman. It is his "pearl of great price," in comparison with which all other jewels are but gew-gaws. It is his prime duty to preserve the integrity of this substance. He must not allow its quality to be impaired either by malnutrition or by disease. He must not destroy it like Origen and Klingsor. He must not waste it like Onan.

But physiology informs us that we are bound to waste it, no matter what be our continence, so long as we are liable to sleep; and nature, whether by precaution or by prodigality, provides us with so great an excess of the substance that the reproduction of the human race need not slacken, though the proportion of men and women were no more than 3 to 1000. The problem of efficiency consequently appears practically insoluble.

We are now struck with the fact that Nuit commands us to exercise the utmost freedom in our choice of the method of utilizing the services of this our first, our finest and our fieriest talisman; the license appears at first sight unconditioned in the most express and explicit terms that it is possible to employ. The caveat, "But always unto me," sounds like an afterthought. We are almost shocked when, in the following verse, we discover a menace, none the less dread because of the obscurity of its terms.

Our first consideration only adds to our sense of surprised repugnance. It becomes evident that one type of act is forbidden, with the penalty of falling altogether from the law of liberty to the code of crime; and our amazement and horror only increase as we recognize that this single gesture which is held damnable, is the natural exercise of the most fatidical function of nature, the most innocent indulgence of irresistable impulse. We glance back to the previous verse—we examine our charter. We are permitted to take our fill and will of love as we will, when, where and with whom we will, but there is nothing said about why we will. On the contrary, despite the infinite variety of lawful means, there is one and only one end held lawful, and not more than one. The act has only one legitimate object; it must be performed unto Nuit. Further reflection reassures us to some extent, not directly, in the manner of the jurist, but indirectly, by calling our attention to the facts of nature which underlie the ethics of the question. Nuit is that from which we have come, that to which we must return. Evasion of the issue is no more possible than was alternation of the antecedent. *From* Nuit we received this talisman, which conveys our physical identity through the ages of time. *To* Nuit, therefore, we owe it; and to defile any portion of that purest and divinest quintessence of ourselves is evidently the supreme blasphemy. Nothing in nature can be misapplied. It is our first duty to ourselves to preserve the treasure entrusted to us: "What shall it profit a man if he gain the whole world and lose his own soul?"

The nature of man is individual. No two faces are identical, still less are two individuals. Unspeakable is the variety of form and immeasurable the diversity of beauty, but in all is the seal of unity, inasmuch as all cometh from the womb of Nuit—to it returneth all. The apprehension of this sublimity is the mark of divinity. Knowing this, all is liberty; ignorant of this, all is bondage. As no two individuals are identical, so also, there can be no identity between the quintessential expressions of the will of any two persons; and the expression of each person, in the first instance, as his purely physical prerogative, is his sexual gesture.

One cannot say that any significance of that gesture is forbidden, for "there is no law beyond Do what thou wilt." But this may and shall be said, that a significance which indicates ignorance or forgetfulness of the central truth of the universe, is an acquiesence in that opacity caused by the confusion of the veils which conceal the soul from the consciousness, and thus create the illusion which the aspirant calls sorrow, and the uninitiate, evil.

The sexual act, even to the grossest of mankind, is the agent which dissipates the fog of self for one ecstatic moment. It is the instinctive feeling that the physical spasm is symbolic of that miracle of the Mass, by which the material wafer, composed of the passive elements, earth and water, is transmuted into the substance of the Body of God, that makes the wise man dread lest so sublime a sacrament suffer profanation. It is this that has caused him, in half-instinctive, half-intellectual, half-comprehension of the nature of the truth, which has driven him to fence the act about with taboos. But a little knowledge is a dangerous thing, his fear has created phantoms, and his malobservation suggested precautions scarce worthy to be called empirical. We see him combat analogous difficulties in a precisely similar manner. History shows us the physician defending mankind against plague, with exorcisms on the one hand and useless herbs on the other. A charred stake is driven through the heart of a vampire, and his victim is protected with garlic. The strength of God, who can doubt? The strength of taste and of smell are known facts. So they measured strength against strength without considering whether the one was appropriate to the other, any more than as if one were to ward off the strength of steel swords by the strength of the color of one's armor. Modern science, by correct classification, has expounded the doctrine of the magical link. We no longer confuse the planes.

We manipulate physical phenomena by physical means; mental by mental. We trace things to their true causes, and no longer seek to cut the Gordian knot of our ignorance by the sword of a postulated pantheon.

Physiology leaves us in no doubt as to the power of our inherited talisman. And modern discoveries in psychology have made it clear enough that the sexual peculiarities of people are hieroglyphs, obscure yet not unintelligible, revealing their histories in the first place, in the second, their relations with environment in the present, and in the third, their possibilities with regard to the modification of the future.

In these supremely important verses of *The Book of the Law,* it becomes clear that Nuit is aware of all these facts, and that she regards them as no less than the combination of the lock of the strong room of the future. "This [doctrine] shall regenerate the world, the little world, my sister." The misunderstanding of sex, the ignorant fear like a fog, the ignorant lust like a miasma, these things have done more to keep back humanity from the realization of itself, and from intelligent cooperation with its destiny, than any other dozen things put together. The vileness and falseness of religion itself have been the monsters aborted from the dark womb of its infernal mystery.

There is nothing unclean or degrading in any mainfestation whatsoever of the sexual instinct, because, without exception, every act is an impulsively projected image of the will of the individual who, whether man or woman, is a star; the Pennsylvanian with his pig no less than the Spirit with Mary; Sappho with Atthis and Apollo with Hyacinth as perfect as Daphnis with Chloe or as Galahad vowed to the Graal. The one thing needful, the all-perfect means of purification, consecration, and sanctification, is independent of the physical and moral accidents circumstantial of the particular incident, is the realization of love as a sacrament. The use of the physical means as a magical operation, whose formula is that by uniting two opposites, by dissolving both, annihilating both, to create a third thing which transcends that opposition, the phase of duality which constitutes the consciousness of imperfection, is perceived as the absolute negative whose apprehension is identical with that duality, is the accomplishment of the Great Work.

The anacephalepsis of these considerations is this: 1.) The accidents of any act of love, such as its protagonists and their peculiarities of expression on whatever plane, are totally immaterial to the magical import of the act. Each person is responsible to himself, being a star, to travel in his own orbit, composed of his own elements, to shine with his own light, with the color proper to his own nature, to revolve and to rush with his own inherent motion, and to maintain his own relation with his own galaxy in its own place in the universe. His existence is his sole and sufficient justification for his own matter and manner. 2.) His only possible error is to withdraw himself from this consciousness of himself as both unique in himself and necessary to the norm of nature.

To bring down this doctrine to a practical rule for every man or woman by which they may enjoy, in perfection, their sexual life and make it what it rightly is, the holiest part of the religious life (I say "Holiest" because it redeems even physical grossness to partake with spiritual saintship)—the intention of the Book of the Law is perfectly simple.

Whatever your sexual predelictions may be, you are free, by the Law of Thelema, to be the star you are, to go your own way rejoicing. It is not indicated here in this text, though it is elsewhere implied, that only one symptom warns that you have mistaken your True Will, and that is, if you should imagine that in pursuing your way you interfere with that of another star. It may, therefore, be considered improper, as a general rule, for your sexual gratification to destroy, deform, or displease any other star. Mutual consent to the act is the condition thereof. It must, of course, be understood that such consent is not always explicit. There are cases when seduction or rape may be emancipation or initiation to another. Such acts can only be judged by their results.

The most important condition of the act, humanly speaking, is that the attraction should be spontaneous and irresistible; a leaping up of the will to create with lyrical frenzy. This first condition once recognized, it should be surrounded with every circumstance of worship. Study and experience should furnish a technique of love. All science, all art, every elaboration should emphasize and adorn the expression of the enthusiasm. All strength and all skill should be flung with a spendthrift gesture on the counter of the merchant of madness. On the steel of your helmet let there be gold inlaid with the motto "Excess."

The above indications are taken from a subsequent passage of the third chapter of this Book.

The supreme and absolute injunction, the crux of your knightly oath, is that you lay your lance in rest to the glory of your Lady, the Queen of the Stars, Nuit. Your knighthood depends upon your refusal to fight in any lesser cause. That is what distinguishes you from the brigand and the bully. You give your life on Her altar. You make yourself worthy of Her by your readiness to fight at any time, in any place, with any weapon, and at any odds. For Her, from Whom you come, of Whom you are, to Whom you go, your life is no more and no less than one continuous sacrament. You have no word but her praise, no thought but love of Her. You have only one cry, of inarticulate ecstasy, the intense spasm, possession of Her, and Death, to Her. You have no act but the priest's gesture that makes your body Hers. The wafer is the disk of the Sun, the Star in Her Body. Your blood is spilt from your heart with every beat of your pulse into her cup. It is the wine of Her life crushed from the grape of your sun-ripened wine. On this wine you are drunk. It washes your corpse that is as the fragment of the Host, broken by you, the Priest, into Her golden chalice. You, Knight and Priest, of the Order of the Temple, saying Her mass become God in Her, by love and death. This act of love, though in its form it be with a horse like Caligula, with a mob like Messalina, with a giant like Heliogabalus, with a pollard like Nero, with a monster like Baudelaire, though with de Sade it gloat on blood, with Sacher-Masoch crave for whips and furs, with Yvette Guilbert crave the glove, or dote on babes like E. T. Reed of "Punch"; whether one love oneself disdaining every other like Narcissus, offer oneself loveless to every love like Catherine, or find the body so vain as to enclose one's lust in the soul and make one lifelong spinthria unassuaged in imagination like Aubrey Beardsley, the means matter no whit. Bach takes one way, Keats one, Goya one. The end is everything: that by the act, whatever it is, one worships, loves, possesses, and becomes Nuit.

The acts of love can no more "trammel up the consequences" than any other act. As long as you possess the talisman, it must be used from time to time, whether you will or no. If you injure the quality, or diminish the quantity, of that quintessence, you blaspheme yourself, and betray the trust reposed in you when you accepted the obligation of that austerely chivalrous order called manhood. The powers of the talisman are irresistible like every other natural force. Every time they are used a child must be begotten. This child must be in your own image, a symbol of your nature, being transformed. It is contrary to nature that a man, with potentialities which can transform the face of the earth, should become nothing but inert carrion when he happens to die. Everything that he was must inevitably persist; and if the manifestation be not to one set of senses, why then, to another! The idea of creation from nothing of something and the destruction of something to nothing, exploded with the theory of phlogiston.

It stands plain, even to skeptical reason—indeed, most of all to the skeptic—that our talisman, one microscopic serpent of which can build for itself such a house as to rule man's bodies for a generation like Alexander, or their minds for an epoch like Plato, cannot be destroyed or diminished by any conceivable force.

When this talisman comes forth from its fortress, its action begins. The ancient Jewish rabbis knew this, and taught that before Eve was given to Adam, the demon Lilith conceived by the spilth of his dreams, so that the hybrid races of satyrs, elves and the like began to populate those secret places of the earth which are not sensible by the organs of the normal man.

I take it as certain that every offering of this talisman infallibly begets children on one plane or anogher of this our cosmos, whose matter is so varied in kind. Such a child must partake of its father's nature; and its character will be determined partly by the environment in which it is bred to manifestation, lives, and ultimately changes in what we call death, and partly by the inmost will of the father, perhaps modified to some extent by his conscious will at the time of his slipping the leash.

This being so, it becomes tremendously important to a man that he should become conscious of his true, inmost will, of his essential nature. This is the Great Work whose attainment constitutes adeptship, provided that the consciousness recognizes that its own dependence on circumstance makes it no more than a troubled image in foul water of the sun which is that Silent Self. If such a man wants to develop his powers, he must use this tremendous talisman to create in his own image.

Although this talisman has such miraculous might, it is also intensely sensitive. Put in an unsuitable environment, it may produce grotesque or malignant perversions of its father's word. We are all aware that fine children are born of healthy mothers who are true and worthy mates of their husbands. The children of hate, of debauch, of sickness, nearly always bear witness in body and mind to the abuse of the talisman. Not only the sins of the father but those of the mother, yea, more, those of their social surroundings, are visited on the children to the third and fourth generation. Nay, more, the mischief can never be mended. A man can destroy in a minute his kingdom, inherited from unnumbered dynasties of biological prudence.

It will also be admitted, without reference to magick, that the abuse of the talisman leads to moral, mental and spiritual misfortune. Crime and insanity, as well as disease and debility, are constantly seen as the direct result of mismanaging the sexual life, either tactically, strategically or both.

The Book of the Law emphasizes the importance of these considerations. The act of love must be spontaneous, in absolute freedom. The man must be true to himself. Romeo must not be thrust on Rosaline for family, social or financial reasons. Desdemona must not be barred from Othello for reasons of race or religion. The homosexual must not blaspheme his nature and commit spiritual suicide by suppressing love or attempting to pervert it, as ignorance and fear, shame and weakness, so often induce him to do.

Whatever the act which expresses the soul, that act and no other is right.

But, on the other hand, whatever the act may be, it is

always a sacrament; and, however profaned, it is always efficient. To profane it is only to turn food into poison. The act must be pure and passionate. It must be held as the union with God in the heart of the Holy of Holies. One must never forget that a child will be born of that deed. One must choose the environment appropriate to the particular child which one wills to create. One must make sure that the conscious will is written, on the pure waters of a mind unstirred, in letters of fire, by the sun of the soul. One must not create confusion in the talisman which belongs to the Silent Self, by letting the speaking self deny the purpose which produced it. If one's True Will, the reason of one's incarnation, be to bring peace on earth, one must not perform an act of love with motives of jealousy or emulation.

One must fortify one's body to the utmost, and protect it from every disaster, so that the substance of the talisman may be as perfect as possible. One must calm the mind, increasing its knowledge, organizing its powers, resolving its tangles, so that it may truly apprehend the Silent Self, judge partial pleas and unbalanced opinions, while supporting the concentration of the will by its fortified frontiers, and, with unanimous enthusiasm, acclaiming the lordship of the thought which expresses the act. The will must seal itself upon the substance of the talisman. It must be, in alchemical language, the sulfur which fixes the mercury which determines the nature of the salt. The whole man, from his inmost Godhead to the tip of his tiniest eyelash, must be one engine, cumbered with nothing useless, nothing inharmonious; a thunderbolt from the hand of Jove. It must give itself utterly in the act of love. It must cease to know itself as anything but the will.

Last of all, the act must be supreme. It must do and it must die. From that death it must rise again, purged of that will, having accomplished it so perfectly that nothing is left therof in its elements. It must have emptied itself into the vehicle. So shall the child be whole of spirit.

But this is not enough. The ground in which the seed is cast must be suitable for its reception. The climate must be favorable, the soil must be prepared, and the enemies of the young child that seek its life must be driven beyond range of malice. These points are obvious enough, if applied to the ordinary affair of breeding children. One needs the right woman, and the right conditions for her. It applies even more closely to other acts, for woman is protected by generations of biological adaptation, whereas spiritual children are more easily diseased and deformed, being of subtler and more sensitive matter. So infinitely varied are the possibilities of creation that each Adept must work out each problem for himself as best he can. There are magical methods of making a link between the force generated and the matter on which it desired to act; but these are, for the most part, best communicated by private instruction and developed by personal practice. The crude description is a bare framework, and (even so) more often misleads than not.

But the general rule is to arrange all the conditions beforehand with intent to facilitate the manifestation of the thing willed, and to prevent the danger of abortion by eliminating discordant elements.

For instance: a man seeking to regain health should assist his magical will by taking all possible hygienic and medical measures proper to amend his malady. A man wishing to develop his genius as a sculptor will devote himself with beautiful forms, and, if possible, live in a place where nature herself testifies to the touch of the thumb of the Great Architect.

He will choose the object of his passion at the nod of his Silent Self. He will not allow the prejudice, either of sense, emotion, or rational judgment, to obscure the sun of his soul. In the first place, mutual magnetism, despite the masks of mind, should be unmistakable. Unless it exists, a puissant purity of passion, there is no magical basis for the sacrament. Yet, such magnetism is only the first condition. Where two people become intimate, each crisis of satisfaction between the terminals leaves them in a proximity which demands mutual observation; and the intense clarity of the mind which results from the discharge of the electric force makes such observation abnormally critical. The higher the type of mind, the more certain this is, and the greater the danger of finding some antipathetic trifle which experience tells us will one day be the only thing left to observe; just as a wart on the nose is remembered when the rest of the face is forgotten.

The object of love must therefore be one with the lover in something more than the will to unite magnetically; it must be in the passionate partnership with the will of which the will-to-love is only the magical symbol. Perhaps no two wills can be identical, but at least they can be so sympathetic that the manifestations are not likely to clash. It is not enough to have a relationship with a partner of the passive type who bleats, "Thy will be done"—a relationship that ends in contempt, boredom and distrust. One wants a passion that can blend with one's own. Where this is the case, it does not matter so much whether the mental expression is syndromic; it is, indeed, better when two entirely different worlds of thought and experience have led to sister conclusions. But it is essential that the habit of mind should be sympathetic, that the machinery should be constructed on similar principles. The psychology of the one should be intelligible to the other.

Social position and physical appearance and habits are of far less importance, especially in a society which has accepted the Law of Thelema. Tolerance itself produces suavity, and suavity soon relieves the strain on tolerance. In any case, most people, especially women, adapt themselves adroitly enough to their environemnt. I say "especially women" for women are nearly always conscious of an important part of their True Will, the bearing of children. To them nothing else is serious in comparison, and they dismiss questions which do not bear on this as trifles, adopting the habits required of them in the interest of domestic harmony which they recognize as a condition favorable to reproduction.

I have outlined ideal conditions. Rarely indeed can we realize even a third of our possibilities. Our magical engine is mighty indeed when its efficiency reaches fifty percent of its theoretical horsepower. But the enormous majority of mankind have no idea whatever of taking love as a sacred and serious thing, of using the eye of the microscopist, or the heart and brain of the artist. Their ignorance and their shame have made love a carcass of pestilence; and love has avenged the outrage by crushing their lives when they pull down the temple upon themselves.

The chance of finding a suitable object of love has been reduced well nigh to zero by substituting for the actual conditions, as stated in the above paragraphs, a totally artificial and irrelevant series; the restrictions on the act itself, marriage, opinion, the conspiracy of silence, criminal laws, financial fetters, selections limited by questions of race, nationality, caste, religion, social and political cliqueishness, even family exclusiveness. Out of the millions of humanity, the average person is lucky if he can take his pick of a couple of score of partners.

I will here add one further pillar to my temple. It happens only too often that two people, absolutely fitted in every way to love each other, are totally debarred from expressing themselves by sheer ignorance of the technique of the act. What nature declares as the climax of the Mass, the manifestation of God in the flesh, when the flesh is begotten, is so gross, clumsy and brutal that it disappoints and disgusts. They are horribly conscious that something is wrong. They do not know how to amend it. They are ashamed to discuss it. They have neither the experience to guide nor the imagination to experiment. Countless thousands of delicate-minded lovers turn against love and blaspheme him. Countless millions, not quite so fixed in refinement, accept the fact, acquiesce in the foulness, till love is degraded to guilty grovelling. They are dragged in the dirt of the night-cart which ought to have been their "chariot of fire and the horses thereof."

This whole trouble comes from humanity's horror of love. For the last hundred years, every first-rate writer on morals has sent forth his lightnings and thunders, hailstones and coals of fire, to burn up Gomorrah and Sodom where love is either shameful and secret, or daubed with the dung of sentiment in order that the swinish citizens may recognize their ideal therein. We do not tell the artist that his art is so sacred, so disgusting, so splendid and so disgraceful that he must not on any account learn the use of the tools of his trade, and study in school how to see with his eye, and record what he sees with his hand. We do not tell the man who would heal disease that he must not know his subject, from anatomy to pathology; or bid him undertake to remove an appendix from a valued archbishop the first time he takes scalpel in hand.

But love is an art no less than Rembrandt's, a science no less than Lister's. The mind must make the heart articulate, and the body the temple of the soul. The animal instinct in man is the twin of the ape's, of the bull's. Yet this is the one thing lawful in the code of the bourgeois. He is right to consider the act, as he knows it, degrading. It is, indeed, for him, an act ridiculous, obscene, gross, beastly; a wallowing unworthy either of the dignity of man or of the majesty of the God within him. So is the guzzling and the swilling of the savage as he crams his enemy's raw liver into his mouth, or tilts the bottle of trade gin, and gulps. Because his meal is loathely, must we insist that any methods but his are criminal? How did we come to Laperouse and Nichol from the cannibal's cauldron unless by critical care and vigorous research?

The act of love, to the bourgeois, is a physical relief like defecation, and a moral relief from the strain of the drill of decency; a joyous relapse into the brute he has to pretend he despises. It is a drunkenness which drugs his shame of himself, yet leaves him deeper in disgust. It is an unclean gesture, hideous and grotesque. It is not his own act, but forced on him by a giant who holds him helplessly; he is half madman, half automaton when he performs it. It is a gawky stumbling across a foul black bog, oozing a thousand dangers. It threatens him with death, disease, disaster in all manner of forms. He pays the coward's price of fear and loathing when peddler sex holds out his rat-poison in the lead-paper wrapping he takes for silver; he pays again with vomiting and with colic when he has gulped it in his greed.

All this he knows, only too well; he is right, by his own lights, to loathe and fear the act, to hide it from his eyes, to swear he knows it not. With tawdry rags of sentiment, sacksful of greasy clouts, he swathes the corpse of love, and, smirking, sputters that love had never a naked limb; then as the brute in him stirs sleepily, he plasters love with mire, and leering grunts that love was never a god in the temple man, but a toothsome lump of carrion in the corner of his sty.

But we of Thelema, like the artist, the true lover of love, shameless and fearless, seeing God face to face alike in our own souls within and in all nature without, though we use, as the bourgeois does, the word love, we hold not the word "too often profaned for us to profane it"; it burns inviolate in its sanctuary, being reborn immaculate with every breath of life. But by "love" we mean a thing which the eye of the bourgeois hath not seen, nor his ear heard; neither hath his heart conceived it. We have accepted love as the meaning of change, change being the life of all matter whatsoever in the universe. And we have accepted love as the mode of motion, of the will to change. To us every act, as implying change, is an act of love; life is a dance of delight, its rhythm an infinite rapture that never can weary or stale. Our personal pleasure in it is derived not only from our own part in it, but from our conscious apprehension of its total perfections. We study its structure, we expand ourselves as we lose ourselves in understanding it, and so becoming one with it. With the Egyptian initiate we exclaim, "There is no part of us that is not of the Gods," and add the antistrophe, "There is no part of the Gods that is not also of us."

Therefore, the love that is Law is no less love in the petty personal sense; for love that makes two one is the engine whereby even the final two, self and not-self, may become one, in the mystic marriage of the bride, the soul, with Him appointed from eternity to espouse her; yea, even the Most High, God All-in-All, the Truth.

Therefore we hold Love holy, our heart's religion, our mind's science. Shall He not have His ordered rite, His priests and poets, His makers of beauty in color and form to adorn Him, His makers of music to praise Him? Shall not His theologians, divining His nature, declare Him? Shall not even those who but sweep the courts of His temple, partake thereby of His person? And shall not our science lay hands on Him, measure Him, discover the depths, calculate the heights, and decipher the laws of His nature?

Also, to us of Thelema, thus having trained our hearts and minds to be expert engineers of the sky-cleaver love, the ship to soar to the sun, to us the act of love is the consecration of the body to love. We burn the body on the altar of love, that even the brute may serve the will of the soul. We must then study the art of bodily love. We must not balk or bungle. We must be cool and competent as surgeons; brain, eye and hand the perfectly trained instruments of will.

We must study the subject openly and impersonally, we must read textbooks, listen to lectures, watch demonstrations, earn our diplomas ere we enter practice.

We do not mean what the bourgeois means when we say "the act of love." To us it is not the gross gesture as of a man in a seizure, a snorting struggle, a senseless spasm, and a sudden revulsion of shame, as it is to him.

We have an art of expression; we are trained to interpret the soul and the spirit in terms of the body. We do not deny the existence of the body, or despise it; but we refuse to regard it in any other light than this: it is the organ of the self. It must nevertheless be ordered according to its own laws; those of the mental or moral self do not apply to it. We love; that is, we will to unite; then the one must study the other, divine every butterfly thought as it flits, and offer the flower it most fancies. The vocabulary of love is small, and its terms are hackneyed; to seek new words and phrases is to be affected, stilted. It chills.

But the language of the body is never exhausted; one may talk for an hour by means of an eyelash. There are intimate, delicate things, shadows of the leaves of the tree of the soul that dance in the breeze of love, so subtle that neither Keats nor Heine in words, neither Brahms nor Debussy in music, could give them body. It is the agony of every artist—the greater he, the more fierce his despair—that he cannot compass expression. And what they cannot do, not once in a life of ardor, is done in all fullness by the body that, loving, hath learned the lesson of how to love.

Addendum: More generally, any act whatsoever may be used to attain any end whatsoever by the magician who knows how to make the necessary links.

---

53. This shall regenerate the world, the little world my sister, my heart & my tongue, unto whom I send this kiss. Also, o scribe and prophet, though thou be of the princes, it shall not assuage thee nor absolve thee. But ecstasy be thine and joy of earth; ever To me! To me!

OLD COMMENT
53. The prophet is retained as the link with the lower. Again the word "assuage" is used in a sense unintelligible to me.

NEW COMMENT
It is clear that this "kiss" (i.e., this Book) will regenerate earth by establishing the law of liberty. "My heart and my tongue" seems a mere phrase of endearment; but has possibly some deep significance which at present escapes me.

The second paragraph [sentence] is perhaps in answer to some unspoken thought of my own that my work was accomplished. No: though I be "of the princes" with the right to enter into my reward, it is my destiny to continue my Work.*

"Assuage thee": satisfy thine aspiration to attainment. "Absolve thee": relieve thee from further duty.

54. Change not as much as the style of a letter; for behold! thou, o prophet, shall not behold all these mysteries hidden therein.

NEW COMMENT

The subject changes most abruptly, perhaps answering some unspoken comment of the scribe on the capital "T's" in "To me."

This injunction was most necessary, for had I been left to myself, I should have wanted to edit the Book ruthlessly. I find in it what I consider faults of style, and even of grammar; much of the matter was at the time of writing most antipathetic. But the Book proved itself greater than the scribe; again and again have the "mistakes" proved themselves to be devices for transmitting a wisdom beyond the scope of ordinary language.

55. The child of thy bowels, he shall behold them.

56. Expect him not from the East, nor from the West; for from no expected house cometh that child. Aum! All words are sacred and all prophets true; save only that they understand a little; solve the first half of the equation, leave the second unattacked. But thou hast all in the clear light, and some, though not all, in the dark.

OLD COMMENT

54-56. to the word "child": A prophecy, not yet (May, 1909, o.s.) fulfilled, so far as I know. I take it in its obvious sense.

56. From the word "Aum": All religions have some

truth. We possess all intellectual truth, and some, not all, mystic truth.

NEW COMMENT

All previous systems have been sectarian, based on a traditional cosmography both gross and incorrect. Our system is based on absolute science and philosophy. We have "all in the clear light," that of reason, because our mysticism is based on an absolute skepticism. But at the time of this writing I had very little mystical expericnce indeed, as my record shows. The fact is that I was far, far from the grade even of Master of the Temple.

So I could not properly understand this Book; how then could I effectively promulgate it? I comprehended but dimly that it contained my word; for the Grade of Magus then seemed to me unthinkably high above me. Also, let me say that the true secrets of this grade are unfathomable and awful beyond all expression; the process of initiation thereto was continuous over years, and contained the most sublime mystical experiences—beyond any yet recorded by man—as mere incidents in its terrific pageant.

The "equation" is the representation of Truth by Word.

---

57. Invoke me under my stars! Love is the law, love under will. Nor let the fools mistake love; for there are love and love. There is the dove, and there is the serpent. Choose ye well! He, my prophet, hath chosen, knowing the law of the fortress, and the great mystery of the House of God.

All these old letters of my Book are aright, but צ is not the Star. This also is secret: my prophet shall reveal it to the wise.

OLD COMMENT

57. Invoke me, etc., I take literally, See *Liber NV* for this ritual.

Love under will—no casual pagan love; nor love under fear, as the Christians do. But love magically directed, and used as a spiritual formula.

The fools (not here implying א fools, for III, 57, says, All fools despise) may mistake.

This love, then should be the serpent love, the awakening of the Kundalini. The further mystery is of פ and unsuited to the grade in which this comment is written.

The last paragraph confirms the Tarot attributions as given in 777. With one secret exception.

NEW COMMENT

"Love is the law, love under will," is an interpretation of the general law of will. It is dealt with fully in the *Book Aleph*. I here insert a few pertinent passages from that book:

> This is the evident and final solvent of the knot philosophical concerning fate and free will, that it is thine own self, omniscient and omnipotent, sublime in eternity, that first didst order the course of thine own orbit, so that that which befalleth thee by fate is indeed the necessary effect of thine own will. These two, then, that like gladiators have made war in philosophy through these many centuries, are made one by the love under will which is the Law of Thelema.

> O my Son, there is no doubt that resolveth not in certainty and rapture at the touch of the wand of our Law, and thou apply it with wit. Do thou grow constantly in the assimilation of the Law, and thou shalt be made perfect.

> Behold, there is a pageant of triumph as each star, free from confusion, sweepeth free in its right orbit; all heaven acclaimeth thee as thou goest, transcendental in joy and splendor; and thy light is as a beacon to them that wander afar, strayed in the night. Amoun.

The "old comment" covers the rest of this verse sufficiently for the present purpose.

I see no harm in revealing the mystery of Tzaddi to "the wise"; others will hardly understand my explanations. Tzaddi is the letter of the Emperor, the Trump IV, and Heh is the Star, the Trump XVII. Aquarius and Aries are therefore counterchanged, revolving on the pivot of Pisces, just as in the Trumps VIII and XI, Leo and Libra, do about Virgo. This last revelation makes our Tarot attributions sublimely, perfectly, flawlessly symmetrical.

The fact of its so doing is a most convincing proof of the superhuman wisdom of the author of this Book to those who have labored for years, in vain, to elucidate the problems of the Tarot.

---

58. I give unimaginable joys on earth: certainty, not faith, while in life, upon death: peace unutterable, rest, ecstasy; nor do I demand aught in sacrifice.

OLD COMMENT
58. The Grace of our Lady of the Stars.

NEW COMMENT
These joys are principally (1) the Beatific Vision, in which Beauty is constantly present to the recipient of Her

grace, together with a calm and unutterable joy; (2) the Vision of Wonder, in which the whole mystery of the universe is constantly understood and admired for its ingenium and wisdom. (1) is referred to Tiphareth, the grade of Adept; (2) to Binah, the grade of Master of the Temple.

The certainty concerning death is conferred by the magical memory, and various experiences without which life is unintelligible. "Peace unutterable" is given by the trance in which matter is destroyed; "rest" by that which finally equilibrates motion. "Ecstasy" refers to a trance which combines these.

"Nor do I demand aught in sacrifice": the ritual of worship is Samadhi. But see later, v.61.

---

59. My incense is of resinous woods & gums; and there is no blood therein: because of my hair the trees of Eternity.

OLD COMMENT
59. "Because," etc. This mystical phrase doubtless refers to some definite spiritual experience connected with the knowledge of Nuit.

NEW COMMENT
It seems possible that Our Lady describes Her hair as "the trees of Eternity" because of the tree-like structure of the cosmos. This is observed in the 'Star-Sponge' vision. I must explain this by giving a comparatively full account of this vision.

The 'Star-Sponge' Vision
There is a vision of a peculiar character which has been

of cardinal importance in my interior life, and to which constant reference is made in my magical diaries. So far as I know, there is no extant description of this vision anywhere, and I was surprised on looking through my records to find that I had given no clear account of it myself. The reason apparently is that it is so necessary a part of myself that I unconsciously assume it to be a matter of common knowledge, just as one assumes that everybody knows that one possesses a pair of lungs, and therefore abstains from mentioning the fact directly, although perhaps alluding to the matter often enough.

It appears very essential to describe this vision as well as is possible, considering the difficulty of language, and the fact that the phenomena involved logical contradictions, the conditions of consciousness being other than those obtaining normally.

The vision developed gradually. It was repeated on so many occasions that I am unable to say at what period it may be called complete. The beginning, however, is clear enough in my memory.

I was on a retirement in a cottage overlooking Lake Pasquaney in New Hampshire. I lost consciousness of everything but a universal space in which were innumerable bright points, and I realized this as a physical representation of the universe, in what I may call its essential structure. I exclaimed: "Nothingness, with twinkles!" I concentrated upon this vision, with the result that the void space which had been the principal element of it diminished in importance; space appeared to be ablaze, yet the radiant points were not confused, and I thereupon completed my sentence with the exclamation, "But what Twinkles!"

The next stage of this vision led to an identification of the blazing points with the stars of the firmament, with ideas, souls, etc. I perceived also that each star was connected by a ray of light with each other star. In the world of ideas, each thought possesses a necessary relation with each other thought; each such relation is of course a thought in itself; each such ray is itself a star. It is here that logical difficulty first presents itself. The seer has a direct perception of infinite series. Logically, therefore, it would appear as if the entire space must be filled up with a homogenous blaze of light. This, however, is not the case. The space is completely full; yet the monads which fill it are perfectly distinct. The ordinary reader might well exclaim that such statements exhibit symptoms of mental confusion. The subject demands more than cursory examination. I can do no more than refer the critic to the Hon. Bertrand Russell's *Introduction to Mathematical Philosophy,* where the above position is thoroughly justified, as also certain positions which follow. At the time I had not read this book; and I regard it as a striking proof of the value of mystical attainment, that its results should have led a mind such as mine, whose mathematical training was of the most elementary character, to the immediate consciousness of some of the most profound and important mathematical truths; to the acquisition of the power to think in a manner totally foreign to the normal mind, the rare possession of the greatest thinkers in the world.

A further development of the vision brought the consciousness that the structure of the universe was highly organized, that certain stars were of greater magnitude and brilliancy than the rest. I began to seek similes to help me to explain myself. Several such attempts are mentioned later in this note. Here again are certain analogies with some of the properties of infinite series. The reader must not be shocked at the idea of a number which is not increased by addition or multiplication, a series of infinite series, each one of which may be twice as long as its predecessor, and so on. There is no "mystical humbug" about this. As Mr. Russell shows, truths of this order are more certain than the most universally accepted axioms; in fact, many axioms accepted by the intellect of the average man are not true at all. But in order to appreciate these truths, it is necessary to educate the mind to thought of an order which is at first sight incompatible with rationality.

I may here digress for a moment in order to demonstrate how this vision led directly to the understanding of the mechanism of certain phenomena which have hitherto been dismissed with a shrug of the shoulders as incomprehensible.

Example No. 1: I began to become aware of my own mental processes; I thought of my consciousness as the commander-in-chief of an army. There existed a staff of specialists to deal with various contingencies. There was an intelligence department to inform me of my environment. There was a council which determined the relative importance of the data presented to them—it required only a slight effort of imagination to think of this council as in debate; I could picture to myself some tactically brilliant proposal being vetoed by the quartermaster-general. It was only one step to dramatize the scene, and it flashed upon me in a moment that here was the explanation of "double personality": that illusion was no more than a natural personification of internal conflict, just as the savage attributes consciousness to trees and rocks.

Example No. 2: While at Montauk I had put my sleeping bag to dry in the sun. When I went to take it in, I remarked, laughingly, "Your bedtime, Master Bag," as if it were a small boy and I its nurse. This was entirely frivolous, but the thought flashed into my mind that after all the bag was in one sense a part of myself. The two ideas came together with a snap, and I understood the machinery of a man's delusion that he is a teapot.

These two examples may give some idea to the reader of the light which mystical attainment throws upon the details of the working of the human mind.

Further developments of this vision emphasized the identity between the universe and the mind. The search for similes deepened. I had a curious impression that the thing I was looking for was somehow obvious and familiar. Ultimately it burst upon me with fulminating conviction that the simile for which I was seeking was the nervous system. I exclaimed: "The mind is the nervous system," with all the enthusiasm of Archimedes, and it only dawned on me later, with a curious burst of laughter at my naivete, that my great discovery amounted to a platitude.

From this I came to another discovery: I perceived why platitudes were stupid. The reason was that they represented the summing up of trains of thought, each of which was superb in every detail at one time. A platitude was like a wife after a few years; she had lost none of her charms, and yet one prefers some perfectly worthless woman.

I now found myself able to retrace the paths of thought which ultimately come together in a platitude. I would start with some few simple ideas and develop them. Each stage in the process was like the joy of a young eagle soaring from height to height in ever-increasing sunlight as dawn breaks, foaming, over the purple hem of the garment of ocean; and, when the many colored rays of rose and gold and green gathered themselves together and melted into the orbed glory of the sun, with a rapture that shook the soul with unimaginable ecstasy, that sphere of rushing light was recognized as a commonplace idea, accepted unquestioningly and treated with drab indifference because it had so long been assimilated as a natural and necessary part of the order of nature. At first I was shocked and disgusted to discover that a series of brilliant researches should culminate in a commonplace. But I soon understood that what I had done was to live over again the triumphant career of conquering humanity; that I had experienced in my own person the succession of winged victories that had been sealed by a treaty of peace whose clauses might be summed up in some such trite expression as "Beauty depends upon form."

It would be quite impracticable to go fully into the subject of this vision of the Star-Sponge, if only because its ramifications are omniform. It must suffice to reiterate that it has been the basis of most of my work for the last five years, and to remind the reader that the essential form of it is "Nothingness with twinkles."

---

60. *My number is 11, as all their numbers who are of us. The Five Pointed Star, with a Circle in the Middle, & the circle is Red. My color is black to the blind, but the blue & gold are seen of the seeing. Also I have a secret glory for them that love me.*

61. *But to love me is better than all things: if under the night-stars in the desert thou presently burnest mine incense before me, invoking me with a pure heart, and the Serpent flame therein, thou shalt come a little to lie in my boson. For one kiss wilt thou then be willing to give all; but whose gives one particle of dust shall lose all in that hour. Ye shall gather goods and store of woman and spices; ye shall wear rich jewels; ye shall exceed the nations of the earth in splendor and pride; but always in the love of me, and so shall ye come to my joy. I charge you earnestly to come before me in a single robe, and covered with a rich headdress. I love you! I yearn to you! Pale or purple, veiled or voluptuous, I who am all pleasure and purple, and drunkenness of the innermost sense, desire you. Put on the wings and arouse the coiled splendour within you: come unto me!*

62. At all my meetings with you shall the priestess say—and her eyes shall burn with desire as she stands bare and rejoicing in my secret temple—To me! To me! calling forth the flame of the hearts of all in her love-chant.

OLD COMMENT

60. Nu=56 and 5+6=11.

The Circle in the Pentagram? See *Liber VN.*

The uninitiated perceive only darkness in night: the wise perceive the golden stars in the vault of azure.

Concerning that secret glory it is not here fitting to discourse.

61. Practical and literal, yet it may be doubted whether "to lose all in that hour" may not refer to the supreme attainment, and that therefore to give one particle of dust (perhaps the ego, or the central atom, Hadit, her complement) is the act to achieve.

62-63. Again practical and literal. Yet the "Secret Temple" refers also to a knowledge incommunicable—save by experience.

NEW COMMENT

It is evident that Our Lady, in her personality, contemplates some more or less open form of worship suited for the laity. With the establishment of the Law, something of this sort may become possible. It is only necessary to kill out the sense of "sin," with its false shame and its fear of nature.

P.S. The *Gnostic Mass* is intended to supply this need. *Liber XV* (it has been said continuously in California for some years).

63. Sing the rapturous love-song unto me! Burn to me perfumes! Wear to me jewels! Drink to me, for I love you! I love you!

NEW COMMENT

All those acts which excite the divine in man are proper to the rite of invocation.

Religion, as understood by the vile Puritan, is the very opposite of all this. He—it—seems to wishes to kill his—its—soul by forbidding every expression of it, and every practice which might awaken it to expression. To hell with this verbotenism!

In particular, let me exhort all men and all women, for they are stars! Heed well this holy verse!

True religion is intoxication, in a sense. We are told elsewhere to intoxicate the innermost, not the outermost; but I think that the word "wine" should be taken in its widest sense as meaning that which brings out the soul. Climate, soil, and race change conditions; each man or woman must find and choose the fit intoxicant. Thus hashish in one or other of its forms seems to suit the Moslem, to go with dry heat; opium is right for the Mongol; whiskey for the dour temperament and damp cold climate of the Scot.

Sexual expression, too, depends on climate and so on, so that we must interpret the Law to suit a Socrates, a Jesus, and a Burton, or a Marie Antoinette and a de Lambelle, as well as our own Don Juans and Faustines.

With this expansion, to the honour and glory of Them, of Their Natures, we acclaim therefore our helpers, Dionysus, Aphrodite, Apollo; Wine, Woman, and Song.

Intoxication, that is, *ecstasy, is the key to reality*. It is explained in *Energized Enthusiasm* (*The Equinox* Vol. 1, No. 9) that there are three Gods whose function is to bring the soul to the realization of its own glory: Dionysus, Aphrodite, Apollo; Wine, Woman, and Song.

The ancients, both in the highest civilizations, as in Greece and Egypt, and in the most primitive savagery, as among the Buriats and the Papuans, were well aware of this, and made their religious ceremonies "orgia," *works.* Puritan foulness, failing to understand what was happening, degraded the word "orgies" to mean debauches. It is the old story of the fox who lost his tail. If you cannot do anything, call it impossible; or, if that be evidently absurd, call it wicked!

It is critics who deny poetry, people without capacity for ecstasy and will who call mysticism moonshine and magick delusion. It is manless old cats, geldings, and psychopaths, who pretend to detest love, and persecute free women and free men.

Verbotenism has gone so far in certain slave-communities that the use of wine is actually prohibited by law!

I wish here to emphasize that the Law of Thelema definitely enjoins us, as a necessary act of religion, to "drink sweet wines and wines that foam." Any free man or woman who resides in any community where this is verboten has a choice between two duties: insurrection and emigration.

The furtive disregard of restriction is not freedom. It tends to make men slaves and hypocrites, and destroy respect for law.

Have no fear: two years after vodka was verboten, Russia, which had endured a thousand lesser tyrannies with patience, rose in revolution.

Religious ecstasy is necessary to man's soul. Where this is attained by mystical practices, directly, as it should be, people need no substitutes. Thus the Hindus remain contentedly sober, and care nothing for the series of invaders who have occupied their country from time to time and governed them. But where the only means of obtaining this ecstasy, or a simulacrum of it, known to the people, is alcohol, they must have alcohol. Deprive them of wine, or beer, or whatever their natural drink may be, and they replace it by morphia, cocaine, or something easier to conceal, and to take without detection.

Stop that, and it is revolution. As long as a man can get rid of his surplus energy in enjoyment, he finds life easy, and submits. Deprive him of pleasure, of ecstasy, and his mind begins to worry about the way in which he is exploited and oppressed. Very soon he begins furtively to throw bombs; and, gathering strength, to send his tyrants to the gallows.

---

64. I am the blue-lidded daughter of Sunset; I am the naked brilliance of the voluptuous night-sky.

65. To me! To me!

66. The Manifestation of Nuit is at an end.

OLD COMMENT

64. The supreme affirmation.

65. The supreme adjuration.

66. The end.

COMMENTARY
ON

The Book
of The Law

BY
ALEISTER CROWLEY
666

Part Two

Part Two

---

1. Nu! the hiding of Hadit.

OLD COMMENT

1. Cf. I, 1. As Had, the root of Hadit, is the manifestation of Nuit, so Nu, the root of Nuit, is the hiding of Hadit.

NEW COMMENT

We see again set forth the complementary character of Nuit and Hadit. Nu conceals Had because He is everywhere in the Infinite, and She manifests Him for the same reason. See verse 3. Every individual manifests the whole; and the whole conceals every individual. The soul interprets the universe; and the universe veils the soul. Nature understands herself by becoming self-conscious in her units; and the consciousness loses its sense of separateness by dissolution in Her.

There has been much difficulty in the orthography (in sacred languages) of these names. Nu is clearly stated to be 56, ןן; but Had is only hinted obscurely. This matter is discussed later more fully; verses 15 and 16.

2. Come! all ye, and learn the secret that hath not yet been revealed. I, Hadit, am the complement of Nu, my bride. I am not extended, and Khabs is the name of my House.

OLD COMMENT

2. Nuit is infinite extension; Hadit, infinite contraction. Khabs is the house of Hadit, even as Nuit is the house of the Khu, and the Khabs is in the Khu (I, 8). These theologies reflect mystic experiences of infinite contraction and expansion, while philosophically they are the two opposing infinities whose interplay gives finity.

NEW COMMENT

Khabs—"a star"—is a unit of Nuit, and therefore Nuit Herself. This doctrine is enormously difficult to apprehend, even after these many years of study.

Hadit is the "core of every star," verse 6. He is thus the impersonal identity within the individuality of "every man and every woman." He is "not extended"; that is, he is without condition of any sort in the metaphysical sense. Only in the highest trances can the nature of these truths be realized. It is indeed a suprarational experience not dissimilar to that characteristic of the "Star-Sponge" vision previously described which can help us here. The trouble is that the truth itself is unfitted to the dualistic reason of "normal" mankind. Hadit seems to be the principle of motion which is everywhere, yet is not extended in any dimension except as it chances to combine with "matter," which is Nuit. There can evidently be no manifestation apart from this conjunction. A "Khabs" or star is apparently any nucleus where this conjunction has taken place. The real philosophical difficulty about this cosmogony is not concerned with any particular equation, or even with the original equation. We can understand x=ab, $x_1 = a_1 b_1$ etc; and also 0-pa=qb, whether pa+qb=0 or not. But we ask how the homogeneity of both Nuit and Hadit can ever lead to even the illusion of "difference." The answer appears to be that this difference appears naturally with the self-realization of Nuit as the totality of possibilities; each of these, singly and in combination, is satisfied or set in motion by Hadit, to compose a particular manifestation. Zero degrees could possess no significance at all, unless there were diverse dimensions wherein it had no extension. "Nothing" means nothing save from the point of view of "two," just as "two" is monstrous unless it is seen as a mode of "nothing."

The above explanation appears somewhat disingenuous, since there is no means whatever of distinguishing any union of H+N=R from another. We must postulate a further stage.

R (Ra-Hoor-Khuit), Kether, Unity, is always itself; but we may suppose that a number of such homogeneous positive manifestations may form groups differing from each other as to size and structure so as to create the illusion of diversity.

---

3. *In the sphere I am everywhere the centre, as she, the circumference, is nowhere found.*

OLD COMMENT

3. A further development of higher meaning. In phrasing this verse is suggested by an old mystical definition of God: "He Whose centre is everywhere and Whose circumference nowhere."

NEW COMMENT

This is again interesting as throwing light on the thesis:

every man and every woman is a star. There is no place whatsoever that is not a centre of light.

This truth is to be realized by direct perception, not merely by intellection. It is axiomatic; it cannot be demonstrated. It is to be assimilated by experience of the vision of the "Star-Sponge."

---

4. Yet she shall be known & I never.

OLD COMMENT

4. The circumference of Nuit touches Ra-Hoor-Khuit, Kether; but her centre Hadit is forever concealed above Kether. Is not Nu the *hiding* of Hadit, and Had the *manifestation* of Nuit? (I later—September, 1911—dislike this note, and refer the student to *Liber XI,* and *Liber DLV.*)

NEW COMMENT

See later, verse 13, "Thou [i.e., the Beast, who is here the mask, or "persona" of Hadit] wast the knower." Hadit possesses the power to know, Nuit that of being known. Nuit is not unconnected with the idea of Nibbana, the "shoreless sea," in which knowledge is not.

Hadit is hidden in Nuit, and knows Her, She being an object of knowledge; but He is not knowable, for He is merely that part of Her which She formulates in order that She may be known.

5. Behold! the rituals of the old time are black. Let the evil ones be cast away; let the good ones be purged by the prophet! Then shall this Knowledge go aright.

OLD COMMENT

5. A reference to certain magical formulae known to the scribe of this book. The purification of said rituals is in progress at this time, An. V.

NEW COMMENT

The "old time" is the Aeon of the Dying God. Some of his rituals are founded on an utterly false metaphysic and cosmogony; but others are based on Truth. We mend these, and end those. This "Knowledge" is the initiated wisdom of this Aeon of Horus. See *Book 4, Part III*, for an account of the new principles of magick.

Note that Knowledge is Daath, Child of Chokmah by Binah, and crown of Microprosopus; yet he is not one of the Sephiroth, and his place is in the Abyss. By this symbolism we draw attention to the fact that knowledge is by nature impossible; for it implies duality, and is therefore relative. Any proposition of knowledge may be written "ARB": "A has the relation R to B." Now if A and B are identical, the proposition conveys no knowledge at all. If A is not identical with B, ARB implies "A is identical with BC"; this assumes that not less than three distinct ideas exist. In every case, we must proceed either to the identity which means ultimately "nothing," or to divergent diversities which only seem to mean something so long as we refrain from pushing the analysis of any term to its logical elements. For example, "Sugar is sugar" is obviously not knowledge. But no more is this: "Sugar is a sweet white crystalline carbohydrate." For each of these four terms describes a sensory impression on ourselves; and we define our impressions only in terms of such things as sugar. Thus "sweet" means "the quality ascribed by our taste to honey, sugar, etc."; "white" is "what champaks, zinc oxide, sugar, etc., report to our eyesight"; and so on. The proposition is ultimately an identity, for all our attempts to evade the issue by creating complications. "Knowledge" is therefore not a "thing-in-itself"; it is rightly denied a place upon the Tree of Life; it pertains to the Abyss.

Besides the above considerations, it may be observed that knowledge, so far as it exists at all, even as a statement of relation, is no more than a momentary phenomenon of consciousness. It is annihilated in the instant of its creation. For no sooner do we assent to ARB than ARB is absorbed in our conception of A. After the nine-days' wonder of "The earth revolves around the sun," we modify our former idea of earth. "Earth" is intuitively classed with other solar satellites. The proposition vanishes automatically as it is assimilated. Knowledge, while it exists as such, is consequently *sub judice*, at the best.

What, then, may we understand by this verse, with its capital K for "Knowledge?" What is it, and how shall it "go aright?" The key is in the word "go." It cannot "be," as we have seen above. It is the fundamental error of the "Black Brothers" in their policy of resisting all change, to try to maintain it as fixed and absolute. But (as the Tree of Life indicates) knowledge is the means by which the conscious mind, Microprosopus, reaches to Understanding and to Wisdom, its mother and father, which reflect respectively Nuit and Hadit from the Ain and Kether. The process is to use each new item of knowledge to correct and increase one's comprehension of the subject of the proposition. Thus ARB should tell us: A is (not A, as we supposed but) A. This facilitates the discovery A, R, C leading to A, is A_2; and so on. In practice, everything that we learn about, e.g., "horse" helps us to understand—to enjoy—the idea. The difference between the scholar and the schoolboy is that the former glows and exults when he is reminded of some word like "Thalassa." Ourselves: What a pageant of passion empurples our minds whenever we think of the number 93! Most of all, each new thing that we know about ourselves helps us to realize what we mean by our "star."

Now, "the rituals of the old time," are no longer valid vehicles. Knowledge cannot "go aright" until they are adapted to the Formula of the New Aeon. Their defects are due principally to two radical errors. (1) The universe was conceived as possessing a fixed center, or summit; an absolute standard to which all things might be referred; a Unity, or God. (Mystics were angry and bewildered, often enough, when attaining to "union with God" for they found him equally in all.) This led to making a difference between one thing and another, and so to the ideas of superiority, of sin, etc., ending by absurdities of all kinds, alike in theology, ethics, and science. (2) The absolute antithesis between the pairs of opposites. This is really a corollary of (1). There was an imaginary "absolute evil" which made Manicheeanism necessary—despite the cloaks of the casuists—and meant "That which leads one away from God." But each man, while postulating an absolute "God" defined Him unconsciously in terms of Freudian phantasms created by his own wish-fulfillment machinery. Thus "God" and "evil" were really expressions of personal prejudice. A man who "bowed humbly to the authority of" the Pope, or the Bible, or the Sanhedrim, or the Oracle of Apollo, or the tribal Medicine-Man, nonetheless expressed truly his own wish to abdicate responsibility.

In the light of this Book, we now know that the centre is everywhere, the circumference nowhere; that "every man and every woman is a star," a "Khabs," the name of the house of Hadit; that "the word of sin is restriction." To us, then, "evil" is a relative term; it is "that which hinders one from fulfilling his True Will." (E.g., rain is "good" or "bad" for the farmer according to the requirements of his crops.)

The Osirian rituals inculcating self-sacrifice to an abstract ideal, mutilation to appease an *ex cathedra* morality, fidelity to a priori formulae, etc., teach false and futile methods of acquiring false knowledge; they must be "cast away" or "purged." The schools of initiation must be reformed.

---

6. I am the flame that burns in every heart of man, and in the core of every star. I am Life, and the giver of Life, yet therefore is the knowledge of me the knowledge of death.

OLD COMMENT

6. Hadit is the ego or Atman in everything, but of course a loftier and more secret thing than anything understood by the Hindus. And of course the distinction between ego and ego is illusion. Hence Hadit, who is the life of all that is, if known, becomes the death of that individuality.

NEW COMMENT

It follows that, as Hadit can never be known, there is no death. The death of the individual is his awakening to the impersonal immortality of Hadit. This applies less to physical death than to the Crossing of the Abyss; for which see *Liber 418,* Fourteenth Aethyr. One may attain to be aware that one is but a particular "child" of the play of Hadit and Nuit; one's personality is then perceived as being a disguise. It is not only not a living thing, as one had thought; but a mere symbol without substance, incapable of life. It is the conventional form of a certain cluster of thoughts, themselves the partial and hieroglyphic symbols of an "ego." The conscious and sensible "man" is to his self just what the printed letters on this page are to me who have caused them to manifest themselves in color and form. They are arbitrary devices for conveying my thought; I could use French or Greek just as well. Nor is this thought, here conveyed, more than one ray of my orb; and even that whole orb is but the garment of me. The analogy is precise; therefore when one becomes "the knower," it involves the "death" of all sense of the ego. One perceives one's personality precisely as I now do these printed letters; and they are forgotten, just as, absorbed in my thought, the trained automatism of my mind and body expresses that thought in writing, without attention on my part, still less with identification of the extremes involved in the process.

---

7. I am the Magician and the Exorcist. I am the axle of the wheel, and the cube in the circle. "Come unto me" is a foolish word: for it is I that go.

OLD COMMENT

7. Hadit is both the maker of illusion and its destroyer. For though His interplay with Nuit results in the production of the finite, yet his withdrawing into Himself is the destruction thereof.

"The axle of the wheel": another way of saying that He is the core of things. "The cube in the circle": cf. *Liber 418, The Vision and the Voice,* 30th Aethyr. "Come unto me" is a foolish word; for it is I that go. That is, Hadit is everywhere; yet, being sought, he flies. The ego cannot be found, as meditation will show.

NEW COMMENT

"It is I that go." *Liber Aleph* must be consulted for a full demonstration of this truth. We may here say briefly that Hadit is motion, that is, change or "love." The symbol of Godhead in Egypt was the Ankh, which is a sandalstrap, implying the power to go; and it suggests the Rosy Cross, the fulfillment of love, by its shape.

The wheel and the circle are evidently symbols of Nuit; this sentence insists upon the conception of lingam-yoni. But beyond the obvious relation, we observe two geometrical definitions. The axle is a cylinder set perpendicularly to the plane of the wheel; thus Hadit supplies the third dimension to Nuit. It suggests that matter is to be conceived as two-dimensional; that is, perhaps, as possessed of two qualities, extension and potentiality. To these Hadit brings motion and position. The wheel moves; manifestation now is possible. Its perception implies three-dimensional space, and time. But note that the Mover is Himself not moved.

The "cube in the circle" emphasizes this question of dimensions. The cube is rectilinear (therefore phallic no less than the axle); its unity suggests perfection projected as a "solid" for human perception; its square faces affirm balance, equity, and limitation; its six-sidedness sets it among the solar symbols. It is thus like the Sun in the Zodiac, which is no more than the field for His fulfillment in His going. He, by virtue of his successive relations with each degree of the circle, clothes Himself with an appearance of "matter in motion," although absolute motion through space is a meaningless expression (Eddington, *op. cit.*). Nonetheless, every point in the cube has an unique relation with every point in the circle exactly balanced against an equal and opposite relation. We have thus matter that both is and is not, motion that both moves and moves not, interacting in a variety of ways which is infinite to manifest individuals, each of which is unlike any other, yet is symmetrically supported by its counterpart. Note that even at the center of gravity of the cube no two rays are identical except in mere length. They differ as to their point of contact with the circle, their right ascension, and their relation with the other points of the cube.

Why is Nuit restricted to two dimensions? We usually think of space as a sphere. "None—and two": extension and potentiality are Her only projections of naught. It is strange, by the way, to find that modern mathematics says that "spherical space is not very easy to imagine" (Eddington, *op. cit.* p. 158) and prefers to attribute a geometrical form whose resemblance to the Kteis is most striking. For Nuit is, philosophically speaking, the archetype of the Kteis, giving appropriate form to all being, and offering every possibility of fulfillment to every several points that it envelops. But Nuit cannot be symbolized as three-dimensional, in our system; each unit has position by one temporal, and three spatial coordinates. It cannot exist, in our consciousness, with less, as a reality. Each "individual" must be a "point-interval"; he must be the product of some part of the matter of Nuit (with special possibilities) and of the motion of Hadit (with special energies), determined in space by his relations with his neighbors, and in time by his relations with himself.

It is evidently "a foolish word" for Hadit to say, "Come unto me," as did Nuit naturally enough, meaning, "Fulfill thy possibilities"; for who can "come unto" motion itself, who can draw near unto that which is in very truth his innermost identity?

8. *Who worshipped Heru-pa-kraath have worshipped me;*
ill, for I am the worshipper.

OLD COMMENT

8. He is symbolized by Harpocrates, crowned child upon
the lotus, whose shadow is called silence. Yet his silence is
the act of adoration; not the dumb callousness of heaven
toward man, but the supreme ritual, the silence of supreme
orgasm, the stilling of all voices in the perfect rapture.

NEW COMMENT

Harpocrates is also the dwarf-soul, the Secret Self of
every man, the serpent with the lion's head. Now Hadit
knows Nuit by virtue of his "going" or "love." It is therefore
wrong to worship Hadit; one is to be Hadit, and worship Her.
This is clear even from His instruction "to worship me" in
verse 22 of this chapter. Cf., Cap. I, v.9. We are exhorted to
offer ourselves unto Nuit, pilgrims to all her temples.

It is bad magick to admit that one is other than one's
inmost self. One should plunge passionately into every
possible experience; by doing so one is purged of those
personal prejudices which we took so stupidly for ourselves,
though they prevented us from realizing our True Wills and
from knowing our names and natures. The aspirant must well
understand that it is no paradox to say that the annihilation
of the ego in the Abyss is the condition of emancipating the
true self, and exalting it to unimaginable heights. So long as
one remains "one's self," one is overwhelmed by the
universe; destroy the sense of self, and every event is equally
an expression of one's will, since its occurrence is the result
of the concourse of the forces which one recognizes as one's
own.

9. Remember all ye that existence is pure joy; that all the sorrows are but as shadows; they pass & are done; but there is that which remains.

OLD COMMENT

9. Hence we pass naturally and easily to the sublime optimism of verse 9. The lie is given to pessimism, not by sophistry, but by a direct knowledge.

NEW COMMENT

This verse is very thoroughly explained in *Liber Aleph*. "All in this kind are but shadows" says Shakespeare, referring to actors. The universe is a puppet play for the amusement of Nuit and Hadit in their nuptials; a veritable *Midsummer Night's Dream.* So then we laugh at the mock woes of Pyramus and Thisbe, the clumsy gambols of Bottom; for we understand the truth of things, how all is a dance of ecstasy. "Were the world understood, Ye would know it was good, a Dance to a lyrical measure!" The nature of events must be "pure joy"; for, obviously, whatever occurs is the fulfillment of the will of its master. Sorrow thus appears as the result of any unsuccessful—therefore, ill-judged—struggle. Acquiesence in the order of nature is the ultimate wisdom.

One must understand the universe perfectly, and be utterly indifferent to its pressure. These are the virtues which constitute a Master of The Temple. Yet each man must act what he will; for he is energized by his own nature. So long as he works "without lust of result" and does his duty for its own sake, he will know that "the sorrows are but shadows." And he himself is "that which remains"; for he can no more be destroyed, or his True Will be thwarted, than matter diminish or energy disappear. He is a necessary unit of the universe, equal and opposite to the sum total of all the others; and his will is similarly the final factor which completes the equilibrium of the dynamical equation. He cannot fail if he would; thus, his sorrows are but shadows—he could not see them if he kept his gaze fixed on his goal, the Sun.

10. O prophet! thou hast ill will to learn this writing.

OLD COMMENT

10. The prophet who wrote this was at this point angrily unwilling to proceed.

NEW COMMENT

As related in *The Equinox,* Vol. 1, No. 7, I was at the time of this revelation, a rationalistic Buddhist, very convinced of the first noble truth: "Everything is sorrow." I supposed this point of view to be an absolute and final truth—as if Apemantus were the only character in Shakespeare!

It is also explained in that place how I was prepared for this work by that period of dryness. If I had been in sympathy with it, my personality would have interfered. I should have tried to better my instructions.

See, in *Liber 418,* the series of visions by which I actually transcended sorrow. But the considerations set forth in the comment on verse 9 lead to a simpler, purer, and more perfect attainment for those who can assimilate them in the subconscious mind by the process described in the comment on verse 6.

It may encourage certain types of aspirants if I emphasize my personal position. Aiwaz made no mistake when he spoke this verse—and the triumphant contempt of his tone still rings in my ear! After seventeen years of unparalleled spiritual progress, of unimaginably intense ecstasies, of beatitudes prolonged for whole months, of initiations indescribably exalted, of proof piled on proof of His power, His vigilance, His love, after being protected and energized with incredible aptness, I find myself still only too ready to grumble, nay even to doubt. It seems as if I resented the whole business. There are times when I feel that the amoeba, the bourgeois, and the cow represent the ABC of enviable creatures. There may be a melancholic strain in me, as one might expect in a case of renal weakness such as mine. In any event, it is surely a most overwhelming proof that Aiwaz is not myself, but my master, that He could force me to write verse 9, at a time when I was both intellectually and spiritually disgusted with, and despairing of, the universe, as well as physically alarmed about my health.

11. I see thee hate the hand & the pen; but I am stronger.

OLD COMMENT

11. He was compelled to do so.

NEW COMMENT

This compulsion was that of true inspiration. It was the karma of countless incarnations of struggle towad the light. There is a sharp repulsion, physical and mental, toward any initiation, like that towards death.

The above paragraph states only a part of the truth. I am not sure that it is not an attempt to explain away the verse, which humiliates me. I remember clearly enough the impulse to refuse to go on, and the fierce resentment at the refusal of my muscles to obey me. Reflect that I was being compelled to make an abject recantation of practically every article of my creed, and I had not even Cranmer's excuse. I was proud of my personal prowess as a poet, hunter, and mountaineer of admittedly dauntless virility; yet I was being treated like a hypnotized imbecile, only worse, for I was perfectly aware of what I was doing.

12. Because of Me in Thee which thou knewest not.

OLD COMMENT
12. For the God was in him, albeit he knew it not.

NEW COMMENT
The use of capitals "Me" and "Thee" emphasizes that Hadit was wholly manifested in the Beast. It is to be remembered that the Beast had agreed to follow the instructions communicated to Him only in order to show that "nothing would happen if you broke all the rules." Poor fool! The way of mastery is to break all rules—but you have to know them perfectly before you can do this; otherwise you are not in a position to transcend them.

Aiwaz here explains that his power over me depended upon the fact that Hadit is verily "the core of every star." As is well known, there is a limit to the power of the hypnotist; he cannot overcome the resistance of the unconscious of his patient. My own unconscious was thus in alliance with Aiwaz; taken between two fires, my conscious self was paralyzed so long as the pressure lasted. It will be seen later—verses 61 to 69—that my consciousness was ultimately invaded by the Secret Self, and surrendered unconditionally, so that it proclaimed, loudly and gladly, from its citadel, the victory of its rightful Lord. The mystery is indeed this, that in so prosperous and joyous a city, there should still be groups of malcontents whose grumblings are occasionally audible.

13. for why? Because thou wast the knower, and me.

OLD COMMENT

13. For so long as any answer remains, there is nothing known. Knowledge is the loss of the knower in the known.

"And me" (not "and I"): Hadit was passive, which could not arise because of the existence of the knower; "and" implying further duality, which is ignorance.

NEW COMMENT

Hadit had to overcome the silly "knower," who thought everything was sorrow. Cf. "Who am I?"—"Thou knowest" in Chapter I.

I am far from satisfied with either of the above interpretations of this verse. We shall see a little later, verses 27 *et seq.*, a general objection to "Because" and "why." Then how is it that Hadit does not disdain to use those terms? It must be for the sake of my mind. Then, "for why" is detestably vulgar; and no straining of grammar excuses or explains the "me."

We have two alternatives. The verse may be an insult to me. My memory tells me, however, that the tone of voice of Aiwaz was at this point low, even and musical. It sounded like a confidential, almost deferential, clarification of the previous verse, which had rung out with joyful crescendo.

The alternative is that the verse contains some Qabalistic proof of the authority of Aiwaz to lay down the law in so autocratic a manner. Just so, one might add weight to one's quotation from Sappho, in the English, by following it up with the original Greek. The absence of all capital letters favors this theory. Such explanation, if discovered, will be given in the Appendix.

However, simply enough, the solution begins with the idea that the small initial of "because" would be explained by a colon preceding it instead of a note of interrogation, which may have been due to my haste, ignorance, and carelessness. Then "for why" may be understood: "for the benefit of this Mr. Why—to satisfy your childish clamor for a reason—I will not repeat my remarks in an alternative form such that even your stupidity can scarcely fail to observe that I have sealed my psychological explanation in cipher."

We find accordingly that the arising "of Me in Thee'. constitutes a state wherein "thou knewest not." By "Knewest" we may understand the function of Hadit, intellectually and conjugally united with Nuit. (See *Book 4, Part III*, for *gn*, the root meaning both "to know" and "to beget.") And "not" is Nuit, as in Cap. I. Now this idea explains that the arising "of Me [Hadit] in Thee [the Beast] is the fulfillment of the magical formula of Hadit and Nuit. And to know Nuit is the very definition of "joy." The next verse confirms this "thou [the Beast] wast the knower [Hadit] and [united with] me [Nuit, as in Cap. I., verse 51 and others]." Finally, Nuit is indicated by two different symbols: "not" (Gk. ΟΥ) and "me" (Gk. ΜΗ). Now ΟΥ ΜΗ was my motto in the grade of Adeptus Exemptus; Aiwaz thus subtly reminds me that I was pledged to deny the assertions of my intellectual and moral consciousness.

He combines in these few words (a) a correct psychological explanation of the situation, (b) a correct magical explanation of that explanation, (c) a personal rebuke to which I had no possible reply, involving a knowledge of my own mental state which was superior to my own.

These two verses are sufficient in themselves to demonstrate the preterhuman qualities of the author of this book.

14. Now let there be a veiling of this shrine; now let the light devour men and eat them up with blindness!

OLD COMMENT
14. Enough has been said of the nature of Hadit; now let a riddle of L.V.X. be propounded.

NEW COMMENT
The subject changes. Hadit will give an exordium upon Himself in the next two verses. Then He will propound an ethical doctrine so terrible and strange that men will be "devoured and eaten up with blindness" because of it.

For I am perfect, being Not; and my number is nine by the fools; but with the just I am eight, and one in eight: Which is vital, for I am none indeed. The Empress and the King are not of me; for there is a further secret.

OLD COMMENT

15. I am perfect, being not (31 אל or 61 אין). My number is Nine by the fools (IX the Hermit ♍ and ☿). With the just I am Eight, VIII, Justice ♎ Maat ל , and One in Eight, א. Which is vital, for I am None indeed, לא. The Empress ד III, the King ה IV, are not of me. III + IV = VII.

NEW COMMENT

See Appendix.

I am The Empress & the Hierophant. Thus eleven, as my bride is eleven.

OLD COMMENT

16. I am the Empress and the Hierophant (ד V) III+V=VIII and VIII is XI, both because of the 11 letters in Abrahadabra (=418=חית=ח=8), the key word of all this ritual, and because VIII is not ♌ but ♎, Justice, in the Tarot (see *Tarot Lecture* and 777).

NEW COMMENT

See Appendix.

---

17. *Hear me, ye people of sighing!*
The sorrows of pain and regret
Are left to the dead and the dying,
The folk that not know me as yet.
18. *These are dead, these fellows; they feel not. We are not for the poor and sad; the lords of the earth are our*

kinsfolk.

19. Is a God to live in a dog? No! but the highest are of us. They shall rejoice, our chosen: who sorroweth is not of us.

20. Beauty and strength, leaping laughter and delicious languor, force and fire, are of us.

21. We have nothing with the outcast and the unfit: let them die in their misery. For they feel not. Compassion is the vice of kings: stamp down the wretched & the weak: this is the law of the strong: this is our law and the joy of the world. Think not, o king, upon that lie: That Thou Must Die: verily thou shalt not die, but live. Now let it be understood: If the body of of the King dissolve, he shall remain in pure ecstacy for ever. Nuit! Hadit! Ra-Hoor-Khuit! The Sun, Strength & Sight, Light; these are for the servants of the Star & the Snake.

OLD COMMENT

17-21. This passage was again very painful to the prophet, who took it in its literal sense. But "the poor and the outcast" are the petty thoughts and the Qliphothic thoughts and the sad thoughts. These must be rooted out, or the ecstasy of Hadit is not in us. They are the weeds in the garden that starve the flower.

NEW COMMENT

17. The dead and the dying, who know not Hadit, are in the illusion of sorrow. Not being Hadit, they are shadows, puppets, and what happens to them does not matter. If you insist upon identifying yourself with Hecuba, your tears are natural enough.

There is no contradiction here, by the way, with verses 4 and 5. The words "know me" are used loosely as is natural in a stanza? or, more likely, are used (as in the English Bible) to suggest the root *gn*, identity in transcendental ecstasy. Possibly "not" and "me" are once more intended to apply to Nuit. With "know" itself, they may be "Nothing under its three forms" of negativity, action, and individuality.

18. This idea is confirmed. Those who sorrow are not real people at all, not "stars"—for the time being. The fact of their being "poor and sad" proves them to be "shadows," who "pass and are done." The "lords of the earth" are those who are doing their will. It does not necessarily mean people with coronets and automobiles; there are plenty of such people who are the most sorrowful slaves in the world. The sole test of one's lordship is to know what one's True Will is, and to do it.

19. A god living in a dog would be one who was prevented from fulfilling his function properly. The highest are those who have mastered and transcended accidental environment. They rejoice, because they do their will; and if any man sorrow, it is clear evidence of something wrong with him. When machinery creaks and growls, the engineer knows that it is not fulfilling its function, doing its will, with ease and joy.

20. As soon as one realizes one's self as Hadit, one obtains all His qualities. It is all a question of doing one's will. A flaming harlot, with red cap and sparkling eyes, her foot on the neck of a dead king, is just as much a star as her predecessor, simpering in his arms. But one must be a flaming harlot—one must let oneself go, whether one's star be twin with that of Shelley, or of Blake, or of Titian, or of Beethoven. Beauty and strength come from doing one's will; you have only to look at any one who is doing it to recognize the glory of it.

21. There is a good deal of the Nietzschean standpoint in this verse. It is the evolutionary and natural view. Of what

use is it to perpetuate the misery of tuberculosis, and such diseases, as we now do? Nature's way is to weed out the weak. This is the most merciful way, too. At present all the strong are being damaged, and their progress hindered by the dead weight of the weak limbs and the missing limbs, the diseased limbs and the atrophied limbs. The Christians to the lions!

Our humanitarianism, which is the syphilis of the mind, acts on the basis of the lie that the king must die. The king is beyond death; it is merely a pool where he dips for refreshment. We must therefore go back to Spartan ideas of education; and the worst enemies of humanity are those who wish, under pretext of compassion, to continue its ills through the generations. The Christians to the lions!

Let weak and wry productions go back into the melting-pot, as is done with flawed steel castings. Death will purge, reincarnation will make whole, these errors and abortions. Nature herself may be trusted to do this, if only we will leave her alone. But what of those who, physically fitted to live, are tainted with rottenness of soul, cancerous with the sin-complex? For the third time I answer: The Christians to the lions!

Hadit calls himself the star, the star being the unit of the macrocosm; and the snake, the snake being the symbol of going or love, and the chariot of life. He is Harpocrates, the dwarf-soul, the spermatazoon of all life, as one may phrase it. The sun, etc., are external manifestations or vestures of this soul, as a man is the garment of an actual spermatazoon, the tree sprung of that seed, with power to multiply, and to perpetuate that particular nature, though without necessary consciousness of what is happening.

In a deeper sense, the word "death" is meaningless apart from the presentation of the universe as conditioned by "time." But what is the meaning of time? There is great confusion of thought in the use of the word "eternal," and the phrase "forever." People who want "eternal happiness" mean by that a cycle of varying events all effective in stimulating pleasant sensations; i.e., they want time to continue exactly as it does with themselves released from the contingencies of accidents such as poverty, sickness and death.

An eternal state is, however, a possible experience, if one interprets the term sensibly. One can kindle *"flamman aeternae caritatis,"* for instance; one can experience a love which is in truth eternal. Such love must have no relation with phenomena whose condition is time. Similarly, one's "immortal soul" is a different kind of thing altogether from one's mortal vesture. This soul is a particular star, with its own peculiar qualities, of course; but these qualities are all "eternal," and part of the nature of the soul. This soul being a monistic consciousness, it is unable to appreciate itself and its qualities, as explained in a previous entry; so it realizes itself by the device of duality, with the limitations of time, space and causality. The "happiness" of wedded love or eating marrons glaces is a concrete external, non-eternal expression of the corresponding abstract internal, eternal idea, just as any triangle is one partial and imperfect picture of the idea of a triangle. (It does not matter whether we consider the idea of a triangle as an unreal thing invented for the convenience of including all actual triangles, or vice versa. Once the idea, triangle, has arisen, actual triangles are related to it as above stated.)

One does not want even a comparatively brief extension of these "actual" states. Wedded love, though licensed for a lifetime, is usually intolerable after a month; and marrons glaces pall after the first five or six kilograms have been consumed. But the "happiness," eternal and formless, is not less enjoyable because these forms of it cease to give pleasure.

What happens is that the idea ceases to find its image in those particular images; it begins to notice the limitations, which are not itself and indeed deny itself, as soon as its original joy in its success at having become conscious of itself wears off. It becomes aware of the external imperfection of marrons glaces; they no longer represent its infinitely varied nature. It therefore rejects them, and creates a new form of itself, such as nightgowns with pale yellow ribbons or amber cigarettes.

In the same way a poet or painter, wiching to express the idea of beauty, is impelled to choose a particular form; with luck, this is at first able to recompense in him what he feels; but sooner or later he finds that he has failed to include certain elements of himself, and he must embody these in a new poem or picture. He may know that he can never do more than present a part of the possible perfection, and that in imperfect imagery; but at least he may utter his utmost within the limits of the mental and sensory instruments of his similarly inadequate symbol of the Absolute, his vehicle of human incarnation.

These suffer from the same defects as the other forms; ultimately, "happiness" wearies itself in the effort to invent fresh images, and become disheartened and doubtful of itself. Only a few people have wit enough to proceed to generalization from the failure of a few familiar figures of itself, and recognize that all "actual" forms are imperfect; but such people are apt to turn with disgust from the whole procedure, and to long for the "eternal" state. This state, however, is incapable of realization, as we know; and the soul, understanding this, can find no good but in "cessation" of all things, its creation no more than its own tendencies to create. It therefore sighs for Nibbana.

But there is one other solution, as I have endeavored to show. We may accept (what after all it is absurd to accuse and oppose) the essential character of existence. We cannot extirpate or even alter in the minutest degree either the matter of manner of any element of the universe, here each item is equally inherent and important, each consubstantial and coherent, each equipollent, independent, and interdependent.

We may thus acquiesce in the fact that it is apodeictically implicit in the Absolute to apprehend itself by self-expression as positive and negative in the first place, and to combine these primary opposites in an infinite variety of finite forms.

We may thus cease either (1) to seek the Absolute in any of its images, knowing that we must abstract every one of their qualities from every one of these equally if we would unveil it; or (2) to reject all images of the Absolute, knowing that attainment thereof would be the signal for the manifestation of that part of its nature which necessarily formulates itself in a new universe of images.

Realizing that these two courses (the materialist's and the mystic's) are equally fatuous, we may engage in either or both of two other plans of action, based on assent to actuality.

We may (1) ascertain our own particular properties as partial projections of the Absolute; we may allow every image presented to us to be of equally intrinsic and essential entity with ourselves, and its presentation to us a phenomenon necessary in nature; and we may adjust our apprehension to the actuality that every event is an item in the account which we render to ourselves of our own estate. We dare not desire to omit any single entry, lest the balance be upset. We may react with elasticity and indifference to each occurrence, intent only on the idea that the total, intelligently appreciated, constitutes a perfect knowledge not indeed of the Absolute but of that part thereof which is ourselves. We thus adjust one imperfection accurately to another, and remain contented in the appreciation of the righteousness of the relation.

This path, the "Way of the Tao," is perfectly proper to all men. It does not attempt either to transcend or to tamper with Truth; it is loyal to its own laws, and therefore no less perfect than any other truth. The equation five plus six is eleven is of the same order of perfection as "ten million times ten times ten thousand million is one billion." In the universe formulated by the Absolute, every point is equally the centre; every point is equally the focus of the forces of the whole.

(In any system of three points, any two may be considered solely with reference to the third, so that even in a finite universe the sum of the properties of all points is the same, though no two properties may be common to any two points. Thus a circle, BCD, may be described by the revolution of a line AB in a plane about the point A; but also from the point C, or indeed any other point, by the application of the proper analysis and construction. We calculate the motion of the solar system in heliocentric terms for no reason but simplicity and convenience; we could convert our tables to a geocentric basis by mere mechanical manipulation without affecting their truth, which is only the truth of the relations between a number of bodies. All are alike in motion, but we have arbitrarily chosen to consider one of them as stationary, so that we may more easily describe the movements of the others in regard to it, without complicating our calculations by introduction of the movements of the whole system as such. And for this purpose the sun is a more convenient standard than the earth.)

There is another Way that we may take, if we will; I say "another," though it seems perhaps to some no more than a development of the other which happens to be proper to some people. Even in the first Way, it is of all things necessary to begin by exploring one's own nature, so as to discover what its peculiarities are. This is accomplished partly by introspection, but principally by right recollection of the whole phantasmagoria presented to it by experience; for since every event of life is a symbol of part of the structure of the soul, the totality of experience must be the "name" of the whole of that part of the soul which has so far uttered itself. Now then, let us suppose that some soul, having penetrated thus far, should discover in its "name" that it is a son truly begotten by the spirit of being upon the body of form, and that it has power to understand itself and its father, with all that such heirship implies. Suppose further that it has come to puberty, will it not be impelled to assert itself as its father's son? Will it not shake itself free from the form that bore and nourished and trained it, and turn from its brothers and sisters and playmates? Will it not glow and ache with the impulse to be utterly itself, and find a form fit to impress with its image, even as did its father before?

If such a soul be indeed its father's son, he will not fear to show lack of filial reverence, or presumption, if he forget its family in the fervor of founding one of his own, of begetting boys not better or braver indeed than his brothers, girls not softer or sweeter indeed than his sisters, but wholly his own, with his own defects and desires evoked by enchantment of ecstasy when he dies to himself in the womb of the witch who lusts for his life, and buys it with the coin that bears his image and superscription.

Such is the secret of the soul of the artist. He knows that he is a God; he has no fear or shame in showing himself of the seed of his father. He is proud of that father's most precious privilege, and he honors him no less than himself by using it. He accepts his family as of his own royal stock; every one is as princely as he is himself. But he were not his father's son unless he found for himself a form fit to express himself by multiple reproductions of his image. He must admire himself in many costumes, each emphatic of some elected elegance or excellence in himself which would otherwise elude his homage by being hidden and hushed in the harmony of his heart. This form which shall serve him must be softness; self to his impress, with exact elasticity adapting itself to the strongest and subtlest salients, yet like steel to resist all other stress than his own, and to retain and reproduce surely and sharply the image that his acid bites into its surface. There must be no flaw, no irregularity, no granulation, no warp in its substance; it must be smooth and shining, pure metal of true temper.

And he must love this chosen form, love it with a fearful fervor; it is the face of his fate that craves his kiss, and in her eyes enigma blazes and smolders; she is his death, her body is his coffin where he may rot and stink, or writhe in damned dreams, self-slain, or rise in incorruption self-renewed, immortal and identical, fulfilling himself wholly in and by her, splashing all space with sparkling stars, his sons and daughters, each star an image of his own infinity made manifest, mood after mood, by her magick to mold him when his passion makes molten her metal.

Thus, then, must every artist work. First, he must find himself. Next, he must find the form that is fitted to express himself. Next, he must love that form, as a form, adoring it, understanding it, and mastering it, with most minute attention, until it (as it seems) adapts itself to him with eager elasticity, and answers accurately and aptly, with the unconscious automatism of an organ perfected by evolution, to his most subtlest suggestion, to his most giant gesture.

Next, he must give himself utterly in every act of love, laboring day and night to lose himself in lust for it, so that he leaves no atom unconsumed in the furnace of their frenzy, as did of old his father that begat him. He must realize himself wholly in the integration of the infinite pantheon of images; for if he fail to formulate one facet of himself, by lack thereof will he know himself falsely.

There is of course no ultimate difference between the artist as here delineated and him who follows the "Way of Tao," though the latter finds perfection in his existing relation with his environment, and the former creates a private perfection of a peculiar and secondary character. We might call one the son, and the other the daughter, of the Absolute.

But the artist—though his work, the images of himself in the form that he loves, is less perfect than the Work of his Father, since he can but express one particular point of view and that by means of one type of technique—is not to be thought useless on that account, any more than an atlas is useless because it presents by means of certain crude conventions a fraction of the facts of geography.

The artist calls our attention away from Nature, whose immensity bewilders us so that she seems incoherent, and unintelligible, to his own interpretation of himself, and his relations with various phenomena of nature expressed in a language more or less common to us all.

The smaller the artist, the narrower his view, the more vulgar his vocabulary, the more familiar his figures, the more readily is he recognized as a guide. To be accepted and admired, he must say what we all know, but have not told each other till it is tedious, and say it in simple and clear language, a little more emphatically and eloquently than we have been accustomed to hear; and he must please and flatter us in the telling by soothing our fears and stimulating our hopes and our self-esteem.

When an artist—whether in astronomy like Copernicus, anthropology like Ibsen, or anatomy like Darwin—selects a set of facts too large, too recondite, or too "regrettable" to receive instant assent from everybody; when he presents conclusions which conflict with popular credence or prejudice; when he employs a language which is not generally intelligible to all; in such cases he must be content to appeal to the few. He must wait for the world to awake to the value of his work.

The greater he is, the more individual and the less intelligible he will appear to be, although in reality he is more universal and more simple than anybody. He must be indifferent to anything but his own integrity in the realization and imagination of himself.

---

22. I am the Snake that giveth Knowledge & Delight and bright glory, and stir the hearts of men with drunkenness. To worship me take wine and strange drugs whereof I will tell my prophet, & be drunk thereof! They shall not harm ye at all. It is a lie, this folly against self. The exposure of innocence is a lie. Be strong, o man! lust, enjoy all things of sense and rapture: fear not that any God shall deny thee for this.

OLD COMMENT
22. Hadit now identifies himself with the Kundalini, the central magical force in man.

This privilege of using wine and strange drugs has been confirmed; the drugs were indeed revealed. (P. S. And they have not harmed those who have used them in this law.)

There follows a curse against the cringing altruism of Christianity, the yielding of the self to external impressions, the smothering of the Babe of Bliss beneath the flabby old nurse Convention.

NEW COMMENT

Drunkenness is a curse and a hindrance only to slaves. Shelley's couriers were "drunk on the wind of their own speed." Any one who is doing his True Will is drunk with the delight of Life.

Wine and strange drugs do not harm people who are doing their will; they only poison people who are cancerous with original sin. In Latin countries, where sin is not taken seriously, and sex-expression is simple, wholesome, and free, drunkenness is a rare accident. It is only in Puritan countries, where self-analysis, under the whip of a coarse bully like Billy Sunday, brings the hearer to "conviction of sin," that he hits first the "trail" and then the "booze." Can you imagine an evangelist in Taormina? It is to laugh.

This is why missionaries, in all these countries, have produced no conversions whatever save among the lowest types of Negro, who resemble the Anglo-Saxon in this possession of the "fear-of-God" and "sin" psychopathies.

Truth is so terrible to these detestable mockeries of humanity that the thought of self is a realization of hell. Therefore they fly to drink and drugs as to an anesthetic in the surgical operation of introspcetion.

The craving for these things is caused by the internal misery which their use reveals to the slave-souls. If you are really free, you can take cocaine as simply as salt-water taffy. There is no better rough test of a soul than its attitude to drugs. If a man is simple, fearless, eager, he is all right; he will not become a slave. If he is afraid, he is already a slave. Let the whole world take opium, hashish, and the rest; those who are liable to abuse them were better dead.

For it is in the power of all so-called intoxicating drugs to reveal a man to himself. If this revelation declare a star, then it shines brighter ever after. If it declare a Christian—a thing not man nor beast, but a muddle of mind—he craves the drug, no more for its analytical but for its numbing effect. Lytton has a great story of this in "Zanoni." Glyndon, an uninitiate, takes an elixir, and beholds not Adonai the glorious, but the Dweller on the Threshold; cast out from the sanctuary, he becomes a vulgar drunkard.

"This folly against self"; altruism is a direct assertion of duality, which is division, restriction, sin, in its vilest form. I love my neighbor because love makes him part of me; not because hate divides him from me. Our law is so simple that it constantly approximates a truism.

"The exposure of innocence." Exposure means "putting out" as in a shop-window. The pretense of altruism and so-called virtue "is a lie"; it is the hypocrisy of the Puritan, which is hideously corrupting both to the hypocrite and to his victim.

To "lust" is to grasp continually at fresh aspects of Nuit. It is the mistake of the vulgar to expect to find satisfaction in the objects of sense. Disillusion is inevitable; when it comes, it leads only too often to an error which is in reality more fatal than the former, the denial of "materiality" and of "animalism." There is a correspondence between these two attitudes and those of the "once-born" and "twice-born" of William James (*Varieties of Religious Experience*). Thelemites are "thrice-born"; we accept everything for what it is, without "lust of result," without insisting upon things conforming with a priori ideas, or regretting their failure to do so. We can therefore "enjoy" all things of sense and rapture according to their true nature.

For example, the average man dreads tuberculosis. The Christian Scientist flees this fear by pretending that the disease is an illusion in "mortal mind." But the Thelemite accepts it for what it is, and finds interest in it for its own sake. For him it is a necessary part of the universe; he makes "no difference between it and any other thing." The artist's position is analogous. Rubens, for instance, takes a gross pleasure in female flesh, rendering it truthfully from lack of imagination and analysis. Idealist painters like Bougereau, awake to the divergence between nature and their academic standards of beauty, falsify the facts in order to delude themselves. The greatest, like Rembrandt, paint a gallant, a hag, and a carcass with equal passion and rapture; they love the truth as it is. They do not admit that anything can be ugly or evil; its existence justifies itself. This is because they know themselves to be part of a harmonious unity; to disdain any item of it would be to blaspheme the whole. The Thelemite is able to revel in any experience soever; in each he recognizes the tokens of ultimate Truth.

It is surely obvious, even intellectually, that all phenomena are interdependent, and therefore involve each other. Suppose abc-d = a-d-b-c just as much as b-d-c-a. It is senseless to pick out one equation as "nice," and another as "nasty." Personal predilections are evidence of imperfect vision. But it is even worse to deny reality to those facts which refuse to humor such predilections. In the charter of spiritual sovereignty it is written that the charcoal-burner is no less a subject than the duke. The structure of the state includes all elements; it would be stupid and suicidal to aim at homogeneity, or to assert it. Spiritual experience soon enables the aspirant to assimilate these ideas, and he can enjoy life to the full, finding his True Self alike in the contemplation of every element of existence.

23. I am alone: there is no God where I am.

OLD COMMENT

23. The atheism of God. "Allah's the atheist! He owns no Allah" (*Bagh-i-Muattar*). To admit God is to look up to God, and so not to be God. The curse of duality.

NEW COMMENT

This refers to the spiritual experience of identity. When one realizes one's truth, there is no room for any other conception.

It also means that the God-idea must go with other relics of the fear born of ignorance into the limbo of savagery. I speak of the idea of God as generally understood: God being "something *not ourselves* that makes for righteousness," as Matthew Arnold Victorianatically phrased his definition. The whiskered wowser! Why this ingrained conviction that self is unrighteous? It is the heritage of the whip, the brand of the born slave. Incidentally, we cannot allow people who believe in this "God"; they are troglodytes, as dangerous to society as any other thieves and murderers. The Christians to the lions!

Yet, in the reign of Good Queen Victoria Matthew Arnold was considered rather hot stuff as an infidel! *Tempora mutantur, p.d.q.,* when a magus gets on the job.

The quintessence of this verse is, however, its revelation of the nature of Hadit as a self-conscious and individual being, although impersonal. He is an ultimate independent, and unique element in nature, impenetrably aloof. The negative electron seems to be his physical analogue. Each such electron is indistinguishable from any other; yet each is determined diversely by its relations with various positive complementary electrons.

The verse is introduced at this juncture in order to throw light on the passage which follows. It is important to understand Hadit as the "core of every star" when we come to consider the character of these stars, his "friends" or sympathetic ideas grouped about him, who are "hermits," individualities eternally isolated in reality though they may appear to be lost in their relations with external things.

24. Behold! these be grave mysteries; for there are also of my friends who be hermits. Now think not to find them in the forest or on the mountain; but in beds of purple, caressed by magnificent beasts of women with large limbs, and fire and light in their eyes, and masses of flaming hair about them; there shall ye find them. Ye shall see them at rule, at victorious armies, at all the joy; and there shall be in them a joy a million times greater than this. Beware lest any force another, King against King! Love one another with burning hearts; on the low men trample in the fierce lust of your pride, in the day of your wrath.

OLD COMMENT

24. Hermits. See v.15. Our ascetics enjoy, govern, conquer, love and are not to quarrel (but see vv.59, 60. Even their combats are glorious).

NEW COMMENT

The Christians to the lions!

A hermit is one who dwells isolated in the desert, exactly as a soul, a star, or an electron in the wilderness of space-time. The doctrine here put forth is that the initiate cannot be polluted by any particular environment. He accepts and enjoys everything that is proper to his nature. Thus, a man's sexual character is one form of his self-expression; he unites Hadit with Nuit sacramentally when he satisfies his instinct for physical love. Of course, this is only one partial projection; to govern, to fight, and so on, must fulfill other needs. We must not imagine that any form of activity is *ipso facto* incapable of supplying the elements of an Eucharist; *suum cuique*. Observe, however, the constant factor in this enumeration of the practices proper to "hermits": it is ecstatic delight.

Let us borrow an analogy from chemistry. Oxygen has two hands (so to speak) to offer to other elements. But contrast the cordial clasp of hydrogen or phosphorus with the weak reluctant greeting of chlorine! Yet hydrogen and chlorine rush passionately to embrace each other in monogamic madness! There is no "good" or "bad" in matter; it is the enthusiastic energy of union, as betokened by the disengagement of heat, light, electricity, or music, and the stability of the resulting compound, that sanctifies the act. Note also that the utmost external joy in any phenomenon is surpassed a millionfold by the internal joy of the realization that self-fulfillment in the sensible world is but a symbol of the universal sublimity of the formula, "love under will."

The last two sentences demand careful attention. There is an apparent contradiction with vv.59-60. We must seek reconcilement in this way: do not imagine that any king can die (v.21) or be hurt (v.59); strife between two kings can therefore be nothing more than a friendly trial of strength. We are all inevitably allies, even identical in our variety; to "love one another with burning hearts" is one of our essential qualities.

But who then are the "low men" since "every man and every woman is a star?" The *causus belli* is this: there are people who are veiled from themselves so deeply that they resent the bared faces of us others. We are fighting to free them, to make them masters like ourselves. Note v.60, "to hell with them"; that is, let us drive them to the "hell" or secret sanctuary within their consciousness. There dwells "the worm that dieth not and the fire that is not quenched"; that is, "the secret serpent coiled about to spring" and "the flame that burns in the heart of every man": Hadit. In other words, we take up arms against falsehood; we cannot help it if that falsehood forces the king it has imprisoned to assent to its edicts, even to believe that his interests are those of his oppressor, and to fear truth as once Jehovah did the serpent.

25. Ye are against the people, o my chosen!

OLD COMMENT

25. The cant of democracy condemned. It is useless to pretend that men are equal; facts are against it. And we are not going to stay, dull and contented as oxen, in the ruck of humanity.

NEW COMMENT

By "the people" is meant that canting, whining, servile breed of whipped dogs which refuses to admit its deity. The mob is always afraid for its bread and butter—when its tyrants let it have any butter—and now and then the bread has 60 percent substitutes of cattle-fodder. (Beast-food, even the *New York Times* of November 13, 1918, e.v., has it.) So, being afraid, it dare not strike. And when the trouble begins, we aristocrats of freedom, from the castle or the cottage, the tower or the tenement, shall have the slave mob against us. The newspapers will point out to us that "the people" prefer to starve, and thank John D. Rockefeller for the permission to do so.

Still deeper, there is a meaning in this verse applicable to the process of personal initiation. By "the people" we may understand the many-headed and mutable mob which swarms at the mercy of a mass of loud and vehement emotions, without discipline or even organization. They sway with the mood of the moment. They lack purpose, foresight, and intelligence. They are moved by ignorant and irrational instincts, many of which affront the law of self-preservation itself, with suicidal stupidity. The moral idea which we call "the people" is the natural enemy of good government. He who is "chosen" by Hadit to kingship must consequently be "against" the "people" if he is to pursue any consistent policy. The massed maggots of "love" devoured Mark Antony as they did Abelard. For this reason the first task of the aspirant is to disarm all his thoughts, to make himself impregnably above the influence of any one of them. This he may accomplish by the methods given in *Liber Aleph, Liber Jugorum, Thien Tao,* and elsewhere. Secondly, he must impose absolute silence upon them, as may be done by the "yoga" practices taught in *Book 4, Part I, Liber XVI,* etc. He is then ready to analyze them, to organize them, to drill them, and so to take advantage of the properties peculiar to each one by employing its energies in the service of his imperial purpose.

26. I am the secret Serpent coiled about to spring; in my coiling there is joy. If I lift up my head, I and my Nuit are one. If I droop down mine head, and shoot forth venom, then is rapture of earth, and I and the earth are one.

OLD COMMENT

26. The Kundalini again. The mystic union is to be practiced both with spirit and with matter.

NEW COMMENT

The magical power is universal. The free man directs it as he will. Leave him alone, or he will make you sorry you tried to interfere!

There is here a reference to the two main types of the orgia of magick; I have already dealt with this matter in the old comment. Observe that in the "mystic" work, the union takes place spontaneously; in the other, venom is shot forth. This awakes the earth to rapture; not until then does union occur. For, in working on the planes of manifestation, the elements must be consecrated and made "God" by virtue of a definite rite.

27. *There is great danger in me; for who doth not understand these runes shall make a great miss. He shall fall down into the pit called Because; and there he shall perish with the dogs of Reason.*

OLD COMMENT

27. The importance of failing to interpret these verses. Unspirituality leads us to the bird-lime of intellect. The hawk must not perch on any earthly bough, but remain poised in the ether.

NEW COMMENT

Humanity errs terribly when it gets "education," in the sense of ability to read newspapers. Reason is rubbish;

race-instinct is the true guide. Experience is the great teacher; and each one of us possesses millions of years of experience, the very quintessence of it, stored automatically in our subconscious minds. The intellectuals are worse than the bourgeoisie themselves; *à la lanterne!* Give us men!

Understanding is the attribute of the Master of the Temple, who has crossed the Abyss (or "pit") that divides the true self from its conscious instrument. (See *Liber 418*, *"Aha"!* and *Book 4, Pt. III.*) We must meditate on the meaning of this attack upon the idea of "because." I quote from my diary the demonstration that Reason is the Absolute, whereof all truths soever are merely particular cases. The theorem may be stated roughly as follows:

> The universe must be expressible either as $\pm$ n, or as zero. That is, it is either unbalanced or balanced. The former theory (theism) is unthinkable; but zero, when examined, proves to contain the possibility of being expressed as n-n, and this possibility must in its turn be considered as $\pm$ p.

This thesis appears to me a *reductio ad absurdum* of the very basis of our mathematical thinking.

We knew before, of course, that all reasoning is bound to end in some mystery or some absurdity; the above is only one more antimony, a little deeper than Kant's perhaps, but of the same character. Mathematicians would doubtless agree that all signs are arbitrary, the elaboration of an abacus, and that all "truth" is merely our name for statements that content our reason; so that it is lower than reason, and within it; not higher and beyond, as transcendentalists argue. I seem never to have seen this point before, though "men of sense" instinctively affirm it, I suppose. The pragmatists are mere tradesmen with their definition of truth as "the useful to be thought"; but why not "the necessary to be thought?" There is a sort of Berkeleyan subjectivity in this view; we might put it: "All that we can know of truth is "that which we are bound to think." The search for the truth amounts, then to the result of the analysis of the mind; and here let us remember my fear of the results of that analysis as I expressed it a month ago. This analysis is the right method after all.

Now, are we justified in assuming, as we always do, that our reason is either correct or incorrect? That if any proposition can be shown to be congruous with "A is A" it is "true" and so on? Does the "reason" of the oyster comply with the same canon as man's? We assume it. We make the necessity in our thought the standard of the laws of nature; and thus implicitly declare Reason to be the Absolute. This has nothing to do with the weakness or error in any one mind, or in all minds; all that we rely on is the existence of some purely mental standard by which we could correct our thinking, if we knew how. It is then this power which constrains our thought, to which our minds owe fealty, that we call "truth"; and this "truth" is not a proposition at all, but a "law!" We cannot think what it is, obviously, as it is a final condition of philosophical thought in the same way as space and time are conditions of phenomenal thought.

But, can there be some third type of thought which can escape the bonds of that as that can of this? "Samadhic realization," one is tempted to rush in and answer—while angels hesitate. All my philosophic thought, as above, is direct reflection upon the meaning of Samadhic experience. Is it simply that the reflections are distorted and dim? I have shown the impossibility of any true zero, and thus destroyed every axiom, blown up the foundations of my mind. In failing to distinguish between none and two, I cannot even cling to the straw of "phases," since time and space are long since perished without conditions; and therefore it is a positive idea, and we are just as right to inquire how it came to be as in the case of Haeckel's monad, or one's aunt's umbrella. We are, however, this one small step advanced by our initiations, that we can be quite sure this "none = two" is, since all possible theories of ontology simplify out to it.

Nevertheless, with whatever we try to identify this absolute, we cannot escape from the fact that it is in reality merely the formula of our own Reason. The idea of space arises from reflection upon the relations of our bodily gestures with the various objects of our senses. (Poincare—I note after reading him, months later, as I revise this note—explains this fully.) So that a "yard" is not a thing in itself, but a term in the equations which express the laws according to which we move our muscles. My knowledge consists exclusively of the mechanics of my own mind. All that I know is the nature of its norm. The judgments of the reason are arbitrary, and can never be verified. Truth and reality are simply the substance of the reason itself. My demonstration that "none = two" is the formula of the universe should then preferably be restated thus: "The mind of the Beast 666 is so constituted that it is compelled to conceive of a universe whose formula is none = two."

I note that Laotze makes no attempt to announce a Tao which is truly free from Teh. Teh is the necessary quality of Tao, even though Tao, withdrawing Teh into itself, seems to ignore the fact. The only pause I make is this, that mine own Holy Guardian Angel, Aiwaz—whose crown is Thelema; whose robe, Agape; whose body the Lost Word that He declared to me—spake in Book Seven and Twenty, saying: "Here is Nothing under its three forms." Can there then be not only Nothing Manifested, Teh or Two, a Nothing Unmanifested, Tao or Naught, but also a Nothing Absolute?

But there is nothing incompatible with the terms of this verse. The idea of "because" makes everything dependent on everything else, contrary to the conception of the universe which this Book has formulated. It is true that the concatenation exists; but the chain does not fetter our limbs. The actions and reactions of illusion are only appearances; we are not affected. No series of images matters to the mirror. What, then, is the danger of making "a great miss?" We are immune—that is the very essence of the doctrine. But error exists in this sense, that we may imagine it; and when a lunatic believes that Mankind is conspiring to poison him, it is no consolation that others know his delusion for what it is. Thus, we must "understand these runes," we must become aware of our true selves. If we abdicate our authority as absolute individuals, we are liable to submit to law, to feel ourselves the puppets of determinism, and to suffer the agonies of impotence which have afflicted the thinker, from Gautama to James Thomson.

Now then, "there is great danger in me"—we have seen what it is; but why should it lie in Hadit? Because the process of self-analysis involves certain risks. The profane are protected against those subtle spiritual perils which lie in ambush for the priest. A Bushman never has a nervous breakdown. (See Cap. 1, v.31.) When the aspirant takes his first oath, the most trivial things turn into transcendental terrors, tortures, and temptations. (*Book 4, pts. II-III,* elaborate this thesis at length.) We are so caked with dirt that the germs of disease cannot reach us. If we decided to wash, we must do it well; or we may have awakened some sleeping dogs, and set them on defenseless areas. Initiation stirs up the mud. It creates unstable equilibrium. It exposes our elements to unfamiliar conditions. The France of Louis XVI had to pass through the Terror before Napoleon could teach it to find itself. Similarly, any error in reaching the realization of Hadit may abandon the aspirant to the ambitions of every frenzied faction of his character, the masterless dogs of the Augean kennel of his mind.

---

28. Now a curse upon Because and his kin!

29. May Because be accursed for ever!

30. If Will stops and cries Why, invoking Because, then Will stops & does nought.

31. If Power asks why, then is Power weakness.

OLD COMMENT

28-31. The great curse pronounced by the supernals against the inferiors who arise against them.

Our reasoning faculties are the toils of the labyrinth within which we are all caught. Cf. *Lib. LXV,* v.59.

NEW COMMENT

28. This is against these intellectuals aforesaid. There are no "standards of right." Ethics are balderdash. Each star must go on its own orbit. To hell with "moral principle";

there is no such thing; that is a herd-delusion, and makes men cattle. Do not listen to the rational explanation of How Right It All Is, in the newspapers.

We may, moreover, consider "Because" as involving the idea of causality, and therefore of duality. If cause and effect are really inseparable, as they must be by definition, it is mere clumsiness to regard them as separate; they are two aspects of one single idea, conceived as consecutive for the sake of (apparent) convenience, or for the general purpose previously indicated of understanding and expressing ourselves in finite terms.

Shallow indeed is the obvious objection to this passage that *The Book of the Law* itself is full of phrases which imply causality. Nobody denies that causality is a category of the mind, a form or condition of thought which, if not quite a theoretical necessity, is yet inevitable in practice. The very idea of any relation between any two things appears as causal. Even should we declare it to be causal, our minds would still insist that causality itself was the effect of some cause. Our daily experience hammers home this conviction; and a man's mental excellence seems to be measurable almost entirely in terms of the strength and depth of his appreciation thereof as the soul of the structure of the universe. It is the spine of science which has vertebrated human knowledge above the slimy mollusc whose principle was faith.

We must not suppose for an instant that *The Book of the Law* is opposed to reason. On the contrary, its own claim to authority rests upon reason, and nothing else. It disdains the arts of the orator. It makes reason the autocrat of the mind. But that very fact emphasizes that the mind should attend to its own business. It should not transgress its limits. It should be a perfect machine, an apparatus for representing the universe accurately and impartially to its master. The self, its will, and its apprehension, should be utterly beyond it. Its individual peculiarities are its imperfections. If we identify ourselves with our thoughts or our bodily instincts, we are evidently pledged to partake of their partiality. We make ourselves items of the interaction of our own illusions.

In vv.29-31 we find the practical application of this theorem.

29. Distrust any explanation whatever. Disraeli said: "Never ask any one to dinner who has to be explained." All explanations are intended to cover up lies, injustices, or shames. The truth is radiantly simple.

30. There is no "reason" why a star should continue in its orbit. Let her rip! Every time the conscious mind acts, it interferes with the subconscious, which is Hadit. It is the voice of man, and not of a God. Any man who "listens to reason" ceases to be a revolutionary. The newspapers are Past Masters in the Lodge of Sophistry Number 333. They can always prove to you that it is necessary, and patriotic, and all the rest of it, that you should suffer intolerable wrongs.

The Qabalists represent the mind as a complex of six elements, whereas the will is single, the direct expression as "the word" of the self. The mind must inform the understanding, which then presents a simple idea to the will. This issues its order accordingly for unquestioning execution. If the will should appeal to the mind, it must confuse itself with incomplete and uncoordinated ideas. The clamor of these cries crowns anarchy, and action becomes impossible.

31. It is ridiculous to ask a dog why it barks. One must fulfill one's true nature, one must do one's will. To question this is to destroy confidence, and so to create an inhibition. If a woman asks a man who wishes to kiss her why he wants to do so, and he tries to explain, he becomes impotent. His proper course is to choke her into compliance, which is what she wants anyhow.

Power acts: the nature of the action depends on the information received by the will; but once the decision is taken, reflection is out of place. Power should indeed be absolutely unconscious. Every athlete is aware that his skill, strength, and endurance depend on forbidding mind to meddle with muscle.

Here is a simple experiment. Hold out a weight at arm's length. If you fix your attention firmly on other matters, you can support the strain many times longer than if you allow yourself to think of what your body is doing.

---

32. Also reason is a lie; for there is a factor infinite &
unknown; & all their words are skew-wise.

OLD COMMENT

32. We have insufficient data on which to reason. This passage only applies to "rational" criticism of the things beyond.

NEW COMMENT

The "factor infinite and unknown" is the subconscious will. "On with the revel!" "Their words"—the plausible humbug of the newspapers and the churches. Forget it! *Allons! Marchons!*

It has been explained at length in a previous note that "reason is a lie" by nature. We may here add certain confirmations suggested by the "factor." A and a (not-A) together make up the universe. As a is evidently "infinite and unknown," its equal and opposite A must be no less. Again, from any proposition, S is P, reason deduces "S is not p"; thus the apparent finitude and knowability of S is deceptive, since it is in direct relation with p.

No matter what n may be, the number of the inductive numbers is unaltered by adding or subtracting it. There are just as many odd numbers as there are numbers altogether. Our knowledge is confined to statements of the relations between certain sets of our own sensory impressions; and we are convinced by our limitations that "a factor infinite and unknown" must be concealed within the sphere of which we see but one minute part of the surface. As to reason itself, what is more certain than that its laws are only the conscious expression of the limits imposed upon us by our animal nature; and that to attribute universal validity, or even significance, to them is a logical folly, the raving of our megalomania? Experiment proves nothing; it is surely obvious that we are obliged to correlate all observations with the physical and mental structure whose truth we are trying to test.

Indeed, we can assume an "unreasonable" axiom, and translate the whole of our knowledge into its terms, without fear of stumbling over any obstacle. Reason is no more than a set of rules developed by the race; it takes no account of anything beyond sensory impressions and their reactions to various parts of our being. There is no possible escape from the vicious circle that we can register only the behavior of our own instrument. We conclude from the fact that it behaves at all, that there must be "a factor infinite and unknown" at work upon it. This being the case, we may be sure that our apparatus is inherently incapable of discovering the truth about anything, even in part.

Let me illustrate. I see a drop of water. Distrusting my eyes, I put it under the microscope. Still in doubt, I photograph and enlarge the slide. I compare my results with those of others. I check them by cultivating the germs in the water, and injecting them into paupers. But I have learned nothing at all about the "infinite and unknown," merely producing all sorts of different impressions according to the conditions in which one observes it!

More yet, all the instruments used have been tested and declared "true" on the evidence of those very eyes, distrust of which drove me to the research.

Modern science has at last grown out of the very-young-man cocksureness of the 19th century. It is now admitted that axioms themselves depend upon definitions, and that intuitive certainty is simply one trait of homo sapiens, like the ears of the ass or the slime of the slug. That we reason as we do merely proves that we cannot reason otherwise. We cannot move the upper jaw; it does not follow that the idea of motion is ridiculous. The limitation hints rather that there may be an infinite variety of structures which the jaw cannot imagine. The metric system is not the necessary mode of measurement. It is the mark of an untrained mind to take its own processes as valid for all men, and its own judgments for absolute truth. Our two eyes see an object in two aspects, and present to our consciousness a third which agrees with neither, and is indeed, strictly speaking, not sensible to sight, but to touch! Our senses declare some things at rest and others in motion; our reason corrects the error, firstly by denying that absolute motion possesses any meaning at all.

At the time when this Book was written, official science angrily scouted the "factor infinite and unknown," and clung with pathetic faith to the idea that reason was the touchstone of truth. In a single sentence, Aiwaz anticipates the discoveries by which the greatest minds now incarnate have made the last ten years memorable.

33. Enough of Because! Be he damned for a dog!

OLD COMMENT

33. We pass from the wandering in the jungle of reason to—the awakening. (See next verse.)

NEW COMMENT

This is the only way to deal with reason. Reason is like a woman; if you listen, you are lost; with a thick stick, you have some sort of sporting chance. Reason leads the philosopher to contradiction, the statesman to doctrinaire follies; it makes the warrior lay down his arms, and the lover cease to rave. What is so unreasonable as man? The only "because" in the lover's litany is "because I love you." We want no skeleton syllogisms at our symposium of souls.

Philosophically, "because is absurd." There is no answer to the question, "Why?" The greatest thinkers have been skeptics or agnostics: *Omnia exeunt in mysterium* and *Summa scientia nihil scire* are old commonplaces. In my essays "Truth" (in *Konx Om Pax*), "The Soldier and the Hunchback," "Eleusis" and others, I have offered a detailed demonstration of the self-contradictory nature of reason. The crux of the whole proof may be summarized by saying that any possible proposition must be equally true with its contradictory, for, if not, the universe would no longer be in equilibrium. It is no objection that to accept this is to destroy conventional logic, for that is exactly what it is intended to do. I may also mention briefly one line of analysis.

I ask, "What is, e.g., a tree?" The dictionary defines this simple idea by means of many complex ideas; obviously one gets in deeper with every stroke one takes. The same applies to any "why" that may be posed. The one existing mystery disappears as a consequence of innumerable antecedents, each equally mysterious.

To ask questions is thus evidently worse than a waste of time, so far as one is looking for an answer.

There is also the point that any proposition S is P merely includes P in the connotation of S, and is therefore not really a statement of relation between two things, but an amendment of the definition of one of them. "Some cats are black" only means that our idea of a cat involves the liability to appear black, and that blackness is consistent with those sets of impressions which we recognize as characteristic of cats. All ratiocination may be reduced to syllogistic form; hence, the sole effect of the process is to make each term more complex. Reason does not add to our knowledge; a filing system does not increase one's correspondence directly, though by arranging it one gets a better grasp of one's business. Thus coordination of our impressions should help us to control them; but to allow reason to rule us is as abject as to expect the exactitude of our ledgers to enable us to dispense with initiative on the one hand and actual transactions on the other.

---

34. But ye, o my people, rise up & awake!

NEW COMMENT

We are not to calculate, to argue, to criticize; these things lead to division of will and to stagnation. They are shackles of our going. They hamstring our Pegasus. We are to rise up, to go, to love; we are to be awake, alert:

> *Joyous and eager, Our tresses adorning,*
> *O let us beleaguer the City of Morning.*

The secret of magick is to "enflame oneself in praying."
This is the ready test of a star, that it whirls, flaming, through
the sky. You cannot mistake it for an old maid objecting to
everything. This universe is a wild revel of atoms, men, and
stars, each one a soul of light and mirth, horsed on eternity.

Observe that we must "rise up" before we "awake"!
Aspiration to the Higher is a dream—a wish-fulfillment which
remains a phantasm to wheedle us away from seeking
reality—unless we follow it up by action. Only then do we
become fully aware of ourselves, and enter into right reaction
with the world in which we live.

---

*35. Let the rituals be rightly performed with joy &
beauty.*

OLD COMMENT

Let us be practical persons, not babblers of gossip and
platitude.

NEW COMMENT

A ritual is not a melancholy formality; it is a sacrament,
a dance, a commemoration of the universe. The universe is
endless rapture, wild and unconfined, a mad passion of speed.
Astronomers tell us this of the Great Republic of Stars;
physicists say the same of the Little Republic of Molecules.
Shall not the Middle Republic of Men be like unto them? The
polite ethicist demurs; his ideal is funereal solemnity. His
horizon is bounded by death; and his spy-glass is smeared
with the idea of sin. The New Aeon proclaims Man as
Immortal God, eternally active to do His Will. All's joy, all's
beauty; this Will we celebrate.

In this verse we see how the awakening leads to ordered

and purposeful action. Joy and beauty are the evidence that our functions are free and fit; when we take no pleasure, find nothing to admire, in our work, we are doing it wrong.

36. *There are rituals of the elements and feasts of the times.*

37. *A feast for the first night of the Prophet and his Bride!*

38. *A feast for the three days of the writing of the Book of the Law.*

39. *A feast for Tahuti and the child of the Prophet—secret, O Prophet!*

40. *A feast for the Supreme Ritual, and a feast for the Equinox of the Gods.*

41. *A feast for fire and a feast for water; a feast for life and a greater feast for death!*

42. *A feast for every day in your hearts in the joy of my rapture!*

43. *A feast every night unto Nu, and the pleasure of uttermost delight!*

OLD COMMENT

36-43. A crescendo of ecstasy in the mere thought of performing these rituals; which are in preparation under the great guidance of V.V.V.V.V.

NEW COMMENT

36. Each element—Fire, Earth, Air, Water, and Spirit—possesses its own nature, will and magical formula. Each one may then have its appropriate ritual. Many such in crude form are described in *The Golden Bough*

of Dr. J. G. Frazer, the Glory of Trinity!

In particular the entry of the sun into the cardinal signs of the elements at the equinoxes and solstices are suitable for festivals.

The difference between "rituals" and "feasts" is this: by the one a particular form of energy is generated, while there is a general discharge of one's superfluous force in the other. Yet a feast implies periodical nourishment.

37. There should be a special feast on the twelfth of August in every year, since it was the marriage of the Beast which made possible the revelation of the New Law. (This is not an apology for marriage. Hard cases make bad law.)

38. This is April 8th, 9th and 10th, the feast beginning at high noon.

39. This particular feast is of a character suited only to initiates.

40. The supreme ritual is the Invocation of Horus, which brought about the opening of the New Aeon. The date is March 20.

The Equinox of the Gods is the term used to describe the beginning of a new aeon, or a new magical formula. It should be celebrated at every equinox, in the manner known to Neophytes of the A.A.

41. The feasts of fire and water indicate rejoicings to be made at the puberty of boys and girls respectively.

The feast for life is at a birth; and the feast for death at a death. It is of the utmost importance to make funerals merry, so as to train people to take the proper view of death. The fear of death is one of the great weapons of tyrants, as well as their scourge; and it distorts our whole outlook upon the universe.

42. To him who realizes Hadit this text needs little comment. It is wondrous, this joy of awakening every morning to the truth of one's immortal energy and rapture.

43. To sleep is to return, in a sense, to the bosom of Nuit. But there is to be a particular act of worship of Our Lady, as ye well wot.

44. *Aye! feast! rejoice! there is no dread hereafter. There is the dissolution, and eternal ecstasy in the kisses of Nu.*

OLD COMMENT

Without fear rejoice; death is only a dissolution, a uniting of Hadit with Nu, the Ego with the All, י with א. (Note י 10+ א 1 = 11, Abrahadabra, the word of uniting the 5 and the 6.)

NEW COMMENT

Do not be afraid of "going the pace." It is better to wear out than to rust out. You are unconquerable, and of indefatigable energy. Great men find time for everything, shirk nothing, make reputations in half a dozen different lines, have twenty simultaneous love affairs, and live to a green old age. The milksops and valetudinarians never get anywhere; usually they die early; and even if they lived forever, what's the use?

The body is itself a restriction as well as an instrument. When death is complete as it should be, the individual expands and fulfills himself in all directions; it is an omniform Samadhi. This is of course "eternal ecstasy" in the sense already explained. But in the time-world Karma reconcentrates the elements, and a new incarnation occurs.

45. There is death for the dogs.

OLD COMMENT

Those without our circle of ecstasy do indeed die. Earth to earth, ashes to ashes, dust to dust.

NEW COMMENT

The prigs, the prudes, the Christians, die in a real sense of the word; for although even they are "stars," there is not enough body to them (as it were) to carry on the individuality. There is no basis for the magical memory if one's incarnation holds nothing worth remembering. Count your years by your wounds—*forsitan haec olim meminisse juvabit.* In regard to this question of death I quote from *Liber Aleph*:

De Morte

Thou hast made Question of me concerning Death, and this is mine Opinion, of which I say not: This is the Truth. First: in the Temple called Man is the God, his Soul, or Star, individual and eternal, but also inherent in the Body of Our Lady Nuit. Now this Soul, as an Officer in the High Mass of the Cosmos, taketh on the Vesture of his Office, that is, inhabiteth a Tabernacle of Illusion, a Body and Mind. And this Tabernacle is subject to the Law of Change, for it is complex, and diffuse, reacting to every Stimulus or Impression. If then the Mind be attached constantly to the Body, Death hath not Power to decompose it wholly, but a decaying Shell of the Dead Man, his Mind holding together for a little his Body of Light, haunteth the Earth, seeking (in its Error, that Feareth Change) a new Tabernacle in some other Body. These Shells are broken away utterly from the Star that did enlighten them, and they are Vampires, obsessing them that adventure themselves into the Astral World without Magical Protection, or invoke them, as do the Spiritists. For by Death is Man released only from the Gross Body, at the first, and is complete otherwise upon the Astral Plane, as he was in his Life. But this Wholeness suffereth Stress, and its Girders are loosened, the weaker first, and after that the stronger.

De Adeptis R. C. Eschatologia

Consider now in this Light what shall come to the Adept, to him that hath aspired constantly and firmly to his Star, attuning the Mind unto the Music of its Will. In him, if his Mind be knit perfectly together in itself, and conjoined with the Star, is so strong a Confection that it breaketh away easily not only from the Gross Body, but the Fine. It is this Fine Body which bindeth it to the Astral, as did the Gross to the Material World; so then it accomplisheth willingly the Sacrament of a Second Death, and leaveth the Body of Light. But the Mind, cleaving closely by Right of its Harmony, and Might of its Love, to its Star, resisteth the Ministers of Disruption, for a Season, according to its Strength.

Now, if this Star be of those that are bound by the Great Oath, incarnating without Remission because of Delight in the Cosmic Sacrament, it seeketh a new Vehicle in the Appointed Way, and indwelleth the Foetus of a Child, and quickeneth it. And if at this Time the Mind of its Former Tabernacle yet cling to it, then is there Continuity of Character, and it may be Memory, between the two Vehicles. This, briefly and without Elaboration, is the Way of Asar in Amenti, according to mine Opinion, of which I say not: This is the Truth.

De Nuptiis Summis

Now then to this Doctrine, o my Son, add thou that which thou hast learned in *The Book of the Law*, that Death is the Dissolution in the Kiss of Our Lady Nuit. This is a true Consonance as of Bass with Treble; for here is the Impulse that setteth us to Magick, the Pain of the Conscious Mind. Having then Wit to find the Cause of this Pain in the Sense of Separation, and its Cessation by the Union of Love, it is the Summit of Our Holy Art to present the whole Being of Our Star to Our Lady in the Nuptial of our Bodily Death. We are then to make our whole Engine the true and real Appurtenance of our Force, without Leak, or Friction, or any other Waste or Hindrance to its Action. Thou knowest well how an Horse, or even a Machine propelled by a Man's Feet, becometh as it were an Extension of the Rider, through his Skill and Custom. Thus let thy Star have Profit of thy Vehicle, assimilating it, and sustaining it, so that it be healed of its Separation, and this even in Life, but most especially in Death. Also thou oughtest to increase thy Vehicle in Mass by true Growth in Balance that thou be a Bridegroom comely and well-favoured, a Man of Might, and a Warrior worthy of the Bed of so divine a Dissolution.

---

46. *Dost thou fail? Art thou sorry? Is fear in thine heart?*

OLD COMMENT

The prophet was again perplexed and troubled; for in his soul was compassion for all beings. But though his compassion is a feeling perhaps admirable and necessary for mortals, yet it pertains to the planes of illusion. It is based on a misapprehension.

NEW COMMENT

This verse brings out what is a fact in psychology, the necessary connection between fear, sorrow, and failure. To will and to dare are closely linked powers of the Sphinx, and they are based on knowing. If one have a right apprehension of the universe, if he know himself free, immortal, boundless, infinite force and fire, then may he will and dare. Fear, sorrow and failure are but phantoms.

47. Where I am these are not.

OLD COMMENT

Hadit knows nothing of these things; he is pure ecstasy.

NEW COMMENT

Hadit is everywhere; fear, sorrow, and failure are only "shadows." It is for this reason that compassion is absurd.

It may be objected that "shadows" exist after all; the "pink rats" of an alcoholic are not to be exorcised by Christian Science methods. Very true—they are, in fact, necessary functions of our idea of the universe in its dualistic "shadow-show." But they do not form any part of Hadit, who is beneath all conditions. And they are in a sense less real than their logical contradictories, because they are patently incompatible with the changeless and impersonal. They have their roots in conceptions involving change and personality. Strictly speaking, joy is no less absurd than sorrow, with reference to Hadit; but from the standpoint of the individual, this is not the case. One's fear of death is removed by the knowledge that there is no such thing in reality; but one's joy in life is not affected.

48. *Pity not the fallen! I never knew them. I am not for them. I console not: I hate the consoled & the consoler.*

OLD COMMENT

Hadit has never defiled His purity with the illusion of sorrow, etc. Even love and pity for the fallen is an identification with it, and therefore a contamination.

NEW COMMENT

It is several times shown in this Book that "falling" is in truth impossible. "All is ever as it was." To sympathize with the illusion is not only absurd, but tends to perpetuate the false idea. It is a mistake to spoil a child, or humor a *malade imaginaire.* One must, on the contrary, chase away the shadows by lighting a fire, which fire is: Do what thou wilt!

49. *I am unique & conqueror. I am not of the slaves that perish. Be they damned & dead. Amen. (This is of the 4:there is a fifth who is invisible, & therein am I as a babe in an egg.)*

OLD COMMENT

Continues the curse against the slave-soul."Amen. This is of the 4 . . . " That is, this should be spelled with four letters (the elements), אמתש not אמן. The fifth, who is invisible, is ע, 70, the Eye. Now אמחש = 741 + 70 = 811 = IAO in Greek, and IAO is the Greek form of יהוה, the synthesis of the four elements: אממתש. (This ע is perhaps the O. in N.O.X., *Liber VII.*, I., 40.)

NEW COMMENT

We are to conquer the illusion, to drive it out. The slaves that perish are better dead. They will be reborn into a world where freedom is the air of breath. So then, in all kindness, the Christians to the lions!

The "Babe in the Egg" is Harpocrates; it is his regular image.

I am not very well satisfied with the old comment on this verse. It appears rather as if the "amen" should be the beginning of a new paragraph altogether. "Amen" is evidently a synthesis of the four elements, and the invisible fifth is Spirit. But Harpocrates, the Babe in the Egg, is Virgo in the Zodiac indeed, but Mercury among the planets. Mercury has the winged helmet and heels, and the winged staff about which snakes twine, and it is He That Goeth. Now this letter is ב whose numeration is 2, and אמן is 91, which added to 2 makes 93. Amoun is of course Jupiter in his highest form. To understand this note fully one must have studied "The Paris Working"; also one must be an initiate of the O.T.O.

50. Blue am I and gold in the light of my bride; but the red gleam is in my eyes; & my spangles are purple & green.

OLD COMMENT
Cf. I, 60.

NEW COMMENT
There is here suggested the Image of "the star and the snake."

---

51. Purple beyond purple: it is the light higher than eyesight.

OLD COMMENT
Purple—the ultraviolet (v.51), the most positive of the colors. Green—the most negative of the colors, half-way in the spectrum.

The magical image of Hadit is therefore an eye within a coiled serpent, gleaming red—the spiritual red of the spirit of nature, the letter Shin, not mere fire—at the apex of the triangle in the half circle of Nuit's body, and shedding spangles as of the spectrum of eight colors, including the ultraviolet but not the ultra-red; and set above a black veil, as the next verse indicates.

NEW COMMENT
There is a certain suggestion in this "purple" as connected with "eyesight," which should reveal a certain identity of Hadit with the dwarf-soul to those who possess—eyesight!

52. There is a veil: that veil is black. It is the veil of the modest woman; it is the veil of sorrow, & the pall of death: this is none of me. Tear down that lying spectre of the centuries: veil not your vices in virtuous words: these vices are my service; ye do well, & I will reward you here and hereafter.

OLD COMMENT

This verse is very difficult for anyone, either with or without morality. For what "men" nowadays call "vice" is really virtue—virtue, manliness—and "virtue"—cowardice, hypocrisy, prudery, chastity, and so on, are really vices: *vitia*, flaws.

NEW COMMENT

Mohammed struck at the root of the insane superstition of taboo with his words: "Women are your field; go in unto them as ye will." He only struck half the blow. I say: Go in unto them as ye will and they will. Two-thirds of modern misery springs from woman's sexual dissatisfaction. A dissatisfied woman is a curse to herself and to everybody in her neighborhood. Woman must learn to let themselves enjoy without fear or shame, and both men and women must be trained in the technique of sex. Sex-repression leads to neurosis, and is the cause of social unrest. Ignorance of sexual technique leads to disappointment, even where passion is free and unrestrained. Sex is not everything in life, any more than food is; but until people have got satisfaction of these natural hungers, it is useless to expect them to think of other things. This truth is vital to the statesman, now that women have some direct political power; they will certainly overthrow the republic unless they obtain full sexual satisfaction. Also, women outnumber men; and one man cannot satisfy a woman unless he be skillful and diligent. The New Aeon will have a foundation of happy women. A woman under taboo is loathsome to life, detested by her fellows, and wretched in herself.

The student should study in *Liber Aleph* and *Liber 418*, the connection between "modesty" and the attitude of the "Black Brothers."

53. Fear not, o prophet, when these words are said, thou shalt not be sorry. Thou art emphatically my chosen; and blessed are the eyes that thou shalt look upon with gladness. But I will hide thee in a mask of sorrow; they that see thee shall fear thou art fallen: but I lift thee up.

OLD COMMENT

But the prophet again disliked the writing. The God comforted him. Also he prophesied of his immediate future, which was fulfilled, and is still being fulfilled at the time (1909, Sun in 20 Cancer) of this writing. Even more marked now (1911, Sun in Libra), especially these words, "I lift thee up."

NEW COMMENT

Yes! I was frightened when the God of Things as They Ought to Be told me They Were to Be. I was born under a German queen, and I did not believe in the revolution that I willed. And lo! it is upon us, ere the fifteenth year of the New Aeon has dawned.

Yes! I am lifted up, the Sun being in Scorpio in this fourteenth year of the Aeon (1918).

54. Nor shall they who cry aloud their folly that thou meanest nought avail; thou shall reveal it: thou availest: they are the slaves of because: They are not of me. The stops as thou wilt; the letters? change them not in style or value.

OLD COMMENT

The triumph over the rationalists predicted.

The punctuation of this book was done after its writing; at the time it was mere hurried scribble from dictation.

NEW COMMENT

The second part of the text was in answer to an unspoken query as to the peculiar phrasing.

The first part is clear enough. There are a number of people of shallow wit who do not believe in magick. This is doubtless partly due to the bad presentation of the subject by previous masters. I have identified magick with the art of life. The transcendental superstructure will not overburden those who have laid this right foundation.

There is an elaborate cryptographic meaning in this verse; the words "folly," "nought," "it," and "me" indicate the path of research.

55. Thou shalt obtain the order & value of the English Alphabet; thou shalt find new symbols to attribute them unto.

OLD COMMENT

Done. See *Liber Trigrammaton*, comment (Appendix I in this volume.)

NEW COMMENT

The attribution in *Liber Trigrammaton* is good theoretically; but no Qabalah of merit has arisen therefrom. I am inclined to look further into the question of Sanskrit roots, and into the Enochian records, in order to put this matter in more polished shape.

56. Begone! ye mockers; even though ye laugh in my honour ye shall laugh not long: then when ye are sad know that I have forsaken you.

OLD COMMENT

The God again identifies himself with the essential ecstasy. He wants no reference, but identity.

NEW COMMENT

These passages are certainly very difficult to understand. It seems as if they might have been given to meet some contingency which has not yet arisen. For example, this verse might be appropriate in case of the institution of a false cultus by impostors.

The doctrine is that Hadit is the nucleolus (to borrow a term from biology) of any star-organism. To mock at Hadit is therefore evidently very much what is meant by the mysterious phrase in the "New Testament" with regard to the unpardonable sin, the "blasphemy against the Holy Ghost." A star forsaken by Hadit would thus be in the condition of real death; it is this state which is characteristic of the "Black Brothers," as they are described in other parts of this comment, and elsewhere in the Holy Books of the A. A.

I may here quote *Liber Aleph,* "De Inferno Servorum" and "De Fratribus Nigris":

Now, o my Son, having understood the Heaven that is within thee, according to thy Will, learn this concerning the Hell of the Slaves of the Slave-Gods, that it is a true Place of Torment. For they, restricting themselves, and being divided in Will, are indeed the Servants of Sin, and they suffer, because, not being united in Love with the whole Universe, they perceive not Beauty, but Ugliness and Deformity; and, not being united in Understanding therof, conceive only of Darkness and Confusion, beholding Evil therein. Thus at last they come, as did the Manicheeans, to find, to their Terror, a Division even in the One, not that Division which we know for the Craft of Love, but a Division of Hate. And this, multiplying itself, Conflict upon Conflict, endeth in Hotchpot, and in the Impotence and Envy of Choronzon, and in the Abominations of the Abyss. And of such the Lords are the Black Brothers, who seek by their Sorceries to confirm themselves in Division. Yet in this even is no true evil, for Love conquereth All, and their Corruption and Disintegration is also Victory of BABALON.

O my Son, know this concerning the Black Brothers, them that exult: I am I. This is Falsity and Delusion, for the Law endureth not exception. So then these Brethren are not Apart, as they vainly think being wrought by Error; but are peculiar Combinations of Nature in Her Variety. Rejoice then even in the Contemplation of these, for they are proper to Perfection, and Adornments of Beauty, like a Mole upon the Cheek of a Woman. Shall I then say that were it of thine own nature, even thine, to compose so sinister a complex, thou shouldst not strive therewith, destroying it by Love, but continue in that Way? I deny not this hastily, nor affirm; nay, shall I even utter any Hint of that which I may foresee? For it is in mine own Nature to think that in this Matter the sum of Wisdom is Silence. But this I say, and that Boldly, that thou shalt not look upon this Horror with Fear, or with Hate, but accept this as thou dost all else, as a Phenomenon of Change, that is, of Love. For in a swift Stream thou mayst behold a Twig held steady for awhile by the Play of the Water, and by this Analogue thou mayst understand the Nature of this Mystery of the Path of Perfection.

57. He that is righteous shall be righteous still; he that is filthy shall be filthy still.

OLD COMMENT

A quotation from the Apocalypse. This God is not a Redeemer: He is Himself. You cannot worship Him, or seek Him—He is He. And if thou be He, well.

NEW COMMENT

This, and the first part of the next verse demonstrate the inviolability of Hadit, our Quintessence. Every star has its own nature, which is "right" for it. We are not to be missionaries, with ideal standards of dress and morals, and such hard ideas. We are to do what we will, and leave others to do what they will. We are infinitely tolerant, save of intolerance. It is no good, however, to try to prevent Christians from meddling, save by the one cure: the Christians to the lions.

It is impossible to alter the ultimate nature of any being, however completely we may succeed in transfiguring its external signs as displayed in any of its combinations. Thus, the sweetness, whiteness, and crystalline structure of sugar depend partly on the presence of carbon; so the bitterness, greenness, and resinous composition of hashish. But the carbon is inviolably carbon. And even when we transmute what seem to be elements, as radium to lead, we merely go a step further; there is still an immutable substance—or essence of Energy—which is inevitably itself, the basis of the diversity.

This holds good even should we arrive at demonstrating material monism. It may well be—I have believed so ever since I was fourteen years old—that the elements are all isomers, differentiated by geometrical structure, electrical charge, or otherwise in precisely the same way as ozone from oxygen, red from yellow, and a paraffin from a benzene of identical empirical formula. Indeed, every "star" is necessarily derived from the uniform continuity of Nuit, and is resolvable back into Her Body by proper analytical methods, as the experience of mysticism testifies. But each complex is nonetheless uniquely itself; for the scheme of its construction is part of its existence, so that this peculiar scheme constitutes the essence of its individuality. It is impossible to change a shilling into two sixpences, though the value and the material may be identical; for part of the essence of the shilling is the intention to have a single coin.

The above consideration must be thoroughly assimilated by any mind which wishes to gain a firm intellectual grasp of the truth which lies behind the paradox of existence.

*58. Yea! deem not of change: ye shall be as ye are, &
not other. Therefore the kings of the Earth shall be Kings for
ever: the slaves shall serve. There is none that shall be cast
down or lifted up: all is ever as it was. Yet there are masked
ones my servants: it may be that yonder beggar is a King. A
King may choose his garment as he will: there is no certain
test: but a beggar cannot hide his poverty.*

OLD COMMENT

Yet it does not follow that He (and His) must appear
joyous. They may assume the disguise of sorrow.

NEW COMMENT

Again we learn the permanence of the nature of a star.
We are not to judge by temporary circumstances, but to
penetrate to the true nature.

It has naturally been objected by economists that our
Law, in declaring every man and every woman to be a star,
reduces society to its elements, and makes hierarchy or even
democracy impossible. The view is superficial. Each star has a
function in its galaxy proper to its own nature.

Much mischief has come from our ignorance in insisting,
on the contrary, that each citizen is fit for any and every
social duty. But also our Law teaches that a star often veils
itself from its nature. Thus the vast bulk of humanity is
obsessed by an abject fear of freedom; the principal
objections hitherto urged against my Law have been made by
those people who cannot bear to imagine the horrors which
would result if they were free to do their own wills. The
sense of sin, shame, self-distrust, this is what makes folk cling
to Christianity-slavery. People believe in a medicine just in so
far as it is nasty; the metaphysical root of this idea is in
sexual degeneracy of the masochistic type. Now "the Law is

for all"; but such defectives will refuse it, and serve us who are free with a fidelity the more dog-like as the simplicity of our freedom denotes their abjection.

Even such shallow soapsud-mongers as Sir Walter Besant and Mr. James Rice have had an inkling of these ideas. I quote *Ready-Money Mortiboy*, Cap. XXIII:

> The big-bearded man stood towering over the children, with his right arm waving them out into the world—where? No matter where: somewhere away: somewhere into the good places of the world—not a boy's heart but was stirred within him: and the brave old English blood rose in them as he spoke, in his deep base tones, of the worth of a single man in those far-off lands: —an oration destined to bear fruit in after-days, when the lads, who talk yet with bated breath of the speech and the speaker, shall grow to man's estate.
>
> "Dangerous, Dick," said Farmer John. "What should I do without my labourers?"
>
> "Don't be afraid," said Dick. "There are not ten percent have the pluck to go. Let us help them, and you shall keep the rest."

He might have added that the employer would be better off without that percentage of yeast to ferment his infusion of harmless vegetable humans.

No one is better aware than I am that the labor problem has to be settled by practical and not ideal considerations, but in this case the ideal considerations happen to be extremely practical. The mistake has been in trying to produce a standard article to supply the labor market; it is an error from the point of view of capital and labor alike. Men should not be taught to read and write unless they exhibit capacity or inclination. Compulsory education has aided nobody. It has imposed an unwarrantable constraint on the people it was intended to benefit; it has been asinine presumption on the part of the intellectuals to consider a smattering of mental acquirements of universal benefit. It is a form of sectarian bigotry. We should recognize the fact that the vast majority of human beings have no ambition in life beyond mere ease and animal happiness. We should allow these people to fulfil their destinies without interference. We should give every opportunity to the ambitious, and thereby establish a class of morally and intellectually superior men and women. We should have no compunction in utilizing the natural qualities of the bulk of mankind. We do not insist on trying to train sheep to hunt foxes or lecture on history; we look after their physical well-being, and enjoy their wool and mutton. In this way we shall have a contented class of slaves who will accept the conditions of existence as they really are, and enjoy life with the quiet wisdom of cattle. It is our duty to see to it that this class of people lack for nothing.

The patriarchal system is better for all classes than any other; the objections to it come from the abuses of it. But bad masters have been artificially created by exactly the same blunder as was responsible for the bad servants. It is essential to teach the masters that each one must must discover his own will, and do it. There is no reason in nature for cut-throat competition. All this has been explained previously in other connections; here it is only necessary to emphasize the point. It must be clearly understood that every man must find his own happiness in a purely personal way. Our troubles have been caused by the assumption that everybody wanted the same things, and thereby the supply of those things has become artificially limited; even those benefits of which there is an inexhaustible store have been cornered. For example, fresh air and beautiful scenery. In a world where everyone did his own will none would lack these things. In our present society, they have become the luxuries of wealth and leisure, and yet they are still accessible to anyone who possesses sufficient sense to emancipate himself from the alleged advantages of city life. We have deliberately trained people to wish for things that they do not really want.

It would be easy to elaborate this theme at great length, but I prefer to leave it to be worked out by each reader in the light of his own intelligence; but I wish to call the very particular attention of capitalists and labor leaders to the principles here set forth.

I conclude by quoting four chapters from *Liber Aleph* which bear on the subject:

De Lege Motus

Consider, my Son, that word in the Call or Key of the Thirty Aethyrs: Behold the Face of your God, the Beginning of Comfort, whose eyes are the Brightness of the Heavens, which provided you for the Government of the Earth, and her Unspeakable Variety! And again: Let there be no Creature upon her or within her the same. All her Members let them differ in their Qualities, and let there be no Creature equal with another. Here also is the voice of true Science, crying aloud: Variation is the Key of Evolution. Thereunto Art cometh the third, perceiving Beauty in the Harmony of the Diverse. Know then, O my Son, that all Laws, all Systems, all Customs, all Ideals and Standards which tend to produce Uniformity, being in direct Opposition to Nature's Will to change and to develop through Variety, are accursed. Do thou with all thy Might of Manhood strive against these Forces, for they resist Change, which is Life; and thus they are of Death.

De Legibus Contra Motum

Say not, in thine Haste, that such Stagnations are Unity

even as the last Victory of thy free Will is Unity. For
thy Will moveth through free Function, according to its
particular Nature, to that End of Dissolution of all
Complexities, and the Ideals and Standards are
Attempts to halt thee on that Way. Although for thee
some certain Ideal be upon thy Path, yet for thy
Neighbour it may not be so. Set all men a-horseback;
thou speedest the Foot-soldier upon his way, indeed;
but what hast thou done to the Bird-man? Thou must
have simple Laws and Customs to express the general
Will, and so prevent the Tyranny or Violence of a few;
but multiply them not! Now then herewith I will
declare unto thee the Limits of the Civil Law upon the
Rock of the Law of Thelema.

De Necessitate Communi

Understand first that the Disturbers of the Peace of
Mankind do so by Reason of their Ignorance of their
own True Wills. Therefore, as this Wisdom of mine
increaseth among Mankind, the false Will to Crime must
become constantly more rare. Also, the Exercise of Our
Freedom will cause Men to be born with less and ever
less Affliction from that Dis-ease of Spirit, which
breedeth these false Wills. But, in the While of waiting
for this Perfection, thou must by Law assure to every
Man a Means of satisfying his bodily and his mental
Needs, leaving him free to develop any Superstructure in
accordance with his Will, and protecting him from any
that may seek to deprive him of these vertebral Rights.
There shall be therefor a Standard of Satisfaction,
though it must vary in Detail with Race, Climate, and
other such Conditions. And this Standard shall be based
upon a large Interpretation of Facts biological,
physiologial, and the like.

De Fundamentis Civitatis

Say not, o my Son, that in this Argument I have set Limits to individual Freedom. For each Man in this State which I purpose is fulfilling his own true Will by his eager Acquiescence in the Order necessary to the Welfare of all, and therefore of himself also. But see thou well to it that thou set high the Standard of Satisfaction, and that to every one be a surplus of Leisure and of Energy, so that, his Will of Self-preservation being fulfilled by the Performance of his Function in the State, he may devote the Remainder of his Powers to the Satisfaction of the other Parts of his Will. And because the People are oft-times unlearned, not understanding Pleasure, let them be instructed in the Art of Life: to prepare Food palatable and wholesome, each to his own Taste, to make Clothes according to Fancy, with variety of Individuality, and to practice the manifold Crafts of Love. These Things being first secured, thou mayst afterward lead them into the Heavens of Poesy and Tale, of Music, Painting, and Sculpture, and into the Lore of the Mind itself, with its insatiable Joy of all Knowledge. Thence let them soar!

---

59. *Beware therefore! Love all, lest perchance is a King concealed! Say you so? Fool! If he be a King, thou canst not hurt him.*

OLD COMMENT

Yet, because they are indeed invulnerable, one need not fear for them.

NEW COMMENT

We must abolish the shadows by the radiant light of the Sun. Real things are only thrown into brighter glory by His effulgence. We need have no fear then to throw the Christians to the lions. If there be indeed true men among them, who happen through defect of education to know no better, they will reincarnate all right, and no harm done.

This passage may perhaps be interpreted in a sense slightly different from that assumed in the above paragraph. We should indeed love all—is not the Law "Love under Will"? By this I mean that we should make proper contact with all, for love means union; and the proper condition of union is determined by will. Consider the right attitude to adopt in the matter of cholera. One should love it, that is, study it intimately; not otherwise can one be sure of maintaining the right relation with it, which is, not to allow it to interfere with one's will to live. (And almost everything that is true of cholera is true of Christians.)

---

60. Therefore strike hard & low, and to hell with them, master!

OLD COMMENT

Hit out indiscriminately, therefore. The fittest will survive. The doctrine is therefore contrary to that of Galileo or of Buddha.

NEW COMMENT

The Christians to the lions!

Sol in Libra, 1921: I am reminded of Samuel Butler's observation that the apotheosis of love is to devour the beloved. Indeed, one cannot say that one has perfectly attained to love or hate until the object of that passion is assimilated. The word "hell" is significant in this connection. One must never be so careless as to let oneself think that even "the style of a letter" (how much less a phrase!) in this Book is casual. The expression "to hell with them" is not merely an outburst of colloquial enthusiasm. The word "hell," that and no other, serves the purpose of the speaker. This would naturally be suggested to us, in any case, by the reflection that our Law does not indulge in the frothings of impotent fury, like the priestly frauds of Moses, the Rishis, and Buddha, in the weeping and wailing and gnashing of teeth of the Galilean fishwife. Our Law knows nothing of punishment beyond that imposed by ignorance and the awkwardness of their possessor. The word "hell" must therefore be explained in terms neither of virile vulgarity, or theological blackmail.

I quote *Liber Aleph*; from which the peculiar applicability of the expression to the problem of the text will be evident.

De Nuptiis Mysticis

O my Son, how wonderful is the Wisdom of this Law of Love! How vast are the Oceans of uncharted Joy that lie before the Keel of thy Ship! Yet know this, that every Opposition is in its Nature named Sorrow, and the Joy lieth in the Destruction of the Dyad. Therefore, must thou seek ever those Things which are to thee poisonous, and that in the highest Degree, and make them thine by Love. That which repels, that which disgusts, must thou assimilate in this Way of Wholeness. Yet rest not in the Joy of the Destruction of every Complex in thy Nature, but press on to that ultimate Marriage with the Universe whose Consummation shall destroy thee utterly, leaving only that Nothingness which was before the beginning.

So then the Life of Non-action is not for thee; the Withdrawal from Activity is not the Way of the Tao; but rather the Intensification and making universal of every Unit of thine Energy on every Plane.

De Inferno Palatio Sapientiae

Now then thou seest that this Hell, or Concealed Place within thee, is no more a Fear or Hindrance to Men of a Free Race, but the Treasure-House of the Assimilated Wisdom of the Ages, and the Knowledge of the True Way. Thus are we Just and Wise to discover this Secret in ourselves, and conform the conscious Mind therewith. For that Mind is composed solely (until it be illuminated) of Impressions and Judgments, so that its Will is but directed by the Sum of the shallow Reactions of a most limited Experience. But thy True Will is the Wisdom of the Ages of thy Generations, the Expression of that which hath fitted thee to thine Environment. Thus thy conscious Mind is often times foolish, as when thou admirest an Ideal, and wouldst attain it, but thy true Will letteth thee, so that there is Conflict, and the Humiliation of that Mind. Here will I call to Witness the common Event of "Good Resolutions" that defy the Lightning of Destiny, being puffed up by the Wind of an Indigestible Ideal putrefying within thee. Thence cometh Colic, and presently the Poison is expelled, or else thou diest. But Resolutions of True Will are mighty against Circumstance.

De Vitiis Voluntatis Secretae

Learn moreover concerning this Hell, or Hidden Wisdom, that is within thee, that is it modified, little by little in respect of its Khu, through the Experience of the Conscious Mind, which feedeth it. For that Wisdom is the Expression, or rather Symbol and Hieroglyph, of the true Adjustment of thy Being to its Environment. Now then, that Environment being eroded by Time, this Wisdom is no more perfect, for it is not Absolute, but standeth in Relation to the Universe. So then a Part thereof may become void of use and atrophy, as (I will instance this Case) Man's Wit of Smell; and the bodily Organ corresponding degenerateth therewith. But this is an Effect of much Time, so that in thine Hell thou art like to find Elements vain, or foolish, or contrary to thy present Weal. Yet, o my Son, this Hidden Wisdom is not thy True Will, but only the Levers (I may say so) thereof. Notwithstanding, there lieth therein a Faculty of Balance, whereby it is able to judge whether any Element in itself is presently useful and benign, or else idle and malignant. Here then is a Root of Conflict between the Conscious and the Unconscious, here is a Debate concerning the right Order of Conduct, how the Will may be accomplished.

---

61. There is a light before thine eyes, o prophet, a light undesired, most desirable.

OLD COMMENT

At the ecstasy of this thought the prophet was rapt away by the God. First came a strange new light, His herald.

NEW COMMENT

This chapter now enters upon an entirely new phase. The revelation or "hiding" of Hadit had by now sunk into the soul of the Beast, so that He realized Himself.

62. I am uplifted in thine heart; and the kisses of the stars rain hard upon thy body.

OLD COMMENT

Next, as Hadit himself, did he know the athletic rapture of Nuit's embrace.

NEW COMMENT

"Uplifted in thine Heart": compare *The Book of the Heart Girt with a Serpent* (Sangreal Foundation, Dallas, 1970).

63. Thou art exhaust in the voluptuous fullness of the inspiration; the expiration is sweeter than death, more rapid and laughterful than a caress of Hell's own worm.

OLD COMMENT

Each breath, as he drew it in, was an orgasm; each breath, as it went out, was a new dissolution unto death.

Note that throughout these books, death is always spoken of as a definite experience, a delightful event in one's career.

NEW COMMENT

This verse conceals a certain magical formula of the loftiest initiations. It refers to a method of using the breath, in connection with the appropriate series of ideas, which is perhaps not to be taught directly. But it may be learned by those who have attained the necessary degree of magical technique, suggested automatically to them by nature herself, just as newly hatched chickens pick up corn without instruction.

64. Oh! thou art overcome: we are upon thee; our delight is all over thee: hail! hail: prophet of Nu! prophet of Had! prophet of Ra-Hoor-Khu! Now rejoice! now come in our splendour & rapture! Come in our passionate peace, & write sweet words for the Kings!

OLD COMMENT

The prophet is now completely swallowed up in the ecstasy. Then he is hailed by the gods, and bidden to write on.

NEW COMMENT

"The Kings" are evidently those men who are capable of understanding themselves. This is a consecration of the Beast to the task of putting forth the Law.

"Thou art overcome." The conscious resisted desperately, and died in the last ditch.

65. I am the Master: thou art the Holy Chosen One.

66. Write, & find ecstasy in writing! Work & be our bed in working! Thrill with the joy of life and death! Ah! Thy death shall be lovely: whoso seeth it shall be glad. Thy death shall be the seal of the promise of our agelong love. Come! Lift up thine heart & rejoice! We are one; we are none.

OLD COMMENT

65-66. The division of consciousness having re-arisen, and been asserted, the God continues, and prophesies—of that which I cannot comment. The ecstasy rekindles.

NEW COMMENT

65. It is curious that this verse should be numbered 65, suggesting L.V.X. and Adonai, the Holy Guardian Angel. It seems then that He is Hadit. I have never liked the term "higher self"; True Self is more the idea. For each star is the husk of Hadit, unique and conqueror, sublime in His own virtue, independent of hierarchy. There is an external hierarchy, of course, but that is only a matter of convenience.

66. The first part of this text appears to be a digression in the nature of a prophecy. The word "Come!" is a summons to re-enter the full trance. Its essence is declared in the last six words. Notice that the transition from one to none is instantaneous.

---

67. *Hold! Hold! Bear up in thy rapture; fall not in swoon of the excellent kisses!*

68. *Harder! Hold up thyself! Lift thine head! breathe not so deep—die!*

OLD COMMENT

67-68. So violently does the trance recommence, that the body of the prophet is nigh death.

68. "Harden," not "Harder," as the MS. indicates. The Memory of DCLXVI says, though with diffidence, that the former is correct.

NEW COMMENT

67-68. The instructions in the text of this and the next verse were actual indications as to how to behave, so as to get the full effect of the trance.

This too is a general magical formula, convenient even in the work of the physical image of the Godhead.

It is of the utmost importance to resist the temptation to let oneself be carried away into trance. One should summon one's reserve forces to react against the tendency to lose normal consciousness. More and more of one's being is gradually drawn into the struggle, and one only yields at the last moment. (It needs practice and courage to get the best results.) I quote from the Holy Books:

Liber VII, I, 33

Fall not into death, O my soul! Think that death is the bed into which you are falling!

Liber LXV, III, 38-48

Thou hast brought me into great delight. Thou hast given me of Thy flesh to eat and of Thy blood for an offering of intoxication.

Thou hast fastened the fangs of Eternity in my soul, and the Poison of the Infinite hath consumed me utterly.

I am become like a luscious devil of Italy; a fair strong woman with worn cheeks, eaten out with Hunger for kisses. She hath played the harlot in diverse palaces; she hath given her body to the beasts.

She hath slain her kinsfolk with strong venom of toads; she hath been scourged with many rods.

She hath been broken in pieces upon the Wheel; the hands of the hangman have bound her unto it.

The fountains of water have been loosed upon her; she hath struggled with exceeding torment.

She hath burst in sunder with the weights of the waters; she hath sunk into the awful Sea. So am I, O

Adonai, my lord, and such are the waters of Thine intolerable Essence.

So am I, O Adonai, my beloved, and Thou hast burst me utterly in sunder.

I am shed out like spilt blood upon the mountains; the Ravens of Dispersion have borne me utterly away.

Therefore is the seal unloosed, that guarded the Eighth abyss; therefore is the vast sea as a veil; therefore is there a rending asunder of all things.

Liber LXV, I, 64
Intoxicate the inmost, O my lover, not the outermost!

68. It is remarkable that this extraordinary experience has practically no effect upon the normal consciousness of the Beast. "Intoxicate the inmost, o my God"—and it was His Magical Self, 666, that was by this ecstasy initiated. It needed years for this light to dissolve the husks of accident that shrouded his true seed.

69. Ah! Ah! What do I feel? Is the word exhausted?

OLD COMMENT
The prophet's own consciousness re-awakens. He no longer knows anything at all—then grows the memory of the inspiration past; he asks if it is all. (It is evidently his own interpolation in the dictation.)

NEW COMMENT
This phrase—the "word"—is of deeper significance than at first sight may appear. The question is not merely equivalent

to: "Is the dictation at an end?" For the word is conceived as the act of possession. This is evident from the choice of the word "exhausted." The inspiration has been like an electrical discharge. Language is in itself nothing; it is only the medium of transmitting experience to consciousness. Tahuti, Thoth, Hermes, or Mercury symbolize this relation; the character of this God is declared in very full terms in "The Paris Working," which should be studied eagerly by those who are fortunate enough to have access to the MS.

---

70. *There is help & hope in other spells. Wisdom says: be strong! Then canst thou bear more joy. Be not animal; refine thy rapture! If thou drink, drink by the eight and ninety rules of art: if thou love, exceed by delicacy; and if thou do aught joyous, let there be subtlety therein!*

OLD COMMENT

Also he has the human feeling of failure. It seems that he must fortify his nature in many other ways, in order that he may endure the ecstasy unbearable of mortals. There is also a change that other than physical considerations obtain.

NEW COMMENT

It is absurd to suppose that "to indulge the passions" is necessarily a reversion or degeneration. On the contrary, all human progress has depended on such indulgence. Every art and science is intended to gratify some fundamental need of nature. What is the ultimate use of the telephone and all other inventions on which we pride ourselves? Only to sustain life, or to protect or reproduce it; or to subserve knowledge and other forms of pleasure.

On the other hand, the passions must be understood properly as what they are, nothing in themselves, but the diverse forms of expression employed by the will. One must preserve discipline. A passion cannot be good or bad, too weak or too strong, etc., by an arbitrary standard. Its virtue consists solely in its conformity with the plan of the commander-in-chief. Its initiative and elan are limited by the requirements of his strategy. For instance, modesty may well cooperate with ambition; but also it may thwart it. This verse counsels us to train our passions to the highest degree of efficiency. Each is to acquire the utmost strength and intelligence; but all are equally to contribute their quota towards the success of the campaign.

It is nonsense to bring a verdict of "guilty" or "not guilty" against a prisoner, without reference to the law under which he is living. The end justifies the means: if the Jesuits do not assert this, I do. There is obviously a limit, where "the means" in any case are such that their use blasphemes "the end": e.g., to murder one's rich aunt affirms the right of one's poor nephew to repeat the trick, and so to go against one's own will-to-live, which lies deeper in one's being than the mere will-to-inherit. The judge in each case is not ideal morality, but inherent logic.

This being understood, then, that we cannot call any given passion good or bad absolutely, any more than we can call Knight to King's Fifth a good or bad move in chess without study of the position, we may see more clearly what this verse implies. There is here a general instruction to refine pleasure, not by excluding its gross elements, but by emphasizing all elements in equilibrated development. Thus one is to combine the joys of Messalina with those of Saint Theresa and Isolde in one single act. One's rapture is to include those of Blake, Petrarch, Shelley, and Catullus. *Liber*

Aleph has detailed instructions on numerous points involved in these questions.*

Why "eight and ninety" rules of art? I am totally unable to suggest a reason satisfactory to myself; but 90 is Tzaddi, the "Emperor," and 8, Cheth, the "Charioteer" or Cup-Bearer; the phrase might then conceivably mean "with majesty." Alternatively, 98 = 2 x 49: now two is the number of the will, and seven, of the passive senses. 98 might then mean the full expansion of the senses (7 x 7) balanced against each other, and controlled firmly by the will.

"Exceed by delicacy": this does not mean, by refraining from so-called animalism. One should make every act a sacrament, full of the divinest ecstasy and nourishment. There is no act which true delicacy cannot consecrate. It is one thing to be like a sow, unconscious of the mire, and unable to discriminate between sweet food and sour; another to take the filth firmly and force oneself to discover the purity therein, initiating even the body to overcome its natural repulsion and partake with the soul at this Eucharist. We "believe in the miracle of the mass" not only because meat and drink are actually "transmuted in us daily into spiritual substance," but because we can make the body and blood of God from any materials whatsoever by virtue of our royal and pontifical art of Magick.

Now when Brillat-Savarin (was it not?) served to the king's table a pair of old kid gloves, and pleased the princely palate, he certainly proved himself a master cook. The feat is not one to be repeated constantly, but one should achieve it at least once—that it may bear witness to oneself that the skill is there. One might even find it advisable to practice it occasionally, to retain one's confidence that one's "right hand hath not lost its cunning." On this point hear

*See also *Liber Astarte vel Berylli*, sub figura CLXXV.

furthermore our Holy Books:

Liber LXV, I, 45-46

Go thou unto the outermost places and subdue all things.

Subdue thy fear and thy disgust. Then— Yield!

Liber LXV, II, 7-15

Moreover I beheld a vision of a river. There was a little boat thereon; and in it under purple sails was a golden woman, an image of Asi wrought in finest gold. Also the river was of blood, and the boat of shining steel. Then I loved her; and, loosing my girdle, cast myself into the stream.

I gathered myself into the little boat, and for many days and nights did I love her, burning beautiful incense before her.

Yea! I gave her of the flower of my youth.

But she stirred not; only by my kisses I defiled her so that she turned to blackness before me.

Yet I worshipped her, and gave her of the flower of my youth.

Also it came to pass, that thereby she sickened, and corrupted before me. Almost I cast myself into the stream.

Then at the end appointed her body was whiter than the milk of the stars, and her lips red and warm as the sunset, and her life of a white heat like the heat of the midmost sun.

Then rose she up from the abyss of Ages of Sleep, and her body embraced me. Altogether, I melted into her beauty and was glad.

The river also became the river of Amrit, and the

little boat was the chariot of the flesh, and the sails thereof the blood of the heart that beareth me, that beareth me.

We therefore train our Adepts to make the gold philosophical from the dung of witches, and the elixir of life from Hippomanes; but we do not advocate ostentatious addiction to these operations. It is good to know that one is man enough to spend a month or so at a height of twenty thousand feet or more above sea level; but it would be unpardonably foolish to live there permanently.

This illustrates one case of a general principle. We consider the attainment of various illuminations, incomparably glorious as that is, of chief value for its witness to our possession of the faculty which made success possible. To have climbed alone to the summit of Iztaccihuatl is great and grand; but the essence of one's joy is that one possesses the courage, knowledge, agility, endurance, and self-mastery necessary to have done it.

The goal is ineffably worth all our pains, as we say to ourselves at first; but in a little while we are aware that even that goal is less intoxicating than the Way itself.

We find that it matters little whither we go; the going itself is our gladness. I quote in this connection *Liber LXV*, II, 17-25, one of several similar passages in our Holy Books.

Also the Holy One came upon me, and I beheld a white swan floating in the blue.

Between its wings I sate, and the aeons fled away.

Then the swan flew and dived and soared, yet no whither we went.

A little crazy boy that rode with me spake unto the swan, and said:

Who art thou that dost float and fly and dive and soar

in the inane? Behold, these many aeons have passed; whence camest thou? Whither wilt thou go?

And laughing I chid him, saying: 'No whence! No whither!'

The swan being silent, he answered: 'Then, if with no goal, why this eternal journey?'

And I laid my head against the Head of the Swan, and laughed, saying: 'Is there not joy ineffable in this aimless winging? Is there not weariness and impatience for who would attain to some goal?'

And the swan was ever silent. Ah! but we floated in the infinite Abyss. Joy! Joy!

'White Swan, bear thou ever me up between thy wings!'

"Be strong!" We need healthy robust bodies as the mechanical instruments of our souls. Could Paganini have expressed himself on the "fiddle for eighteen pence" that someone once bought when he was "young and had no sense?" Each of us is Hadit, the core of our Khabs, our star, one of the company of heaven; but this Khabs needs a Khu or magical image, in order to play its part in the great drama. This Khu, again, needs the proper costume, a suitable "body of flesh," and this costume must be worthy of the play.

We therefore employ various magical means to increase the vigor of our bodies and the energy of our minds, to fortify and to sublime them.

The result is that we of Thelema are capable of enormously more achievement than others, even in terrestrial matters, from sexual orgia to creative art. Even if we had only this one earthlife to consider, we exceed our fellows some thirtyfold, some sixtyfold, some hundredfold.

One most important point, in conclusion. We must doubtless admit that each one of us is lacking in one capacity or another. There must always be some among the infinite possibilities of Nuit which possess no correlative points of contact in any given Khu. For example, the Khu of a male body cannot fulfill itself in the quality of motherhood. Any such lacuna must be accepted as a necessary limit, without regret or vain yearnings for the impossible. But we should beware lest prejudice or other personal passion exclude any type of self-realization which is properly ours. In our initiation the tests must be thorough and exhaustive. The neglect to develop even a single power can only result in deformity. However slight this might seem, it might lead to fatal consequences; the ancient Adepts taught that by the parable of the heel of Achilles. It is essential for the aspirant to make a systematic study of every possible passion, icily aloof from all alike, and setting their armies in array beneath the banner of his will after he has perfectly guaged the capacity of each unit, and assured himself of its loyalty, discipline, courage, and efficiency. But woe unto him who leaves a gap in his line, or one arm unprepared to do its whole duty in the position proper to its peculiar potentialities!

71. But exceed! exceed!

OLD COMMENT

Yet excess is the secret of success.

NEW COMMENT

"The Road of Excess leads to the Palace of Wisdom." "You never know what is enough until you know what is too much." So wrote William Blake.

Progress, as its very etymology declares, means a step

ahead. It is the genius, the eccentric, the man who goes one better than his fellows, who is the savior of the race. And while it is unwise possibly (in some senses) to exceed in certain respects, we may be sure that he who exceeds, in no respect, is a mediocrity.

The key of evolution is right variation.

Excess is evidence at least of capacity in the quality at issue. The golf teacher growls tirelessly: "Putt for the back of the hole! Never up, never in!" The application is universal. Far from me be it to deny that excess is too often disastrous. The athlete who dies in his early prime is the skeleton at every boat supper. But in such cases the excess is almost always due to the desire to excel other men, instead of referring the matter to the only competent judge, the True Will of the body. I myself used to "go all out" on mountains; I hold more world's records of various kinds than I can reckon—for pace, skill, daring, and endurance. But I never worried about whether other people could beat me. For this reason my excesses, instead of causing damage to health and danger to life, turned me from a delicate boy, too frail for football, doomed by my doctors to die in my teens, into a robust ruffian who throve on every kind of hardship and exposure.

On the contrary, every department of life in which, from distaste or laziness, I did not "exceed," is constantly crippling me in one way or another—and I recognize with savage remorse that the weakness which I could have corrected so easily in my twenties is in my forties an incurably chronic complaint.

72. Strive ever to more! and if thou art truly mine—and doubt it not, and if thou art ever joyous!—death is the crown of all.

OLD COMMENT

There is no end to the Path; death itself crowns all.

NEW COMMENT

This striving is to be strenuous. We are not to set our lives at a pin's fee. "Unhand me, gentlemen!" "I'll make a ghost of him that lets me!" Death is the end that crowns the work.

Evolution works by variation. When an animal develops one part of itself beyond the others, it infringes the norm of its type. At first this effort is made at the expense of other efforts, and it seems as if the general balance is being upset, that nature is in danger. (It must obviously appear so to the casual observer—who probably reproaches and persecutes the experimenter.) But when this variation is indended to meet some new, or even foreseen, change in environment, and is paid for by some surplus part, or some part now superfluous, although once useful to meet a quality of the environment which no longer menaces the individual, the adaptation is biologically profitable.

Obviously, the whole idea of exercise, mental or bodily, is to develop the involved organs in a manner physiologically and psychologically proper.

It is deleterious to force any faculty to live by an alien law. When parents insist on a boy's adopting a profession which he loathes, because they themselves fancy it; when Florence Nightingale fought to open hospital windows in India at night; then the ideal mutilates and murders.

Every organ has "no law beyond Do What Thou Wilt."

Its law is determined by the history of its development, and by its present relations with its fellow-citizens. We do not fortify our lungs and limbs by identical methods, or aim at the same tokens of success in training the throat of the tenor and the fingers of the fiddler. But all laws are alike in this: they agree that power and tone come from persistently practicing the proper exercise without overstraining. When a faculty is freely fulfilling its function, it will grow; the test is its willingness to "strive ever to more"; it justifies itself by being "ever joyous." It follows that "death is the crown of all." For a life which has fulfilled all its possibilities ceases to have a purpose; death is its diploma, so to speak; it is ready to apply itself to new conditions of a larger life. Just so a schoolboy who has mastered his work "dies" to school, "reincarnates" in cap and gown, "triumphs" in the tripos, "dies" to the cloisters, and is "reborn" to the world.

Note that the "Death" in the Tarot refers to Scorpio. Its sign is threefold: the scorpion that kills itself with its own poison, when its environment (the ring of fire) becomes intolerable; the serpent that renews itself by shedding its skin, that is crowned and hooded, that moves by undulations like light, and gives man wisdom at the price of toil, suffering and mortality; and the eagle that soars, its lidless eyes bent boldly upon the sun. Death is, to the initiate, an inn by the wayside; it marks a stage accomplished; it offers refreshment, repose, and advice as to his plans for the morrow.

But in this verse, the main point is that death is the "crown" of all. The crown is Kether, the unity; "Love under will" having been applied to all Nuit-possibilities of all Khu-energies of any Hadit-central-star, that star has exhausted itself perfectly, completed one stage of its course. It is therefore crowned by death; and, being wholly itself, lives again by attracting its equal and opposite counterpart, with whom "love under will" is the fulfillment of the

Law, in a sublimer sphere.

But there are no rules until one finds them; a man leaving Ireland for the Sahara does well to discard such "indispensable" and "proper" things as a waterproof and a blackthorn for a turban and dagger.

The "moral" man is living by the no-reason of law, and that is stupid and inadequate even when the laws still hold good; for he is a mere mechanism, resourceless should any danger that is not already provided for in his original design, chance to arise. Respect for routine is the mark of the second-rate man.

The "immoral" man, defying convention by shouting aloud in church, may indeed be "brawling"; but equally he may be a sensitive who has felt the first tremor of an earthquake.

We of Thelema encourage every possible variation; we welcome every new "sport"; its success or failure is our sole test of its value. We let the hen's queer hatching take to water, and laugh at her alarms; and we protect the "ugly duckling," knowing that time will tell us whether it be a cygnet.

Herbert Spencer, inexorably condemning the unfit to the gallows, only echoed the high-priest who protected Paul from the Pharisees. Sound biology and sound theology are, for once, one!

The question of the limits of individual liberty is fully discussed in *Liber CXI (Aleph)*, to which we refer the student. The following chapters will give a general idea of the main principles.

De Vi Disciplinam Colenda

Consider the Bond of a cold Climate, how it maketh a man a Slave; he must have Shelter and Food with fierce Toil. Yet thereby he becometh strong against the

Elements, and his moral Force waxeth, so that he is Master of such Men as live in Lands of Sun where bodily Needs are satisfied without Struggle.

Consider also him that willeth to excel in Speed or in Battle, how, he denieth himself the Food he craveth, and all Pleasures natural to him, putting himself under the harsh Order of a Trainer. So by this Bondage he hath, at the last, his Will.

Now then the one by natural, and the other by voluntary, Restriction have come each to a greater Liberty. This is also a general law of Biology, for all Development is Structuralization; that is, a Limitation and Specialization of an originally indeterminate Protoplasm, which later may therefore be called free, in the definition of a Pendant.

De Ordine Rerum

In the Body every Cell is subordinated to the general physiological Control, and we who will that Control do not ask whether each individual Unit of that Structure be consciously happy. But we do care that each shall fulfil its Function, and the Failure of even a few Cells, or their Revolt, may involve the Death of the whole Organism. Yet even here the Complaint of a few, which we call pain, is a Warning of general Danger. Many Cells fulfil their Destiny by swift Death, and this being their Function, they in no wise resent it. Should Haemoglobin resist the attack of Oxygen, the Body would perish, and the Haemoglobin would not even save itself. Now, o my Son, do then consider deeply of these Things in thine Ordering of the World under the Law of Thelema. For every Individual in the State must be perfect in his own Function, with Contentment, respecting his own Task as necessary and holy, not

envious of another's. For so only mayst thou build up a
Free State, whose directing Will shall be singly directed
to the Welfare of all.

We of Thelema think it vitally aright to let a man take
opium. He may destroy his physical vehicle thereby, but he
may produce another "Kubla Khan." It is his own
responsibility. Also we know well that "if he be a King" it
will not hurt him—in the end. We trust Nature to protect, and
Wisdom to be justified of, their children. It is superficial to
object that a man should be prevented from ruining and
killing himself, for his own sake or for that of "those
dependent on him." One who is unfit to survive ought to be
allowed to die. We want only those who can conquer
themselves and their environment. As for "those dependent
on him" it is one of our chief objects to abolish the very idea
of dependence on others. Women with child, and infants, are
not exceptions, as might seem. They are doing their will, the
one class to reproduce, the other to live; the state should
consider their welfare to be its first duty; for if they are for
the moment dependent on it, it is also dependent on them. A
man might as well cut out his heart because it was weak and
in need of cautious care. But he would be no less foolish if he
tried to prevent the used-up elements from eliminating
themselves from his body. We respect the Will-to-Live; we
should respect the Will-to-Die. The race is auto-intoxicated
by suppressing the excretory process of Nature.

Each case must of course be judged on its merits. His
neighbors do well to assist one who is weak by accident or
misfortune, if he wishes to recover. But it is a crime against
the state and against the individuals in question to hinder the
gambler, the drunkard, the voluptuary, the congenital
defective, from drifting to death, unless they prove by their
own dogged determination to master their circumstances,
that they are fit to pull their weight in the Noah's Ark of

73. Ah! Ah! Death! Death! thou shalt long for death. Death is forbidden, o man, unto thee.

74. The length of thy longing shall be the strength of its glory. He that lives long & desires death much is ever the King among the Kings.

OLD COMMENT

73-74. Yet death is forbidden: work, I suppose must be done before it is earned; its splendor will increase with the years that it is longed for.

NEW COMMENT

73. There is a connection between death, sleep, and Our Lady Nuit. (This is worked out, on profane lines, by Dr. Sigmund Freud, and his school, especially by Jung, in the *Psychology of the Unconscious*, which the reader should consult.) The fatigue of the day's toil creates the toxins whose accumulation is the "will-to-die." All mystic attainment is of this type, as all magick is of the "will-to-live." At times we all want Nibbana, to withdraw into the Silence, and so on. The art of it is to dip deeply into "death," but to emerge immediately, a giant refreshed. This plan is also possible on the larger scale, all life being magick, all death, mysticism.

Then why is death "forbidden"? All things are surely lawful. But we must work "without lust of result," taking everything as it comes without desire indeed, but with all manner of delight! Let thy love-madrigal to death, thy mother-mistress, ripple and swell throughout the years, with all the starry heaven for thine orchestra; but do not imagine that to attain Her is the sole satisfaction. It is the yearning itself that is beatitude.

It may seem that in this verse the word "death" is used in a sense somewhat other than that explained in the previous note. It is forbidden, observe, to "man." That is, then, the formula must not be used by one who is still an imperfect being. Our definition is surely confirmed by this phrase rather than denied, or even modified. To long for death is to aspire to the complete fulfillment of all one's potentialities, and it would evidently be an error to insist upon passing on to one's next life while there were hawsers unhitched from this one. The mere inexplicability of the various jerks would make for bewilderment, irritation and clumsiness.

For this reason, alone, it is all-important to ascertain one's True Will, and to work out every detail of the work of doing it, as early in life as one can. One is apt (at the best) to define one's will dogmatically, and to devote one's life almost puritanically to the task, sternly suppressing all side-issues, and calling this course concentration. This is error, and perilous. For one cannot be sure that a faculty which seems (on the surface) useless, even hostile, to one's work, may not in the course of time, become one of vital value. If it be atrophied—alas! Its suppression may, moreover, have poisoned one's whole system, as a breast debarred from its natural use is prone to cancer. At best, it may be too late to repair the mischief; the lost opportunity may be a life-long remorse.

The one way of safety lies in applying the Law of Thelema with utmost rigor. Every impulse, however feeble, is necessary to the stability of the whole structure; the tiniest flaw may cause the cannon to burst. Every impulse, however opposite to the main motive, is part of the plan; the rifling does not thwart the purpose of the barrel. One should therefore acquiesce in every element of one's nature, and develop it as its own laws demand, with absolute impartiality. One need not fear; there is a natural limit to the growth of any species; it either finds that food fails, or it is choked by its neighbors, or overgrows itself and is transformed. Nor need one fret about the harmony and proportion of one's various faculties; the fit will survive, and the perfection of the whole will be understood as soon as the parts have found themselves, and settled down after fighting the matter out in the balanced stability which represents their right reaction to each other, and to their environment.

It is thus policy for an aspirant to initiation to analyze himself with indefatigable energy, shrewd skill, and accurate subtlety; but then to content himself with observing the interplay of his instincts, instead of guiding them. Not until he is familiar with them all, should he perform the practices which enable him to read the word of his will. And, then having assumed conscious control of himself, that he may do his will, he should make a point of using every faculty in a detached way (just as one inspects one's pistols and fires a few rounds) without expecting ever to need them again, but on the general principle that if they were wanted, one might as well feel confident of the issue.

This theory of initiation is so important to every aspirant that I shall illustrate how my own ignorance bred error and injury. My True Will was, I now know, to be the Beast, 666, a Magus, the Word of the Aeon, Thelema; to proclaim this new Law to mankind.

My passion for personal freedom, my superiority to sexual impulses, my resolve to master physical fear and weakness, my contempt for other people's opinions, my poetic genius: I indulged all these to the full. None of them carried me too far, ousted the other or injured my general well-being. On the contrary, each automatically reached its natural limit, and each has been incalculably useful to me in doing my will when I became aware of it, able to organize its armies, and to direct them intelligently against the inertia of ignorance.

But I suppressed certain impulses in myself. I abandoned my ambitions to be a diplomatist. I checked my ardor for science. I trampled upon my prudence in financial matters. I mortified my fastidiousness about caste. I masked my shyness in bravado, and tried to kill it by ostentatious eccentricity. This last mistake came from sheer panic; but all the rest were quite deliberate sacrifices on the altar of my God, Magick.

They were all accepted, as it then seemed. I attained all my ambitions; yea, and more also. But I know now that I should not have forced my growth and deformed my destiny. To nail geese to boards and stuff them makes *foie gras*, very true; but it does not improve the geese. It may be said that I strengthened my moral character by these sacrifices, and that I was indeed compelled to act as I did. The mad elephant Want-to-be-Magus pulled over the team of oxen. We may put it like that, certainly; but still, I feel that it might have been better had he not been mad.

For today, if I were an ambassador, versed profoundly in science, financially armed and socially stainless, I should be able to execute my will by pressure upon all classes of powerful people, to make this comment carry conviction to thinkers, and to publish *The Book of the Law* in every part of the world. Instead, I am exiled and suspected, despised by men of science, ostracized by my class, and a beggar. If I were in my teens again! I cannot change my mind about these ice-glazed pinnacles nor which ridge I'll climb the mountain by, now when I see, through gashes torn from whirling wreaths of arrowy sleet, the cloud-surpassing summit, not far, not very far. I regret nothing, be sure! I may be even in error to argue that an evident distortion of nature, and its issue in disaster, are proof of imprudence. Perhaps the other road would not have taken me to Cairo, to the climax of my life, to my True Will fulfilled in Aiwaz and made word in this Book. Perhaps it is lingering "lust of result" that whispers hideous lies to daunt me, that urges these plausible arguments to accuse me. It may be that my present extremity is the very condition required for the fulfillment of my work.* Who shall say what is power, what impotence? Who shall be bold to measure the morrow, or declare what causes conjoin to bring forth an effect that no man knoweth?

Was not Lao-Tze thrust forth from his city? Did not Buddha go begging in rags? Did not Mohammed flee for his life into exile? Was not Bacchus the scandal and the scorn of men? The Joseph Smith: had any man less learning? Yet each of these attained to do his will; each cried his word, that all the earth yet echoes it! And each was able to accomplish this by virtue of that very circumstance which seems so cruel. Shall I, who am armed with all their weapons at once, complain that I must go into the fight unfurnished?

74. One does not need to be constantly popping in and out of trance. One ought to do both actions with ever-increasing length and strength of swing. Hence, one's life-periods, where time counts, become gradually larger and more vivid, and one's death periods, though very short, perhaps, may be unfathomably intense.

The whole question of time has been thoroughly investigated already.† The present remarks refer only to the conditions of "normal" consciousness, into which we throw ourselves at recurring intervals. The doctrine here stated should be studied in the light of previous remarks; verses 61 to 74 inclusive form a coherent passage: notice the words "death" in verses 63 and 66, and "die" in verse 68. There is evidently an intention to identify the climax of love with that of life. It is then not unnatural for us to ask: Can "death" have some deeper significance than appears? Scorpio, the zodiacal sign of death, is really the sexual c.

---

*1926. It is now evident that this was the case.

†See also the essay on "Time": Crowley's *Collected Works*, Vol. II, pp. 267-82.

reproductive function of nature. It is the earth-transcending eagle, the self-restoring serpent, and the self-immolating scorpion. In alchemy it is the principle of putrefaction, the "black dragon," whose state of apparent corruption is but a prelude to the rainbow-colored springtide of the man in motley. The nymph of spring, Syrinx, the trembling hollow reed which needs but breath to fill the world with music, attracts Pan, the Goat-God of Ecstatic Lust, by whose work the glory of summer is established anew.

It is obvious that "the length of thy longing" varies with the number of potentialities to be satisfied. In other words, the more complex the Khu of the star, the greater the man, and the keener his sense of his own imperfections of the scope of his work, and of his need to achieve it.

---

75. Aye! listen to the numbers & the words:

76. 4 6 3 8 A B K 2 4 A L G M O R 3 Y X 24 89 R P S T O V A L. What meaneth this, o prophet? Thou knowest not; nor shalt thou know ever. There cometh one to follow thee: he shall expound it. But remember, o chosen one, to be me; to follow the love of Nu in the star-lit heaven; to look forth upon men, to tell them this glad word.

OLD COMMENT

75-76. A final revelation. The revealer to come is perhaps the one mentioned in I. 55 and III. 47. The verse goes on to urge the prophet to identify himself with Hadit, to practice the union with Nu, and to proclaim this joyful revelation unto men.

NEW COMMENT

75-76. Verse 76 appears to be a Qabalistic test (on the regular pattern) of any person who may claim to be the magical heir of the Beast. Be ye well assured all, that the solution, when it is found will be unquestionable. It will be marked by the most sublime simplicity, and carry immediate conviction.

(The above paragraph was written previous to the communication of Charles Stanfeld Jones with regard to the "numbers and the words" which constitute the key to the cipher of this Book. See the Appendix to this comment. I prefer to leave my remark as it originally stood, in order to mark my attitude at the time of writing.)

It is the prophet, the "forth-speaker," who is never to know this mystery. But that does not prevent it from lying within the comprehension of the Beast, kept secret by him in order to prove anyone who should claim sonship. (Cf. the note in brackets to the new comment on v.75.) The last part of this verse presents no difficulty.

1920, Sun in Sagittarius: In the Appendix will be found the Qabalistic proofs referred to in the penultimate paragraph, as supporting the claim of Charles Stanfeld Jones, whose occult names, numbers, dignities and titles are as follows:

PARZIFAL, Knight of the Holy Ghost, etc., X°
ACHAD, or O.I.V.V.I.O. (Omnia in Uno, Unus in Omnibus)
Fra.'. A.'. A.'., 8° = 3
O.T.O., 418, 777, VIO. (Unus in Omnibus)
ARCHTAEON, to be my son by Jeanne Foster
Soror Hilarion.

See Appendix for the technical explanation of this

verse. I may here briefly mention, however, that "Thou knowest not" is one of the cryptographic ambiguities characteristic of this Book. "Thou knowest"—see Chap. I, v.26; and "not" is Nuit. The word "ever," too, may be the object of "know," rather than merely an adverb.

Note "to be me," not "to be I"— an evident reference to Nuit, "not," MH. Cf. v.13 comment. One can only exist by being Nuit, as explained in discussing the general magical theory.

Observe that I am here definitely enjoined to proclaim my Law to men, "to look forth" instead of retiring from the world as mystics are wont to do. I may then be confident that this work is a proper part of my will.

Note: this "one" is not to be confused with the "child" referred to elsewhere in this Book. It is quite possible that O.I V.V.I.). (who took the grade of 8° = 3 by an act of will without going through the lower grades in the regular way) failed to secure complete annihilation in crossing the Abyss; so that the drops of blood which should have been cast into the cup of Babalon should "breed scorpions, and vipers, and the Cat of Slime." In this case he would develop into a Black Brother, to be torn in pieces and reduced to his elements against his will.

---

77. O be thou proud and mighty among men!

78. Lift up thyself! for there is none like unto thee among men or among Gods! Lift up thyself, o my prophet, thy stature shall surpass the stars. They shall worship thy name, foursquare, mystic, wonderful, the number of the man and the name of thy house 418.

OLD COMMENT

77-78. Though the prophet had, in a way, at this time, identified himself with the number 666, he considered the magic square drawn therefrom rather silly and artificial, if indeed it had yet been devised, on which point he is uncertain.

The House of the Prophet, not named by him, was chosen by him before he attached any meaning to the number 418; nor had he thought of attaching any importance to the name of the House. He supposed this passage to be mystical, or to refer to some future house.

Yet on trial we obtain at once: Boleskine—418.

NEW COMMENT

77-78. Pride is the quality of Sol. Tiphareth; Might of Mars, Geburah. Now Leo, my rising sign, combines these ideas, as does Ra-Hoor-Khuit. The Christian ideas of humility and weakness as "virtues" are natural to slaves, cowards and defectives.

The type of tailless simian who finds himself a mere forked radish in a universe of giants clamoring for hors d'oeuvres must take refuge from reality in Freudian fantasies of "God." He winces at the touch of truth; and shivers at his nakedness in nature.

He therefore invents a cult of fear and shame, and makes it presumption and blasphemy to possess courage and self-respect. He burrows in the slime of "reverence and godly fear" and makes himself houses of his own excrement, like the earthworm he is. He shams dead, like other vile insects, at the approach of danger; he tries to escape notice by assuming the color and form of his surroundings, using "protective mimicry" like certain other invertebrates.

He exudes stink or ink like the skunk or the cuttle-fish, calling the one morality and the other decency. He is slippery with hypocrisy, like a slug; and, labeling the totality of his defects perfection, defines God as feces so that he may flatter himself with the epithet divine. The whole maneuver is described as religion.

78. There are certain occult wonders concealed in the first part of this text. (See *Liber CCCLXX.*)

The solution of the last sentence may depend upon the number of the verse, which is that of Mezla, the Influx from the Highest, and of the Book of Thoth, or Tarot.

We may take "thy name" as "the Sun," for Qabalistic reasons given in the Appendix; the verse need not imply the establishment of a new cult with myself as Demigod. (Help!) But they shall worship the group of ideas connected with the Sun, and the magical formula of the number 418, explained elsewhere.

---

79. *The end of the hiding of Hadit; and blessing & worship to the prophet of the lovely Star!*

OLD COMMENT
So mote it be!

NEW COMMENT
So mote it be!

COMMENTARY
ON

The Book
of The Law

BY
ALEISTER CROWLEY
666

Part Three

Part Three

1. Abrahadabra; the reward of Ra-Hoor Khut.

OLD COMMENT

Abrahadabra—the reward of Ra-Hoor-Khuit. We have already seen that Abrahadabra is the glyph of the blending of the 5 and the 6, the rose and the cross. So also the Great Work, the equilibration of the 5 and the 6, is shown in this God; fivefold as a Warrior Horus, sixfold as the solar Ra. Khuit is a name of Khem the Ram-Phallus-two-plume god Amoun; so that the whole God represents in qabalistic symbolism the second triad ("whom all nations of men call the first").

It is the red descending triangle—the sole thing visible For Hadit and Nuit are far beyond.

Note that Ra-Hoor ראהוור=418.

NEW COMMENT

Observe firstly the word "reward," which is to be compared with the words "hiding" and "manifestation" in the former chapters. To "reward" is to "guard again"; this word

Abrahadabra then is also to be considered as a sentinel before the fortress of the God.

Why is the name of Him spelled Khut? We have seen that *st* is the regular honorific termination for a God. Ra is, as shown in the old comment, the Sun, Hoor the Warrior Mars; who is Khu? He is the magical ego of a star. Without the Yod or Iota, Khu-t, we get a human conception; the insertion of that letter makes the transmutation to Godhead. Therefore, when Ra Hoor Khut is rewarded or re-guarded with the magick word of the Aeon, he becomes God. Thus in the next verse: I "raise the spell of Ra-Hoor-Khuit."

The text may also be read as follows. Abrahadabra is the magick formula of the Aeon, by which man may accomplish the Great Work. This formula is then the "reward" given by the God, the largesse granted by Him on his accession to the lordship of the Aeon, just as the *INRI-IAO-LUX* formula of attainment by way of crucifixion was given by Osiris when he came to power in the last Aeon. (See *Book 4, Part III*, and *The Equinox*, Vol. I, No. 3, pp. 208-233.)

I must here say that I find myself in the greatest difficulty, again and again, in the comprehension of this chapter. It might be said roughly that at the end of the first five years of silence (1904-09) I understood Chapter I; at the end of the second five years (1914-18) I understood Chapter II.

---

2. There is division hither homeward; there is a word not known. Spelling is defunct; all is not aught. Beware! Hold! Raise the spell of Ra-Hoor-Khuit!

OLD COMMENT

Suggested by a doubt arising in the mind of the prophet as to the unusual spelling. But the "I" makes a difference in the Qabalistic interpretation of the name.

NEW COMMENT

"Division hither homeward"; a most dour phrase to interpret! Such a curious concatenation is sure to imply profound meaning. "Homeward" must mean "toward the house of" the speaker. He says, then, that there is "division," which (as I take it) prevents man from being God. This is a natural and orthodox meaning, and it goes well with "there [i.e., in verse 1] is a word not known." That word is Abrahadabra, which was not known, it having been concealed by the corrupt spelling "abracadabra."

"Spelling is defunct"; this seems to be an echo of the statement in Cap. II, V.5: "The rituals of the old time are black." (The word "defunct" is decidedly curious; the implication is "no longer able to fulfill its function.") "Spelling" then means "making spells." And it is characteristic of Ra-Hoor-Khuit that He demands not words, but acts. (Compare "The Paris Working.") So then we pass naturally to verse 3. "All is not aught" is an abrogation of all previous law, on the accession of a monarch. He wipes out the past as with a sponge.

This phrase is also an excessively neat cipher or hieroglyph of the great key to this Book. All (Al) is not aught (La). Al is La: that is to say, the phases of the Universe X and O are identical.

"Beware!" as if it were said to a soldier, "Attention." "Hold!" that is, "Steady!" Listen to the proclamation! "Raise the spell of Ra-Hoor-Khuit!" That is "Here, I, the New God, utter my word."

3. Now let it be first understood that I am a God of War and of Vengeance. I shall deal hardly with them.

OLD COMMENT

—end. This whole book seems intended to be interpreted literally. It was so taken by the scribe at the time. Yet a mystical meaning is easy to find—*Exempli gratia;* vv.4-9.

NEW COMMENT

Comment seems hardly necessary. The Great War is a mere illustration of this text. The only nations which have suffered are those whose religion was Osirian, or, as they called it, Christian. The exception is Turkey, which foolishly abandoned the principles of Islam to form an unholy alliance with the Giaour. Abdul Hamid would never have made such an ass of himself as the degenerate gang of "Liberty and Progress"; may jackals defile the pyres of their dog fathers!

(The God of Vengeance is in Greek, Aleister. For some reason which I have not been able to trace, this God became Alastor, the Desert Daemon of the Rabbins, later the "Spirit of Solitude" of Shelley. The attribution is appropriate enough, the root being apparently A λOMAI, "I wander." The idea of "going" is dreadful to the bourgeois, so that a wanderer is "accursed." But, *me judice,* to settle down in life is to abandon the heroic attitude; it is to acquiesce in the stagnation of the brain. I do not want to be comfortable, or even to prolong life; I prefer to move constantly from galaxy to galaxy, from one incarnation to another. Such is my intimate individual will. It seems as though this "God of War and of Vengeance" is then merely one who shall cause men to do their own wills by going as Gods do, instead of trying to check the irresistible course of nature.)

P.S. El Ouid, Algeria, 1924: The terror of Syria in the reign of Oman was the great soldier and administrator, Melekh-al-Astar. Possibly Jewish mothers used to scare their crying babies by threatening them with this "demon of the desert" and the Rabbins incorporated the "Bogey man" in their averse hierarchy.

---

4. Choose ye an island!

5. Fortify it!

6. Dung it about with enginery of war!

7. I will give you a war-engine.

8. With it ye shall smite the peoples; and none shall stand before you.

9. Lurk! Withdraw! Upon them! this is the Law of the Battle of Conquest: thus shall my worship be about my secret house.

OLD COMMENT

4. An island—one of the Cakkrams or nerve-centers in the spine.

5. Fortify it! Concentrate the mind upon it.

6. Prevent any impressions from reaching it.

7. I will describe a new method of meditation by which—

8. Ye shall easily suppress invading thoughts.

9. May mystically describe this method (e.g., *Liber HHH*, Section 3). But the course of history will determine the sense of the passage.

NEW COMMENT

4-9. This is a practical instruction; and, as a "military secret," is not in any way whatsoever to be disclosed. I say only that the plans are complete, and that the first nation to accept the Law of Thelema shall, by my counsel, become the sole mistress of the world.

6. This phrase is curiously suggestive of the "mine-layer" to those who have seen one in action.

7. This suggests the tank, the island chosen being England. But this is probably a forth-shadowing of the *real* Great War, wherein Horus shall triumph utterly.

9. "Lurk! Withdraw! Upon them!" describes the three parts of a certain magical gesture indicative of a formula which has proven very powerful in practical work.

(The events beginning in 1921, Sol in Libra, when I write these words, and ending I do not yet know when, will form a luminous comment on the passage. There is an alternative, taking the beginning as 1914, Sol in Libra, and implying larger periods.)

---

10. *Get the stele of revealing itself; set it in thy secret temple—and that temple is already aright disposed—& it shall be your Kiblah forever. It shall not fade, but miraculous colour shall come back to it day after day. Close it in locked glass for a proof to the world.*

OLD COMMENT

The stele of revealing—see illustration [at the beginning of *The Law Is for All*] .

That temple; it was arranged as an octagon; its length double its breadth; entrances on all four quarters of the temple; enormous mirrors covering six of the eight walls (there were no mirrors in the east or west or in the western halves of the south and north sides.)

There was an altar; and two obelisks in the temple; a lamp above the altar; and other furniture.

Kiblah—any point to which one turns to pray, as Mecca is the Kiblah of the Mohammedan.

11. This shall be your only proof. I forbid argument. Conquer! That is enough. I will make easy to you the abstruction from the ill-ordered house in the Victorious City. Thou shalt thyself convey it with worship, o prophet, though thou likest it not. Thou shalt have danger & trouble. Ra-Hoor-Khu is with thee. Worship me with fire & blood; worship me with swords & with spears. Let the woman be girt with a sword before me: let the blood flow to my name. Trample down the Heathen; be upon them, o warrior, I will give you of their flesh to eat!

OLD COMMENT

"Abstruction." It was thought that this meant to combine the abstruction and construction, i.e., the preparation of a replica, which was done.

Of course, the original is in "locked glass."

NEW COMMENT

The Victorious City is of course* Cairo (Al-Kahira, the victorious), and the ill-ordered house is the museum at Bulak.

Ra-Hoor-Khu; why is the name without its termination? Perhaps to indicate the essence of the force.

The ritual of the adoration of Ra-Hoor-Khuit is, as one might expect, illustrative of His nature. It seems doubtful

---

*Well, is it? Why not Nice (NIKH, Victory)?

whether this ritual can ever be of the type of symbolic celebration; it appears rather as if expeditions against the heathen, i.e., Christians and other troglodytes—but most especially the parasites of man, the Jews—were to be His rite. And it is to be taken that "the woman" is to take arms in His honor. This woman might be the Scarlet Woman, or perhaps woman generally. Remember that in the Scarlet Woman "is all power given"; and I expect a new Semiramis.

---

12. *Sacrifice cattle, little and big: after a child.*

13. *But not now.*

14. *Ye shall see that hour, o blessed Beast, and thou the Scarlet Concubine of his desire!*

15. *Ye shall be sad thereof.*

OLD COMMENT

12-15. This, ill-understood at the time, is now too terribly clear. The 15th verse, apparently an impossible sequel, has justified itself.

NEW COMMENT

12-15. This, read in connection with verse 43, was then fulfilled May 1, 1906. The tragedy was also part of my initiation, as described in the *Temple of Solomon the King.* It is yet so bitter that I care not to write of it.

16. Deem not too eagerly to catch the promises; fear not to undergo the curses. Ye, even ye, know not this meaning all.

OLD COMMENT

Courage and modesty of thought are necessary to the study of this book. Alas! we know so very little of the meaning.

NEW COMMENT

The God wisely refrains from clear expression, so that the event, as it occurs, may justify His word. This progressive illumination of that word has served to keep it alive as no single revelation could have done. Every time that I have dulled to *Liber Legis* something has happened to rekindle it in my heart.

"Know *not* this meaning *all*"; another cipher for LA-AL.

17. Fear not at all; fear neither man, nor Fates, nor gods, nor anything. Money fear not, nor laughter of the folk folly, nor any other power in heaven or upon the earth, or under the earth. Nu is your refuge as Hadit your light; and I am the strength, force, vigour of your arms.

OLD COMMENT

The infinite unity is our refuge, since if our consciousness be in that unity, we shall care nothing for the friction of its component parts. And our light is the inmost point of illuminated consciousness.

And the great red triangle is as a shield, and its rays are far-darting arrows!

NEW COMMENT

The last paragraph is a singular confirmation of the view which I have taken of our hierarchy: compare what has been said on the subject in previous chapters.

---

18. Mercy let be off: damn them who pity! Kill and torture; spare not; be upon them!

OLD COMMENT

An end to the humanitarian mawkishness which is destroying the human race by the deliberate artificial protection of the unfit.

NEW COMMENT

What has been the net result of our fine "Christian" phrases? In the good old days there was some sort of natural selection; brains and stamina were necessary to survival. The race, as such, consequently improved. But we thought we knew, oh! so much better, and we had "Christ's law" and other slush. So the unfit crowded and contaminated the fit, until earth herself grew nauseated with the mess. We had not only a war which killed some eight million men, in the flower of their age, picked men at that, in four years, but a pestilence which killed six million in six months.

Are we going to repeat the insanity? Should we not rather breed humanity for quality by killing off any tainted stock, as we do with other cattle? And exterminating the vermin which infect it, especially Jews and Protestant

Christians? Catholic Christians are really pagans at heart; there is usually good stuff in them, particularly in Latin countries. They only need to be instructed in the true meaning of their faith to reject the false veils.

(1925: After some years spent in Catholic countries, I wish to modify the above. Catholics are dead alike to spirituality and to reason, as bad as Protestants. And the Jew is far from hopeless outside America, where the previous paragraph was written.)

---

19. That stele they shall call the Abomination of Desolation; count well its name, & it shall be to you as 718.

OLD COMMENT
718 is γπομονη, the abstract noun equivalent to Perdurabo. (Sun in 3° Cancer, AnVII.)

NEW COMMENT
The reference appears to be to the old prophecies of "Daniel" and "John." The first Qabalistic allusion is yet (1915) undiscovered.

1921: I think it proper to insert here the account of the true meaning of this verse, though it more properly belongs to the Appendix. But the circumstances are so striking that it is well worth the while of the lay reader to become acquainted with the nature of the reasoning which attests the preterhuman character of the author of this Book.

It follows, in the words in which it was originally written, June 8, 1921 e.v., with no prelimianries, in my magical diary, at the Abbey of Thelema in Cephaloedium of Trinacria.

These verses are very subtly worded. How should I understand this allusion to the Stele; how "count well its name" without knowing it? I tried to count "Abomination of Desolation," but that is what "they shall call" it, not its proper name. It seemed that this name, when found, ought to add to 718, or to be identical with some other word or phrase that did so. More, this name when found must somehow express "the fall of because."

For many years these two verses, despite elaborate research, yielded no meaning whatsoever. At last I chanced upon the abstract noun = 718; it means "persistence," my first magical motto. Of course the Stele had persisted since the 26th Dynasty, but that scarcely justified naming it "Persistence"; also, there was nothing about "the fall of because."

Now, 1921, I was going through the Law in order to repair any details or omissions in the ritual ordained, and found these verses introduced among the instructions. They fascinated me; when I had finished the work in hand, I returned to them and worked for some hours with a lexicon, starting from the word APXH, cause, 709, to find some phrase equal to 718 which would deny cause. I found AZA, 9, a word meaning "dryness," but most especially the dirt or mold upon a disused object. APXH AZA is, therefore, a precise expression of the doctrine expounded in our Law about "because."

So far, so good; but this is in no sense the name of the Stele.

I worked on, and found XOIZA, 718, "yesterday" which might be grasped as a straw if I sank the third time; but I was swimming strongly enough. I found XAIPE A. A. "Hail to the A. A." I gracefully acknowledged the greeting to our Holy Order, but went on with my search. There is no such word as AXPICTA, "unchristlike things"; only blind bigotry could be satisfied with so crude an invention.

Then came ΧΑΡΑΗ, 713, an engraved character. That was a true name for the Stele; if I suffixed AD, 5, it might read "the Mark of Hadit." But I did not feel inwardly that thrill of ecstacy that springs in the heart or that dawn of amazement that kindles the mind, when truth's sheer simplicity takes form. There is a *definite psychological phenomenon* which accompanies any important discovery. It is like first love, at first sight, to the one; like the recognition of a law of nature, to the other. It inflames one with love for the universe, and it explains all its puzzles, in a flash; and it gives an interior conviction which nothing can shake, a living certainty quite beyond one's argued acquiescence; in any newly acquired facts.

I liked this; I knew that I had to seek further. The truth uttered by Aiwaz is hidden with such exquisite art that it is always easy to wring out a more or less plausible meaning by torture. Yet all such learned and ingenious fumblings reveal their own impotence; the right key opens the safe in a second, so simply and smoothly as to make it ridiculous to doubt that the lock was made by a master smith to respond to that key and no other.

The reader will have noticed that all the really important correspondences in this Book are so simple that a child might understand them. There also my own creaking and lumbering scholar-dredgers, not one of which is truly illuminating or even convincing. The real solution, moreover, is almost always confirmed by other parts of the text, or by events subsequent to the writing of the Book.

I worked on: I asked myself for the thousandth time what the Stele could claim with literal strictness as "its name." I scribbled the word CTHΛH and added it up. The result is 546, when Ct counts as 500; or 52, when Ct is 6, a frequent usage, as in CTAYPOS, whose number is thus 777.

Idly enough, my tired pen subtracted 52 from 718. I started up like a magician who, conjuring Satan in vain till faith's lamp sputters, and hope's cloak is threadbare, gropes, heavily leaning on the staff of love, blinking and droning along—and suddenly sees Him!

I did the sum over, this time with my pen like a panther. Too good to be true! I added my figures; yes, 718 past denial. I checked my value of Stele; 52, and no error. Then only I let myself yield to the storm of delight and wonder that rushed up from the hand of Him that is throned in the abyss of my being; and I wrote in my magical record the triumph for which I have warred for over seventeen years.

718
CTHλH 666

No fitter name could be found, that was sure . . . .And then came a flash to confirm me, to chase the last cloud of criticism; the actual name of the Stele, its ordinary name, the only name it ever had until it was called the "Stele of Revealing" in *The Book of the Law* itself. "Its name" in the catalogue of the museum at Boulak was just this: "Stele 666."

I have described this discovery at length because I wish to emphasize its importance. Most of the numbers and words openly mentioned in *The Book of the Law* which conceal secret matters were already at the time possessed of a certain significance for me. Some unconscious cooperation of a mind might be alleged as the determinant factor in the choice of those numbers, their subsequent interconnections, and so on, explained by the commentator's ingenuity, and the confirmation of independent facts by coincidence.

Similarly, the hidden numbers such as 3.141593, 395, 31, 93, may be ascribed to the commentators, and denied to the intention of the text; at least, by that class of pharisee which strains at the butterfly of the soul, preferring to swallow any hippopotamus if it be slimed thickly enough with the miasmal swamp-mire of materialism.

But 718 is expressed openly; its nature is described sufficiently and unambiguously; and it meant nothing to anybody in the world, either then or for seventeen years after.

And now the meaning falls so pat, so natural, so self-justified, so evidently the unique value of the "X" of the equation, that it is impossible to quibble.

The law of probabilities excludes all theories but one. The simple truth is what I have always asserted.

There is a being called Aiwaz, an intelligence discarnate, who wrote this *Book of the Law,* using my ears and hand. His mind is certainly superior to my own in knowledge and in power, for he has dominated me and taught me ever since.

But that apart, the proof of any discarnate intelligence, even of the lowest order, has never before been established. And lack of that proof is the flaw in all the religions of the past; man could not be certain of the existence of "God," because though he knew many powers independent of muscle, he knew of no consciousness independent of nerve.

---

20. Why? Because of the fall of Because, that he is not there again.

OLD COMMENT

In answer to some mental "why" of the prophet, the God gives this sneering answer. Yet perhaps therein is contained some key to enable me one day to unlock the secret of verse 19, at present, 1909, obscure. Now, 1911, clear.

NEW COMMENT

There is here a perception of the profound law which opposes thought to action. We act, when we act aright, upon the instructive wisdom inherited from the ages. Our ancestors survived because they were able to adapt themselves to their environment; their rivals failed to breed, and so "good" qualities are transmitted, while "bad" are sterile. Thus the race-thought, subconscious, tells a man that he must have a son, cost what it may. Rome was founded on the rape of the Sabine women. Would a reasoner have advocated that rape? Was it "justice" or "mercy" or "morality" or "Christianity?"

There is much on the ethics of this point in Chapter II of this Book. Thomas Henry Huxley in his essay, "Ethics and Evolution,"pointed out the antithesis between these two ideas, and concluded that evolution was bound to beat ethics in the long run.

He was apparently unable to see, or unwilling to admit, that his argument proved ethics (as understood by Victorians) to be false. The ethics of *Liber Legis* are those of evolution itself. We are only fools if we interfere. Do what thou wilt shall be the whole of the Law, biologically as well as in every other way.

Let us take an example. I am an anti-vaccinationist in a sense which every other anti-vaccinationist would repudiate. I admit that vaccination protects from small-pox. But I should like everyone to have small-pox. The weak would die; the strong might have pitted faces; but the race would become immune to the disease in a few generations.

On somewhat similar lines, I would advocate, with Samuel Butler, the destruction of all machinery. (I admit the practical difficulties of defining the limits of legitimate devices. The issue is this: how are we to develop human skill? The printing press is admirable in the hands of an Aldus, a Charles T. Jacobi, or even a William Morris. But the cheap mechanical printing of luetic rubbish on rotten pulp with worn types in inferior ink has destroyed the eyesight, putrified the mind, and deluded the passions of the multitude.) For machines are dodges for avoiding hard work; and hard work is the salvation of the race. In *The Time Machine*, H. G. Wells draws an admirable picture of a dichotomized humanity, one branch etiolated and inane, the other brutalized and automatic. Machines have already nearly completed the destruction of individual craftsmanship. A man is no longer a worker, but a machine-feeder. The product is standardized; the result, mediocrity. Nobody can obtain what he will; he must be content with what knavery puts on the market. Instead of every man and every woman's being a star, we have an amorphous pullulation of vermin.

---

21. Set up my image in the East: thou shalt buy thee an image which I will show thee, especial, not unlike the one thou knowest. And it shall be suddenly easy for thee to do this.

OLD COMMENT
This was remarkably fulfilled.

NEW COMMENT
Verses 21-30 seem to refer to the rites of public worship of Ra-Hoor-Khuit.

The word "set" is curious—is there here a reference to Set the God?

With regard to the old comment, I did indeed find an image of the kind implied. But there seems no special importance in this. I am inclined to see some deeper significance in this passage. There has elsewhere been reference to the words "not", "one," "Thou knowest." The word "easy" is moreover suggestive of some mystery; it is used in the same doubtfully intelligible sense in verse 40.

---

22. The other images group around me to support me: let all be worshipped, for they shall cluster to exalt me. I am the visible object of worship; the others are secret; for the Beast & his Bride are they: and for the winners of the Ordeal x. What is this? Thou shalt know.

OLD COMMENT

This first stage was accomplished; but nothing resulted of a sufficiently striking nature to record. The Ordeal "x" is dealt with in private.

NEW COMMENT

There are to be no regular temples of Nuit and Hadit, for They are incommensurables and absolutes. Our religion, therefore, for the people, is the cult of the Sun, who is our particular star of the Body of Nuit, from whom, in the strictest scientific sense, come this earth, a chilled spark of Him, and all our light and life. His vicegerent and representative in the animal kingdom is His cognate symbol, the phallus, representing love and liberty. Ra-Hoor-Khuit, like all true Gods, is therefore a solar-phallic deity. But we regard Him as He is in truth, eternal; the solar-phallic deities of the Old Aeon, such as Osiris, "Christ," Hiram, Adonis,

Hercules, etc., were supposed, through our ignorance of the cosmos, to "die" and "rise again." Thus we celebrated rites of "crucifixion" and so on, which have now become meaningless. Ra-Hoor-Khuit is the Crowned and Conquering Child. This is also a reference to the Crowned and Conquering Child in ourselves, our own personal God. Except ye become as little children, said "Christ," ye shall not enter into the Kingdom of God. The Kingdom is Malkuth, the Virgin Bride, and the Child is the Dwarf-Self, the phallic consciousness, which is the true life of man, beyond his "veils" of incarnation. We have to thank Freud—and especially Jung—for stating this part of the magical doctrine so plainly, as also for their development of the connection of the will of the "child" with the True or Unconscious Will, and so for clarifying our doctrine of the Silent Self or Holy Guardian Angel. They are of course totally ignorant of magical phenomena, and could hardly explain even such terms as "Augoeides"; and they are seriously to blame for not stating more openly that this True Will is not to be daunted or suppressed; but within their limits they have done excellent work.

---

23. *For perfume mix meal & honey & thick leavings of red wine: then oil of Abramelin and olive oil, and afterward soften & smooth down with rich fresh blood.*

OLD COMMENT

23-25. This incense was made; and the prediction most marvellously fulfilled.

NEW COMMENT

Meal: ordinary wheaten flour; leavings: the "beeswing" of port should be good; Oil of Abramelin: take eight parts of oil of cinnamon, four of oil of myrrh, two of oil of galangal, seven of olive oil.

24. The best blood is of the moon, monthly: then the fresh blood of a child, or dropping from the host of heaven: then of enemies; then of the priest or of the worshippers: last of some beast, no matter what.

NEW COMMENT

A: menstrual blood; B: possibly "dragon's blood."

These two kinds of "blood" are not to be confused. The student should be able to discover the sense of this passage by recollecting the Qabalistic statement that "the blood is the life," consulting *Book 4, Part III*, and applying the knowledge which reposes in the sanctuary of the Gnosis of the Ninth Degree of O.T.O. The "child" is "Babalon and the Beast conjoined, the secret saviour," the being symbolized by the egg and serpent hieroglyph of the Phoenician adepts. The second kind is also a form of Baphomet, but differs from the "child" in that it is the lion-serpent in its original form.

The process of softening and smoothing down is thus, in this case, that of vitalizing the eagle. It is inadvisable to word this explanation in terms too intelligible to the profane, since uninitiated attempts to make use of the formidable arcana of magick presented in this passage could lead only to the most fulminating and irremediable disaster.

25. This burn: of this make cakes & eat unto me. This hath also another use; let it be laid before me, and kept thick with perfumes of your orison, it shall become full of beetles as it were and creeping things sacred unto me.

NEW COMMENT

These beetles, which appeared with amazing suddenness in countless numbers at Boleskine during the summer of 1904 e.v., were distinguished by a long single horn; the species was new to the naturalists in London to whom specimens were sent for classification.

26. These slay, naming your enemies; & they shall fall before you.

27. Also these shall breed lust & power of lust in you at the eating thereof.

28. Also ye shall be strong in war.

29. Moreover, be they long kept, it is better; for they swell with my force. All before me.

OLD COMMENT

26-29. These experiments, however, were not made.

NEW COMMENT

26. See *Liber 418*, First Aethyr, final paragraphs.

27. The word "lust" is not necessarily to be taken in the sense familiar to Puritans. It means robustness, "merriment" as of old understood; the Germans have retained the proper force of the term in *lustig*. But even the English retain "lusty."

The Puritan is undoubtedly a marvel. He has even succeeded in attaching a foul connotation to a colorless word like "certain." "In a section of the city with a certain reputation women of a certain class suffering from certain diseases are charged with performing certain acts," is a common enough item in the newspapers. It allows the fullest play to the dirtiest imaginations—which appears to be the aim of the societies for the suppression of vice, and their like.

29. It is not altogether clear whether the beetles of the cakes are referred to in this strange passage. The proper way to discover the truth of this is to experiment.

There is a considerable amount of evidence in my possession which throws light upon this part of the chapter; but no important purpose would be served by producing it at present. These are circumstances when apparent frankness defeats its own ends as well as those of policy.

30. My altar is of open brass work: burn thereon in silver or gold.

OLD COMMENT
Not yet accomplished. (1909.)

NEW COMMENT
There is now such an altar as described; and the due rites are performed daily on it. (1921.)

31. There cometh a rich man from the West who shall pour his gold upon thee.

OLD COMMENT
Not yet accomplished. (1909.)

NEW COMMENT
I do not know whether this is to be taken in a practical sense. The obvious meaning of "from the West" in an Egyptian document would be "from the House of the Dead."

Alternatively, there may be a reference to the name of the person in question. I feel convinced that some event will occur to fit the passage with unmistakable accuracy. (1921.)

32. From gold forge steel.
33. Be ready to fly or to smite!

OLD COMMENT
32-33. Certainly, when the time comes.

NEW COMMENT
32-33. It suggests itself that the foregoing verses may have been fulfilled already in some manner which my feeble understanding of the chapter has hitherto failed to identify.

*34. But your holy place shall be untouched throughout
the centuries: though with fire and sword it be burnt down &
shattered, yet an invisible house there standeth, and shall
stand until the fall of the Great Equinox; when Hrumachis
shall arise and the double-wanded one assume my throne and
place. Another prophet shall arise, and bring fresh fever from
the skies; another woman shall awake the lust & worship of
the Snake; another soul of God and beast shall mingle in the
globed priest; another sacrifice shall stain The tomb; another
king shall reign; and blessing no longer be poured To the
Hawk-headed mystical Lord!*

OLD COMMENT

This prophecy, relating to centuries to come, does not
concern the present writer at the moment. Yet he must
expound it.

The hierarchy of the Egyptians gives us this genealogy:
Isis, Osiris, Horus.

Now the "pagan" period is that of Isis: a pastoral,
natural period of simple magic. Next with Buddha, Christ,
and others there came in the Equinox of Osiris; when sorrow
and death are the principal objects of man's thought, and his
magical formula is that of sacrifice.

Now, with Mohammed perhaps as its forerunner, comes
in the Equinox of Horus, the young child who rises strong and
conquering (with his twin Harpocrates) to avenge Osiris and
bring on the age of strength and splendor. His formula is not
yet fully understood.

Following will arise the Equinox of Maat, the Goddess
of Justice. It may be a hundred or ten thousand years from
now; for the computation of time is not here as there.

NEW COMMENT

Note the close connection between Leo and Libra in the Tarot, the numbers VIII and XI of their Trumps being interchanged with XI and VIII. There is no such violent antithesis as that between Osiris and Horus; Strength will prepare the reign of Justice. We should begin already, as I deem, to regard this Justice as the ideal whose way we should make ready, by virtue of our force and fire.

Taking the "holy Place" to be Boleskine House, it has already been subjected to a sort of destruction. It was presented by me to the O.T.O. and sold in order to obtain funds for the publication of *The Equinox,* Volume III. But the proceeds of the sale were mostly stolen by the then grand treasurer general of the order, one George MacNie Cowie, who became obsessed by the vulgarest form of hate against the Germans, despite my warnings, with reference to v.59 of this chapter. He became insane, and behaved with the blackest treachery, this theft being but a small portion of his infamies. The incident was necessary to my own initiation.

Hrumachis is the Dawning Sun; he therefore symbolizes any new course of events. The "double-wanded one" is "Thmaist of dual form as Thmais and Thmait," from whom the Greeks derived their Themis, goddess of Justice. The student may refer to *The Equinox,* Vol. I., No. 2, pp. 244-261. Thmaist is the Hegemon, who bears a mitre-headed scepter, like Joshua in the royal arch degree of freemasonry. He is the third officer in rank in the neophyte ritual of the G∴D∴ following Horus as Horus follows Osiris. He can then assume the "throne and place" of the Ruler of the Temple when the "Equinox of Horus" comes to an end.

The rhymed section of this verse is singularly impressive and sublime. We may observe that the details of the ritual of

changing officers are the same on every occasion. We may
therefore deduce that the description applies to the
"Equinox of the Gods" itself. How have the conditions been
fulfilled? The introduction to *Book 4, Part IV*, tells us. We
may briefly remind the reader of the principal events,
arranging them in the form of a rubric, and placing against
each the corresponding magical acts of the Equinox previous
to ours, as they are symbolized in the legends of Osiris,
Dionysus, Jesus, Attis, Adonis, and others (see page 291).

It may be presumptuous to predict any details
concerning the next Aeon after this.

35. *The half of the word of Heru-ra-ha, called
Hoor-pa-Kraat and Ra-Hoor-Khut.*

OLD COMMENT

Note, Heru-ra-ha = 418.

NEW COMMENT

Heru-ra-ha combines the ideas of Horus (cf. also "the
great angel Hru" who is set over the Book of Tahuti; see
Liber LXXVIII) with those of Ra and Spirit. For the
Atziluthic or archetypal spelling of He, the Holy Ghost. And
Ha = 6, the number of the Sun. He is also Nuit, H being Her
letter.

The language suggests that Heru-ra-Ha is the "true
Name" of the Unity who is symbolized by the Twins,
Harpocrates and Horus. Note that the *Twin Sign—and the
Child Sign—is Gemini*, whose letter is Zain, a sword.

The doctrine of the dual character of the God is very
important to a proper understanding of Him. "The Sign of

THE RUBRIC	AEON OF HORUS	AEON OF OSIRIS
Another prophet shall arise,	• The Beast 666	• Dionysis and others are names for (perhaps) Apollonius of Tyana. In the conditions then obtaining, several magi were required.
And bring fresh fever from the skies.	• "force and fire" of Horus—"skies" of Nuith.	
Another woman shall awake	• See comment on Chapter I, V.15	• "Venus" of the Adonis legends. We have no clue to her name.
The lust & worship of the Snake,	• The might and worthiness of Hadit within men; also the cult of the spermatozoon.	• The "Holy Ghost" or "Satan" indwelling. The key to magick in the Snake Apophis the Destroyer.
Another soul of God and beast Shall mingle in the globed priest,	• The union of Aiwaz and The Beast in Aleister Crowley. The identification of matter and spirit in our doctrine	• Pan as God & goat; Mary, etc. as Mother of the Son of God, fertilized by the Dove or Bull, Swan, etc. The doctrine of the regenerate incorruptible body.
Another sacrifice shall stain the tomb,	• Love is the magical formula: Sex as the key to life. "The tomb"—the temple of love.	• Crucifixion, etc. as the Magical Formula; Death as the key to life. "The tomb" —the coffin or grave.
Another king shall reign,	• Horus (Ra-Hoor-Khuit, the Crowned Child).	• Osiris (Jesus, etc.) the dying King [dying God formula] (see Frazer).
And blessing no longer be poured to the hawk-headed mystical Lord.	• Blessing—semen.	• Blessing—blood.

the Enterer is always to be followed immediately by the Sign of Silence": such is the imperative injunction to the Neophyte. In *Book 4*, the necessity for this is explained fully.

---

36. *Then said the prophet unto the God:*
37. *I adore thee in the song-*

> *I am the Lord of Thebes, and I*
> > *The inspired forth-speaker of Mentu;*
> *For me unveils the veiled sky,*
> > *The self-slain Ankh-af-na-Khonsu*
> *Whose words are truth. I invoke, I greet*
> > *Thy presence, O Ra-Hoor-Khuit!*

> *Unity uttermost showed!*
> > *I adore the might of Thy breath,*
> *Supreme and terrible God,*
> > *Who makest the gods and death*
> *To tremble before Thee:—*
> > *I, I adore Thee!*

> *Appear on the throne of Ra!*
> > *Open the ways of the Khu!*
> *Lighten the ways of the Ka!*
> > *The ways of the Khabs run through*
> *To stir me or still me!*
> > *Aum! let it fill me!*

38. *So that thy light is in me & its red flame is as a sword in my hand to push thy order. There is a secret door that I shall make to establish thy way in all the quarters, (these are the adorations, as thou hast written), as it is said:*

The light is mine; its rays consume
*   Me: I have made a secret door*
Into the House of Ra and Tum,
*   Of Khephra and of Ahathoor.*
I am thy Theban, O Mentu,
*   The prophet Ankh-af-na-khonsu!*

By Bes-na-Maut my breast I beat;
*   By wise Ta-Nech I weave my spell.*
Show thy star-splendour, O Nuith!
*   Bid me within thine House to dwell,*
O winged snake of light, Hadit!
*   Abide with me, Ra-Hoor-Khuit!*

OLD COMMENT

36-38. Mostly translation from the Stele.

NEW COMMENT

36. This passage appears to be a dramatic presentation of the scene shown in the Stele. The interpretation is to be that Ankh-f-n-Knonsu recorded for my benefit the details of the magical formula of Ra-Hoor-Khuit. To link together the centuries in this manner is nothing strange to the accomplished magician; but in view of the true character of time as it appears to the adept in mysticism, the riddle vanishes altogether.

37. Stanza 3 suggests the Rosicrucian Benediction:

May thy Mind be open unto the Higher!

May thy Heart be the Center of Light!

May thy Body be the Temple of the Rosy Cross!

38. See the translation of the Stele in the Introduction to *Book 4, Part IV* [and in the frontispiece to this book]. Note the four quarters or four solar stations enumerated in

lines 3 and 4 of the first stanza, and compare the ritual given in *Liber Samekh*. (*Book 4, Part III,* Appendix.)

---

39. All this and a book to say how thou didst come hither and a reproduction of this ink and paper for ever—for in it is the word secret & not only in the English—and thy comment upon this the Book of the Law shall be printed beautifully in red ink and black upon beautiful paper made by hand; and to each man and woman that thou meetest, were it to dine or to drink at them, it is the Law to give. Then they shall chance to abide in this bliss or no; it is no odds. Do this quickly!

OLD COMMENT

This is being done; but quickly? No. I have slaved at the riddles in this book for nigh on seven years; and all is not yet clear (1909). Nor yet (1911).

NEW COMMENT

This account is published with this comment itself. The present volume is thus the obedience to this command. "At them" may mean "at their house"; i.e., one must give when one recognizes anyone as a potential king by accepting his hospitality. An alternative meaning is "in their honor."

---

40. But the work of the comment? That is easy; and Hadit burning in thy heart shall make swift and secure thy pen.

OLD COMMENT

I do not think it easy. Though the pen has been swift enough, once it was taken in hand. May it be that Hadit hath indeed made it secure! (I am still [1911] entirely dissatisfied.)

NEW COMMENT

I am less annoyed with myself than when I wrote the "Old Comment," but not wholly content. How is one to write a comment? For whom? One has more than the difficulties of the lexicographer. Each new postulant presents new problems; the degrees and kinds of their ignorance are no less numerous than they. I am always finding myself, sailing along joyously for several months in the belief that my teaching is helping somebody, suddenly awakened to the fact that I have made no way whatever, owing to the object of my solicitude having omitted to learn that Julius Caesar conquered Gaul, or something of the sort, which I had assumed to be a matter of universal knowledge.

41. Establish at thy Kaaba a clerk-house: All must be done well and with business way.

OLD COMMENT

This shall be done as soon as possible.

NEW COMMENT

It is being done now.

42. The ordeals thou shalt oversee thyself, save only the blind ones. Refuse none, but thou shalt know & destroy the traitors. Success is thy proof: argue not; convert not; talk not over much! Them that seek to entrap thee, to overthrow thee, them attack without pity or quarter; & destroy them utterly. Swift as a trodden serpent turn and strike! Be thou deadlier than he! Drag down their souls to awful torment: laugh at their fear: spit upon them!

OLD COMMENT

This shall be attended to.

NEW COMMENT

"Ordeals" refer to the comment on chapter I, v.v. seq.; "Traitors": see *Liber 418,* 1st Aethyr. I quote:

Mighty, mighty, mighty, mighty; yea, thrice and four times mighty art thou. He that riseth up against thee shall be thrown down, though thou raise not so much as thy little finger against him. And he that speaketh evil against thee shall be put to shame, though thy lips utter not the littlest syllable against him. And he that thinketh evil concerning thee shall be confounded in his thought, although in thy mind arise not the least thought of him. And they shall be brought into subjection unto thee, and serve thee, though thou willest it not. And it shall be unto them a grace and a sacrament, and ye shall all sit down together at the supernal banquet, and ye shall feast upon the honey of the gods, and be drunk upon the dew of

immortality—FOR I AM HORUS, THE CROWNED
AND CONQUERING CHILD, WHOM THOU
KNEWEST NOT!

*43. Let the Scarlet Woman beware! If pity and
compassion and tenderness visit her heart; if she leave my
work to toy with old sweetnesses; then shall my vengeance be
known. I will slay me her child: I will alienate her heart: I
will cast her out from men: as a shrinking and despised harlot
shall she crawl through dusk wet streets, and die cold and
an-hungered.*

*44. But let her raise herself in pride! Let her follow me
in my way! Let her work the work of wickedness! Let her
kill her heart! Let her be loud and adulterous! Let her be
covered with jewels, and rich garments, and let her be
shameless before all men!*

*45. Then will I lift her to pinnacles of power: then will I
breed from her a child mightier than all the kings of the
earth. I will fill her with joy: with my force shall she see &
strike at the worship of Nu: she shall achieve Hadit.*

OLD COMMENT
43-45. The two latter verses have become useless, so far
as regards the person first indicated to fill the office of
"Scarlet Woman." In her case the prophecy of v.43 has been
most terribly fulfilled, to the letter; except the last
paragraph. Perhaps before the publication of this comment
the final catastrophe will have occurred. (1909.)

It or an even more terrible equivalent is now in progress.
(1911.)

(P.S.) I sealed up the MS. of this comment and posted it to the printer on my way to the Golf Club at Hoylake. On my arrival at the club, I found a letter awaiting me which stated that the catastrophe had occurred. Let the next upon whom the cloak may fall beware!

NEW COMMENT

43-45. It is impossible to discuss such passages as these until time has furnished the perspective.

The accounts of certain magical experiments in this line will be found in "The Urn."

This "child" is not necessarily to be identified with "him who shall discover the key of it all."

---

46. I am the warrior Lord of the Forties: the Eighties cower before me, and are abased. I will bring you to victory and joy: I will be at your arms in battle and ye shall delight to slay. Success is your proof; courage is your armour; go on, go on, in my strength; and ye shall turn not back for any!

OLD COMMENT

I do not understand the first paragraph.

NEW COMMENT

Forty is Mem, Water, the Hanged Man; and Eighty is Pe, Mars the Blasted Tower. These Trumps refer respectively to the "Destruction of the World by Water" and "by Fire." The meaning of these phrases is to be studied in my rituals of magick, such as *Book 4, Parts II & III.* Its general purport is that He is master of both types of force. I am inclined to opine that there is a simpler and deeper sense in the text than I have so far disclosed.

"At your arms" is a curious turn of phrase. There may be some cryptographic implication, or there may not; at least, there is this, that the use of such un-English expressions makes a clear-cut distinction between Aiwaz and the Scribe. In the inspired Books, such as *Liber LXV, VII, DCCCXIII* and others, written by the Beast 666 directly, not from dictation, no such awkward expressions are to be found. The style shows a well-marked difference.

47. *This book shall be translated into all tongues: but always with the original in the writing of the Beast; for in the chance shape of the letters and their position to one another: in these are mysteries that no Beast shall divine. Let him not seek to try: but one cometh after him whence I say not, who shall discover the Key of it all. Then this line drawn is a Key: then this Circle squared in its failure is a key also. And Abrahadabra. It shall be his child and that strangely. Let him not seek after this; for thereby alone can he fall from it.*

OLD COMMENT

These mysteries are inscrutable to me, as stated in the text. Later (1909) I note that the letters of the Book are the letters of the Book of Enoch; and are stars, or totems of stars. (See 15th Aire in *Liber 418*) so that he shall divine it shall be a Magus, 9 = 2.

NEW COMMENT

I am now (1918) a Magus, 9 = 2; and I agree with the former comment. He need only be a Magister Templi, 8 = 3, whose word is understanding.

"One cometh after him"—"one," i.e., Achad. See Appendix for this and other points of this most "evidential" verse. "The Key of it all"—all, i.e., Al 31 the Key! See MS. for allusion to the "line drawn" and the "circle squared in its failure."

The attribution (in the old comment) of the letters to those of the Book of Enoch is unsupported.

---

48. Now this mystery of the letters is done, and I want to go on to the holier place.

OLD COMMENT

48-62. Appears to be a plain instruction in theology and ethics. I do not understand "Din." Bahlasti = 358, and Ompehda, perhaps, 210. See Appendix.

---

49. I am in a secret fourfold word, the blasphemy against all gods of men.

NEW COMMENT

The evident interpretation of this is to take the word to be "Do what thou wilt," which is a secret word, because its meaning for every man is his own inmost secret. And it is the most profound blasphemy possible against all "gods of men," because it makes every man his own God.

We may then take it that this Solar-Phallic Ra-Ha is each man himself. As each independent cell in our bodies is to us, so is each of us to Heru-Ra-Ha. Each man's "child"—consciousness is a star in the cosmos of the sun, as the sun is a star in the cosmos of Nuit.

---

50. Curse them! Curse them! Curse them!
51. With my Hawk's head I peck at the eyes of Jesus as he hangs upon the cross.

NEW COMMENT

We are to consider carefully the particular attack of Heru-Ra-Ha against each of these "gods" or prophets; for though they be, or represent, the Magi of the past, the curse of their Grade must consume them.

Thus it is the eyes of "Jesus"—his point of view—that must be destroyed; and this point of view is wrong because of his magical gesture of self-sacrifice.

One must not for a moment suppose that this verse supports the historicity of "Jesus." "Jesus" is not, and never was, a man; but he was a "god," just as a bundle of old rags and a kerosene tin on a bush may be a "god." There is a man-made idea, built of ignorance, fear, and meanness, for the most part, which we call "Jesus," and which has been tricked out from time to time with various gauds from Paganism and Judaism.

The subject of "Jesus" is, most unfortunately, too extensive for a note; it is treated fully in my *Book 888*.

---

52. I flap my wings in the face of Mohammed & blind him.

NEW COMMENT

Mohammed's point of view is wrong too; but he needs no such sharp correction as "Jesus." It is his face—his outward semblance—that is to be covered with His wings. The tenets of Islam, correctly interpreted, are not far from our way of life and light and love and liberty. This applies especially to the secret tenets. The external creed is a mere nonsense suited to the intelligence of the peoples among whom it was promulgated; but even so, Islam is magnificent in practice. Its code is that of a man of courage and honor and self-respect; contrasting admirably with the cringing cowardice of the damnation-dodging Christians with their unmanly and dishonest acceptance of vicarious sacrifice, and their currish conception of themselves as "born in sin," "miserable sinners" with "no health in us."

53. With my claws I tear out the flesh of the Indian and Buddhist, Mongol and Din.

NEW COMMENT

"The Indian." The religion of Hindustan, metaphysically and mystically comprehensive enough to assure itself the possession of much truth, is in practice almost as supersititious and false as Christianity, a faith of slaves, liars, and dastards. The same remarks apply roughly to Buddhism.

"Mongol": Presumably the reference is to Confucianism, whose metaphysical and ethical flawlessness has not saved its adherents from losing those ruder virtues which are proper to a fighting animal, and thus yielding at last a civilization coeval with history itself to the barbarous tribes of Europe.

"Din"—"severity" or "Judgment" may refer to the Jewish Law, rather than to the faith (ad "din") of Islam. Assuming this, the six religions whose flesh must be torn out cover the whole globe outside Islam and Christianity.

Why assault their flesh rather than their eyes, as in the other cases? Because the metaphysics, or point of view, is correct—I take Judaism as Qabalistic—but the practice imperfect.

---

54. Bahlasti! Ompehda! I spit on your crapulous creeds.

NEW COMMENT

By sound, Bahlasti, suggests "hurling" or "blasting"; Ompehda is not too fantastically onomatopoetic for an "explosion."

---

55. Let Mary Inviolate be torn upon wheels: for her sake let all chaste women be utterly despised among you!

NEW COMMENT

The name Mary is connected with Mars, Mors, etc., from the Sanskrit *Mr,* "to slay"; and with *mare,* the sea, whose water opposes the fire of Horus. I here quote a passage from *Liber XCVIII* which deals with this fully.

"Let me strictly meditate this hate of the mother. *Mr* is the Sanskrit root "kill," hence Mara, Mors, Maria, and I suppose meer, mere, mer—in short, lots of words meaning "death" or "sea." Note Mordred as the traitor villain in *Morte d'Arthur*. In *Liber Legis* we have "Mary" who is to be "torn upon wheels" apparently because she is "inviolate." *Liber 418* has some explanation of this: "because she hath shut herself up," I seem to remember is the phrase. It appears (I don't remember the Sanskrit) as if a dental *t* or *d* were inserted phallically to give us madar, mater, mother (? meter—measure)."

Does the accent in "mere" conceal a lost dental? I suppose Jung or Freud has this all worked out in detail.

I have thought this before, long ago, but don't get a satisfactory Qabalah. 240 is a doubling of the Pentagram, of course, and is a six-fold of 40, the number of repressive "sealed-up" law. By our R.O.T.A., *Mr* is the sea swallowing the sun and the insertion of a Tau would help this in a certain formula of "he lives in the Sun." But that would only boost the mother, which won't do, for she is the tomb, the eater of flesh, and there's no getting away from it. But apparently she is all right just so far as she is open, to enter or leave at one's pleasure, the gateway of eternal life.

She is Sakti, the Teh, the magical door between the Tao and the manifested world. The great obstacle then is if that door be locked up. Therefore Our Lady must be symbolized as a whore. (Note Daleth, the Door—Venus. The Dove; free-flowing; all this is linked up in the symbol.) Clearly, at last, the enemy is this shutting up of things. Shutting the door is preventing the operation of change, i.e., of love. The objection to Calypso, Circe, Armida, Kundry, and co., is that one is liable to be shut up in their gardens. The whole of *The*

Book of the Dead is a device for opening the closed vehicles, and enabling the Osiris to go in and out at his pleasure. On the other hand, there seems to be a sealing up, for a definite period, in order to allow the change to proceed undisturbed. Thus earth lies fallow; the womb is closed during gestation; the Osiris is plugged with talismans. But it is vital to consider this as a strictly temporary device; and to *cut out the idea of eternal rest.* This Nibbana-idea is the coward—"Mother's Boy" idea; one ought to take a refreshing dip in the Tao, no more. I think this must be brought forward as the cardinal point of Holy Law. Thus, though Nuit cries "to me!" that is balanced by the formula of Hadit. "Come unto me" is a foolish word; for it is I that go.

Now the semen is God (the going-one, as shown by the Ankh or sandal-strap, which He carries) because he goes in at the door, stays there for a specified period, and comes out again, having flowered, and still bearing in him that seed of going. (The birth of a girl is a misfortune everywhere, because the true going-principle is the lion-serpent, or dragon; the egg is only the cavern where he takes refuge on occasions.)

Liber 418 explains this succinctly; 3rd Aethyr.

> Moreover, there is Mary, a blasphemy against Babalon, for she hath shut herself up; and therefore is she the queen of all those wicked devils that walk upon the earth, those that thou sawest even as little black specks that stained the Heaven of Urania. And all these are the excrement of Chorozon.

It is this "shutting up" that is hideous, the image of death. It is the opposite of going, which is God.

Women under Christianity are kept virginal for the market as Strasbourg geese are nailed to boards till their livers putrefy. The nature of woman has been corrupted, her hope of a soul thwarted, her proper pleasure balked, and her mind poisoned, to titillate the jaded palates of senile bankers and ambassadors.

Why do men insist on "innocence" in women?

1. To flatter their vanity.
2. To give themselves the best chance of (a) escaping venereal disease, (b) propagating their noble selves.
3. To maintain power over their slaves by their possession of knowledge.
4. To keep them docile as long as possible by drawing out the debauching of their innocence. A sexually pleased woman is the best of willing helpers; one who is disappointed or disillusioned, a very psychical eczema.
5. In primitive communities, to serve as a guard against surprise and treachery.
6. To cover their secret shame in the matter of sex.

Hence, the pretense that a woman is "pure," modest, delicate, aesthetically beautiful and morally exalted, ethereal and unfleshly, though in fact they may know her to be lascivious, shameless, coarse, ill-shapen, unscrupulous, nauseatingly bestial both physically and mentally. The advertisements of "dress shields," perfumes, cosmetics, anti-sweat preparations, and "beauty treatments" reveal woman's nature as seen by the clear eyes of those who would lose money if they misjudged her; and they are loathsomely revolting to read. Her mental and moral characteristics are those of the parrot and the monkey. Her physiology and pathology are hideously disgusting, a sickening slime of uncleanliness.

Her virgin life is a sick ape's, her sexual life a drunken sow's, her mother life all bulging filmy eyes and sagging udders.

These are the facts about "innocence"; to this has man's

Christian endeavor dragged her when he should rather have made her his comrade, frank, trusty, and gay, the tenderer self of himself, his consubstantial complement even as earth is to the sun.

We of Thelema say that "Every man and every woman is a star." We do not fool and flatter women; we do not despise and abuse them. To us, a woman is herself, absolute, original, independent, free, self-justified, exactly as a man is.

We dare not thwart her going, Goddess she! We arrogate no right upon her will; we claim not to deflect her development, to dispose of her desires, or to determine her destiny. She is her own sole arbiter; we ask no more than to supply our strength to her, whose natural weakness else were prey to the world's pressure. Nay more, it were too zealous even to guard her in her going; for she were best by her own self-reliance to win her own way forth!

We do not want her as a slave; we want her free and royal, whether her love fight death in our arms by night, or her loyalty ride by day beside us in the charge of the battle of life.

"Let the woman be girt with a sword before me"!

"In her is all power given."

So sayeth this our *Book of the Law.* We respect woman in the self of her own nature; we do not arrogate the right to criticize her. We welcome her as our ally, come to our camp as her will, free-flashing, sword-swinging, hath told her. Welcome, thou woman, we hail thee, star shouting to star! Welcome to rout and to revel! Welcome to fray and to feast! Welcome to vigil and victory! Welcome to war with its wounds! Welcome to lust and to laughter! Welcome to peace with its pageants! Welcome to board and to bed! Welcome to trumpet and triumph; welcome to dirge and to death!

It is we of Thelema who truly love and respect woman, who hold her sinless and shameless even as we are; and those who say that we despise her are those who shrink from the flash of our falchion as we strike from her limbs their foul fetters.

Do we call woman whore? Ay, verily and amen, she is that; the air shudders and burns as we shout it, exulting and eager.

O ye! Was not this your sneer, yor vile whisper that scorned her and shamed her? Was not "whore" the truth of her, the title of terror that you gave her in your fear of her, coward comforting coward with furtive glance and gesture?

But we fear her not; we cry whore, as her armies approach us. We beat on our shields with our swords. Earth echoes the clamor!

Is there any doubt of the victory? Your hordes of cringing slaves, afraid of themselves, afraid of their own slaves, hostile, despised and distrusted, your only tacticians the ostrich, the opossum, and the cuttle, will you not break and flee at our first onset, as with leveled lances of lust we ride at the charge, with our allies, the whores whom we love and acclaim, free friends by our sides in the battle of life?

The Book of the Law is the charter of woman; the word Thelema has opened the lock of her "girdle of chastity." Your Sphinx of stone has come to life; to know, to will, to dare and to keep silence.

Yea, I, the Beast, my Scarlet Whore bestriding me, naked and crowned, drunk on her golden cup of fornication, boasting herself my bedfellow, have trodden her in the market place, and roared this word that every woman is a star. And with that word is uttered woman's freedom; the fools and fribbles and flirts have heard my voice. The fox in woman hath heard the lion in man; fear, fainting, flabbiness, frivolity, falsehood—these are no more the mode.

In vain will bully and brute and braggart man, priest, lawyer, or social censor knit his brows to devise him a new tamer's trick; once and for all the tradition is broken;

vanished the vogue of bowstring, sack, stoning, nose-slitting, belt-buckling, cart's tail-tragging, whipping, pillory posting, walling-up, divorce court, eunuch, harem, mind-crippling, house-imprisoning, menial-work-wearying, creed-stultifying, social-ostracism marooning, divine-wrath-scaring, and even the device of creating and encouraging prostitution to keep one class of women in the abyss under the heel of the police, and the other on its brink, at the mercy of the husband's boot at the first sign of insubordination or even failure to please.

Man's torture-chamber had tools inexhaustibly varied; at one end murder crude and direct to subtler, more callous, starvation; at the other moral agonies, from tearing her child from her breast to threatening her with a rival when her service had blasted her beauty.

Most masterful man, yet most cunning was not thy supreme stratagem to band the woman's own sisters against her, to use their knowledge of her psychology and the cruelty of their jealousies to avenge thee on thy slave as thou thyself hadst neither wit nor spite to do?

And woman, weak in body, and starved in mind; woman, morally fettered by her heroic oath to save the race, no care of cost, helpless and hard, endured these things, endured from age to age. Hers was no loud spectacular sacrifice, no cross on a hill-top, with the world agaze, and monstrous miracles to echo the applause the heaven. She suffered and triumphed in most shameful silence; she had no friend, no follower, none to aid or approve. For thanks she had but maudlin flatteries, and knew what cruel-cold scorn the hearts of men scarce cared to hide.

She agonized, ridiculous and obscene; gave all her beauty and strength of maidenhood to suffer sickness, weakness, danger of death, choosing to live the life of a cow—so that mankind might sail the sea of time.

She knew that man wanted nothing of her but service of

his base appetites; in his true manhood-life she had no part nor lot; and all her wage was his careless contempt.

She hath been trampled thus through all the ages, and she hath tamed them thus. Her silence was the token of her triumph.

But now the word of me the Beast is this; not only art thou woman, sworn to a purpose not thine own; thou art thyself a star, and in thyself a purpose to thyself. Not only mother of men art thou, or whore to men; serf to their need of life and love, not sharing in their light and liberty; nay, thou art mother and whore for thine own pleasure; the word I say to man I say to thee no less: Do what thou wilt shall be the whole of the Law!

Ay, priest, ay, lawyer, ay, censor! Will ye not gather in secret once again, if in your hoard of juggler's tricks there be not one untried, or in your cunning and counsel one device new-false to save your pirate ship from sinking?

It has always been so easy up to now! What is the blasting magick in that word, first thesis of *The Book of the Law,* that "every woman is a star."

Alas! it is I the Beast that roared that word so loud, and wakened beauty.

Your tricks, your drowsy drugs, your lies, your hypnotic passes—they will not serve you. Make up your minds to be free men, fearless as I, fit mates for women no less free and fearless! For I, the Beast, have come; an end to the evils of old, to the duping and clubbing of abject and ailing animals, degraded to that shameful state to serve that shameful pleasure.

The essence of my word is to declare woman to be herself, of, to, and for, herself; and I give this one irresistible weapon, the expression of herself and her will through sex, to her on precisely the same terms as to man.

Murder is no longer dreaded; the economic weapon is

powerless since female labor has been found industrially valuable; and the social weapon is entirely in her own hands.

The best women have always been sexually free, like the best men; it is only necessary to remove the penalties for being found out. Let Women's labor organizations support any individual who is economically harried on sexual grounds. Let social organizations honor in public what their members practice in private.

Most domestic unhappiness will disappear automatically, for its chief cause is the sexual dissatisfaction of wives, or the anxiety (or other mental strain) engendered should they take the remedy into their own hands.

The crime of abortion will lose its motive in all but the most exceptional cases. Blackmail will be confined to commercial and political offenses, thus diminishing its frequency by two thirds at least, maybe much more. Social scandals and jealousies will tend to disappear. Sexual disease will be easier to track and to combat, when it is no longer a disgrace to admit it.

Prostitution (with its attendant crimes) will tend to disappear, as it will cease to offer exorbitant profits to those who exploit it. The preoccupation of the minds of the public with sexual questions will no longer breed moral disease and insanity, when the sex appetite is treated as simply as hunger. Frankness of speech and writing on sexual questions will dispel the ignorance which entraps so many unfortunate people; proper precaution against actual dangers will replace unnecessary and absurd precautions against imaginary or artificial dangers; and the quacks who trade on fear will be put out of business.

All this must follow as the light the night as soon as woman, true to herself, finds that she can no longer be false to any man. She must hold herself and her will in honor; and she must compel the world to accord it.

The modern woman is not going to be dupe, slave, and victim anymore; the woman who gives herself up freely to her own enjoyment, without asking recompense, will earn the respect of her brothers, and will openly despise her "chaste" or venal sisters, as men now despise "milksops," "sissies," and "tango lizards." Love is to be divorced utterly and irrevocably from social and financial agreements, especially marriage. Love is a sport, an art, a religion, as you will; ol' clo' emporium.

"Mary inviolate" is to be "torn upon wheels" because tearing is the only treatment for her; and RV, a wheel, is the name of the feminine principle. (See *Liber D.*) It is her own sisters who are to punish her for the crime of denying her nature, not men who are to redeem her, since, as above remarked, it is man's own false sense of guilt, his selfishness, and his cowardice, which originally forced her to blaspheme against herself, and so degraded her in her own eyes, and in his. Let him attend to his own particular business, to redeem himself—he surely has his hands full! Woman will save herself if she be but left alone to do it. I see it, I, the Beast, who have seen—who see—space splendid with stars, who have seen—who see—the Body of our Lady Nuit, all-pervading, and therein swallowed up, to have found—to find—no soul that is not wholly of her. Woman! thou drawest us upward and onward forever; and every woman is among women, of woman; one star of her stars.

I see thee, woman; thou standest alone; High Priestess art thou unto love at the altar of life. And man is the victim therein.

Beneath thee, rejoicing, he lies; he exalts as he dies, burning up in the breath of thy kiss. Yea, star rushes flaming to star; the blaze bursts, splashes the skies.

There is a cry in an unknown tongue. It resounds through the temple of the universe; in its one word is death and ecstasy, and thy title of honor, o thou, to thyself High Priestess, Prophetess, Empress, to thyself the Goddess whose name means mother and whore!

---

56. Also for beauty's sake and love's!

NEW COMMENT

It is obvious to the physiologist that beauty (that is, the fitness of proportion) and love (that is, the natural attraction between things whose union satisfies both) need for fulfillment absolute spontaneity and freedom from restriction. A tree grows deformed if it be crowded by other trees or by masonry; and gunpowder will not explode if its particles are separated by much sand.

If we are to have beauty and love, whether in begetting children or works of art, or what not, we must have perfect freedom to act, without fear or shame or any falsity. Spontaneity, the most important factor in creation, because it is evidence of the magnetic intensity and propriety of the will to create, depends almost wholly on the absolute freedom of the agent. Gulliver must have no bonds or packthread. These conditions have been so rare in the past, especially with regard to love, that their occurrence has usually marked something like an epoch. Practically all men work with fear of result or lust of result, and the "child" is a dwarf or still-born.

It is within the experience of most people that pleasure-parties and the like, if organized on the spur of the moment, are always a success, while the most elaborate entertainments, prepared with all possible care, often fall flat. Now one cannot exactly give rules for producing a "genius" to order, a genius in this sense being one who has the idea, and is fortified with power to enflame the enthusiasm of the crowd, with wit to know, and initiative to seize, the psychological moment.

But one can specify certain conditions, compatible with the manifestation of this spontaneity; and the first of these is evidently absolute freedom from obstacles, internal or external, to the idea of the "genius."

It is clear that a woman cannot love naturally, freely, wholesomely, if she is bound to contaminate the purity of her impulse with thoughts of her social, economical, and spiritual status. When such things restrain her, love may conquer, as often enough it does; but the beauty is usually stunted or made wry, assuming a tragic or cynic mask. The history of the world is full of such stories; it is, one may almost say, the chief motive of romance. I need only mention Tristan, Paolo, Romeo, Othello, Paris, Edward the Second, Abelard, and Tannhauser of old, and recently Mrs. Asquith, Maud Allen, Charles Stuart Parnell, Sir Charles Dilke, Lord Henry Somerset, and Oscar Wilde, down to "Fatty" Arbuckle!

Men and women have to face actual ruin, as well as the probability of scandal and disgust, or consent to love within limits which concern not love in the least. The chance of spontaneity is therefore a small one; and, should it occur and be seized, the lawyers hasten to hide under the bridal bed, while the families, gluing eye to chink and keyhole, intrude their discordant yowls on the duet.

Then, when love dies, as it must if either party have more imagination than a lump of putty, the fetters are fixed. He or she must go through the sordid farce of divorce if the chance of free choice is to be recovered; and even at that the fetters leave an incurable ulcer. It is no good playing the game of respectability after one is divorced.

Thus we find that almost the only love affairs which breed no annoyance, and leave no scar, are those between people who have accepted the Law of Thelema, and broken for good with the taboo of the slave-gods. The true artist, loving his art and nothing else, can enjoy a series of spontaneous liaisons, all his life long, yet never suffer himself, or cause any other to suffer.

Of such liaisons beauty is ever the child; the wholesome attitude of the clean simple mind, free from all complications alien to love, assures it.

Just as a woman's body is deformed and diseased by the corset demanded by Jagannath fashion, so is her soul by the compression of convention, which is a fashion as fitful, arbitrary, and senseless as that of the man-milliner, though they call him God, and his freakish fiat pass for everlasting law.

The English Bible sanctions the polygamy and concubinage of Abraham, Solomon and others, the incest of Lot, the wholesale rape of captured virgins, as well as the promiscuity of the first Christians, the prostitution of temple servants, men and women, the relations of Johannes with his master, and the putting of wandering prophets to stud, as well as the celibacy of such people as Paul. Jehovah went so far as to slay Onan because he balked at fertilizing his brother's widow, condoned the adultery, with murder of the husband, of David, and commanded Hosea to intrigue with a "wife of whoredom." He only drew the moral line at any self-assertion on the part of a woman.

In the past, man has bludgeoned woman into gratifying the lust of her loathed tyrant, and trampled the flower of her own love into the mire; making her rape more beastly by calling her antipathy chastity, and proving her an unclean thing on the evidence of the torn soiled blossom.

She has had no chance to love unless she first renounced

the respect of society, and found a way to drive the world of hunger from her door.

Her chance has come! In any abbey of Thelema any woman is welcome; there she is free to do her will, and held in honor for the doing. The child of love is a star, even as all are stars; but such an one we especially cherish; it is a trophy of battle fought and won!

---

57. Despise also all cowards; professional soldiers who dare not fight, but play: all fools despise!

NEW COMMENT

To fight is the right and duty of every male, as of every woman to rejoice in his strength and to honor and perpetuate it by her love. My primary objection to Christianity is "gentle Jesus, meek and mild," the pacifist, the conscientious objector, the Tolstoyan, the passive resister. When the Kaiser fled, and the Germans surrendered their fleet, they abandoned Nietzsche for Jesus. Rodjestvensky and Gervera took their fleets out to certain destruction. The Irish revolutionists of Easter Week, 1916, fought and died like men; and they have established a tradition.

"Jesus" himself, in the legend, "set his face as a flint to go to Jerusalem," with the foreknowledge of his fate. But Christians have not emphasized that heroism since the crusades. The sloppy sentimental Jesus of the sunday school is the only survivor; and the war killed him, thank Ares!

When the non-conformist Christian churches, especially in America, found the doctrine of eternal punishment no longer tenable, they knocked the bottom out of their religion. There was nothing to fight for. So they degenerated into tame social centers, so that Theosophy with its black brothers, Mrs. Eddy with her mental arsenic experts, the T. K. with his hypnotists and Jesuits, and Billy Sunday with his hell-fire, made people's flesh creep once more, and got both credit and cash.

The Book of the Law flings forth no theological fulminations; but we have quarrels enough on our hands. We have to fight for freedom against oppressors, religious, social, or industrial; and we are utterly opposed to compromise. Every fight is to be a fight to the finish; each one of us for himself, to do his own will; and all of us for all, to establish the law of liberty.

We do not want "professional soldiers," hired bravos sworn to have no souls of their own. They "dare not fight"; for how should a man dare to fight unless his cause be a love mightier than his love of life? Therefore they "play"; they have sold themselves; their will is no more theirs. Life is no longer a serious thing to them; therefore they wander wastrel in clubs and boudoirs and greenrooms; bridge, billiards, polo, petticoats puff out their emptiness; scratched for the great race of life, they watch the derby instead.

Brave such may be; they may well be (in a sense) classed with the rat; but brainless and idle they must be, who have no goal beyond the grave, where, at the best, chance flings fast-withering flowers of false and garish glory. They serve to defend things vital to their country; they are the skull that keeps the brain from harm? Oh foolish brain! Wert thou wiser to defend thyself, rather than to trust to brittle bone that hinders thee from growth?

Let every man bear arms, swift to resent oppression, generous and ardent to draw sword in any cause, if justice or freedom summon him!

"All fools despise." In this last phrase the word "fools" is evidently not to be taken in its deeper mystical sense, the context plainly bearing reference to ordinary life.

But the "fool" is still as described in the Tarot Trump. He is an epicene creature, soft and sottish, with an imbecile laugh and a pretty taste in fancy waistcoats. He lacks virility, like the ox which is the meaning of the letter Aleph which describes the Trump, and his value is zero, its number. He is air, formless and incapable of resistance, carrier of sounds which mean nothing to it, swept up into destructive rages of senseless violence from its idleness, incalculably moved by every pressure or pull. One-fifth is the fuel of fire, the corruption of rust; the rest is inert, the soul of explosives, with a trace of that stifling and suffocating gas which is yet food for vegetable, as it is poison to animal life.

We have here a picture of the average man, of a fool. He has no will of his own, is all things to all men, is void, a repeater of words whose sense he knows nought, a drifter, both idle and violent, compact partly of fierce passions that burn up both himself and the other, but mostly of inert and characterless nonentity, with a little heaviness, dullness, and stupefaction for his only positive qualities.

Such are the "fools" whom we despise. The man of Thelema is vertebrate, organized, purposeful, self-controlled, virile; he uses the air as the food of his blood; so also, were he deprived of fools he could not live. We need our atmosphere, after all; it is only when the fools become violent madmen that we need our cloak of silence to wrap us, and our staff to stay us as we ascend our mountain ridge; and it is only if we go down into the darkness of mines to dig ourselves treasures of earth that we need fear to choke on their poisonous breath.

*58. But the keen and the proud, the royal and the lofty;
ye are brothers!*

NEW COMMENT

"The keen": these are the men whose will is as a sword sharp and straight, tempered and ground and polished its flawless steel; with a wrist and an eye behind it.

"The proud": these are the men who know themselves to be stars, and bend the knee to none. True pride prevents a man from doing aught unworthy of himself.

"The royal": these are the men whose nature is kingly, the men who "can." They know themselves born rulers, whether their halidom be art, or science, or aught else whatsoever.

"The lofty"; these are the men who, being themselves high-hearted, endure not any baseness.

59. As brothers fight ye!

NEW COMMENT

Fight! Fight like gentlemen, without malice, because fighting is the best game in the world, and love the second best! Don't slander your enemy, as the newspapers would have you do; just kill him, and then bury him with honor. Don't keep crying "Foul!" like a fifth-rate pugilist. Don't boast! Don't squeal! If you're down, get up and hit him again! Fights of that sort make fast friends.

There is perhaps a magical second meaning in this verse, a reference to the ritual of which we find hints in the legends of Cain and Abel, Esau and Jacob, Set and Osiris, etc. The "elder brother" within us, the Silent Self, must slay the younger brother, the conscious self, and he must be raised again incorruptible.

---

60. There is no law beyond Do what thou wilt.

NEW COMMENT

There are of course lesser laws than this, details, particular cases of the Law. But the whole of the Law is "Do what thou wilt," and there is no law beyond it. This subject is treated fully in *Liber CXI, Aleph,* and the student should refer thereto.

Far better, let him assume this Law to be the universal key to every problem of life, and then apply it to one particular case after another. As he comes by degrees to understand it, he will be astounded at the simplification of the most obscure questions which it furnishes. Thus he will assimilate the Law and make it the norm of his conscious being; this, by itself, will suffice to initiate him, to dissolve his complexes, to unveil himself to himself; and so shall he attain the knowledge and conversation of his Holy Guardian Angel.

I have myself practiced constantly to prove the Law by many and diverse modes; in many and diverse spheres of thought, until it has become absolutely fixed in me, so much so that it appears an "identical equation," axiomatic indeed, and yet not a platitude, but a very sword of truth to sunder every knot at touch.

As the practical ethics of the Law, I have formulated in words of one syllable my declaration of the rights of man.

RIGHTS OF MAN
DO WHAT THOU WILT
SHALL BE THE WHOLE OF THE LAW
There is no god but Man.

Man has the right to live by his own Law.
Man has the right to live in the way that he wills to do.
Man has the right to dress as he wills to do.
Man has the right to dwell where he wills to dwell.
Man has the right to move as he will on the face of the earth.
Man has the right to eat what he will.
Man has the right to drink what he will.
Man has the right to think as he will.
Man has the right to speak as he will.
Man has the right to write as he will.
Man has the right to mold as he will.
Man has the right to paint as he will.
Man has the right to carve as he will.
Man has the right to work as he will.
Man has the right to rest as he will.
Man has the right to love as he will, when, where and whom
   he will.
Man has the right to die when and how he will.
Man has the right to kill those who would thwart these rights.

This statement must not be regarded as individualism run wild. Its harmony with statecraft is demonstrated in the chapters of *Liber Aleph* already quoted—see comment on Chapter II, v.72.

Modern thought, even that of the shallowest, is compelled by Aiwaz to confirm His Law, without knowing what it is about. For instance: "God's wind from nowhere which is called the will; and is man's only excuse upon this earth," was written by so trivial a fat man as Gilbert Keith Chesterton in "The Flying Inn."

61. There is an end to the word of the God enthroned in Ra's seat, lightening the girders of the soul.

NEW COMMENT

Note that Heru-Ra-Ha is not merely a particular form of Ra, but the God enthroned in Ra's seat. That is, his kingdom on earth is temporary, as explained in v.34. And he is here conceived as the Hierophant, "lightening the girders of the soul," that is, bringing man to initiation.

These "girders" imply the skeletal structure on which the soul is supported, the conditions of its incarnation. Man is the heir of ages of evolutionary experience, on certain lines, so that he is organized on formulae which have determined the type of his development. Of some such formulae we are conscious, but not of all. Thus it is true for all men—empirically—that a straight line is the shortest distance between two points; some savages may not know this consciously, but they base their actions on that knowledge.

Now we cannot doubt that consciousness has developed elsewhere than in man; only a blind megalomaniac or a Christian divine could suppose our infinitesimal mote of a planet the sole habitat of mind, especially as our minds are, at best, totally incompetent to comprehend nature. It is also unlikely that our earth's physical conditions of temperature, atmosphere, density etc., which some still regard as essential to life, are found frequently; we are only one of nine planets ourselves, and it is absurd to deny that life exists on the others, or in the sun himself, just because the conditions of our own life are absent elsewhere.

Such life and mind may therefore be utterly different to anything we know of; the "girders" of their souls in other spheres may be other than ours.

The above argument is a case of a "girder"; we are bound mentally by our race-experience of the environment in which our own lives flourish. A pioneer choosing a camp must look for wood, water, perhaps shelter, perhaps game. In another planet he might not need any of these.

The "girders" which determine the "form" of our souls are therefore limitations to our thought, as well as supports. In the same way, rails help a train to run easily, but confine it to a definite direction. The "laws" of nature and thought, mathematics, logic, and so on, are "girders" of this sort. Our race-inherited conceptions of a space prevented man, until quite recent years, from conceiving a non-Euclidean geometry, or the existence of a fourth dimension. The initiate soon becomes aware of the untruth of many of these limiting laws of his mind; he has to identify being with not-being, to perceive matter as continuous and homogeneous, and so for many another truth, apprehended directly by pure perception, and consequently not to be refuted by syllogistic methods. The laws of logic are thus discovered to be superficial, and their scope only partial.

It is significant in this connection that such advanced thinkers as the Hon. Bertrand Russell have found themselves obliged to refer mathematical laws to logic; it seems to have escaped them that the laws of logic are no more than the statement of the limitations of their own intelligence. I quote *The Book of Lies*:

CHINESE MUSIC

> *Explain this happening!*
> *It must have a 'natural' cause.*
> *It must have a 'supernatural' cause.*
> *Let these two asses be set to grind corn.*

May, might, must, should, probably, may be, we may safely assume, ought, it is hardly questionable, almost certainly—poor hacks! Let them be turned out to grass!

Proof is only possible in mathematics, and mathematics is only a matter of arbitrary conventions.

And yet doubt is a good servant but a bad master; a perfect mistress, but a nagging wife.

"White is white" is the lash of the overseer; "white is black" is the watchword of the slave. The Master takes no heed.

The Chinese cannot help thinking that the octave has 5 notes. The more necessary anything appears to my mind, the more certain it is that I only assert a limitation.

I slept with Faith, and found a corpse in my arms on awaking; I drank and danced all night with Doubt, and found her a virgin in the morning.

Now then consider the man whose soul has thoroughly explored its structure, is actively conscious of its "girders" of axiom. He must find that they confine him like prison bars, when he would gain the freedom of the initiate.

In this verse, therefore, doth the God "enthroned in Ra's seat" declare that his word lightens (or removes) the oppression of these "girders of the soul." The study of this chapter is accordingly a soul-preparatory course for whosoever will become Initiate.

See also the six verses following this; the word increases in value as the reader advances on the path, just as a Rembrandt is a "pretty picture" to the peasant, a "fine work of art" to the educated man, but to the lover of beauty a sublime masterpiece, the greater as he grows himself in greatness.

62. To Me do ye reverence! to me come ye through tribulation of ordeal, which is bliss.

NEW COMMENT

This seems to indicate the means to used in freeing the soul from its "girders."

We have seen that Ra-Hoor-Khuit is in one sense the Silent Self in a man, a name of his Khabs, not so impersonal as Hadit, but the first and least untrue formulation of the ego. We are to reverse this self in us, then, not to suppress it and subordinate it. Nor are we to evade it, but to come to it. This is done "through tribulation of ordeal." This tribulation is that experienced in the process called psychoanalysis, now that official science has adopted—so far as its inferior intelligence permits—the methods of the magus. But the "ordeal" is "bliss"; the solution of each complex by "tribulation"—note the etymological significance of the word!—is the spasm of joy which is the physiological and psychological accompaniment of any relief from strain and congestion.

63. The fool readeth this Book of the Law, and its comment; & he understandeth it not.

NEW COMMENT

The fool is also the great fool, Bacchus Diphues, Harpocrates, the Dwarf-Self, the Holy Guardian Angel, etc. "He understandeth it not"; i.e., he understandeth that it is NOT, LA, 31.

But the above is only the secondary or hieroglyphic magical meaning. The plain English still discusses the technique of initiation. The "fool," is one such as described in my note on v.57. The vain, soft, frivolous, idle, mutable sot will make nothing either of this Book, or of my comment thereon. But this fool is the child Harpocrates, the "Babe in the Egg," the innocent not yet born, in silence awaiting his hour to come forth into light. He is then the uninitiated man, and he has four ordeals to pass before he is made perfect. These ordeals are now to be described.

---

64. Let him come through the first ordeal, & it will be to him as silver.

65. Through the second, gold.

66. Through the third, stones of precious water.

67. Through the fourth, ultimate sparks of the intimate fire.

OLD COMMENT

64-67. This too shall be proven to him who will and can.

NEW COMMENT

64. The "Tree of Life" in the Qabalah represents ten spheres arranged in three pillars, the central one of these containing four, and the others three each. These spheres are attributed to certain numbers, planets, metals, and many other groups of things; indeed all things may be referred to one or another of them. (See *Book 4, Part III* and *Liber 777.*) The four ordeals now to be described, represent the ascent of the aspirant from the tenth and lowest of these spheres, which refers to the earth, unregenerate and confused, in which the aspirant is born. He riseth in the first ordeal to the sphere called the Foundation, numbered 9, and containing, among other ideas, those of the generative organs, air, the moon, and silver. Its secret truth is that stability is identical with change; of this we are reminded by the fact that any multiple of 9 has 9 for the sum of its digits.

The initiate will now perceive that the sum of the motions of his mind is zero, while, below their moon-like phases and their air-like divagations, the sex-consciousness abides untouched, the true foundation of the temple of his body, the root of the Tree of Life that grows from earth to heaven. This Book is now to him "as silver." He sees it pure, white and shining, the mirror of his own being that this ordeal has purged of its complexes. To reach this sphere he has to pass through a path of darkness where the four elements seem to him to be the universe entire. For how should he know that they are no more than the last of the 22 segments of the Snake that is twined on the Tree?

Assailed by gross phantoms of matter, unreal and unintelligible, his ordeal is of terror and darkness. He may pass only by favor of his own silent God, extended and exalted within him by virtue of his conscious act in affronting the ordeal.

65. The next sphere reached by the aspirant is named

Beauty, numbered 6, and referred to the heart, to the sun, and to gold. Here he is called an "Adept." The secret truth in this place is that God is man, symbolized by the hexagram (in which two triangles are interlaced).

In the last sphere he learned that his body was the temple of the Rosy Cross, that is, that it was given him as a place wherein to perform the magical work of uniting the oppositions in his nature. Here he is taught that his heart is the center of light. It is not dark, mysterious, hollow, obscure even to himself, but his soul is to dwell there, radiating light on the six spheres which surround it; these represent the various powers of his mind. This Book now appears to him as gold; it is the perfect metal, the symbol of the Sun itself. He sees God everywhere therein.

To this sphere hath the aspirant come by the path called Temperance, shot as an arrow from a rainbow. He hath beheld the light, but only in division. Nor had he won to this sphere except by temperance, under which name we mask the art of pouring freely forth the whole of our life, to the last spilth of our blood, yet losing never the least drop thereof.

66. Now once again the adept aspires and comes to the sphere called the Crown, numbered 1, referred to the God Ra-Hoor-Khuit himself in man, to the beginning of whirling motions, and the first mode of matter. (See *Liber 777, The Equinox,* and *Book 4* for these attributions.) Its secret truth is that earth is heaven as heaven is earth, and shows the aspirant to himself as being a star. All that seems to him reality is not even to be deemed illusion, but all one light infusing star and star. The many, each of them, are the One; each individual, no twain alike, yet all identical; this he knows and is, for now the word hath lightened his soul's girders. (The logic of the Ruach—the normal intellect—is transcended in spiritual experience. It is, evidently, impossible to "explain" how this can be.)

In the number 6 he saw God interlocked with man, two trinities made one; but here he knows that there was never but one.

Thus now this Book is "stones of precious water"; its light is not the borrowed light of gold, but is shed through the Book itself, clear sparkling, flashed from its facets. Each phrase is a diamond; each is diverse, yet all identical. In each the one light laughs!

Now to this sphere came he by the Path called the High Priestess; She is his Silent Self, virgin beyond all veils, made free to teach him, by virtue of this third ordeal wherein, passing through the abyss, he has stripped from him every rag of falsehood, his last complexes, even his fantasy that he called "I." And so he knows at last how the soiled harlot's dress was mere disguise; naked in moonlight shines the maiden body.

67. Beyond the One, how shall he pass on? What is this One, which is in every place the center of all? Indeed the logic-girders of our souls need lightening, if we would win to freedom of such truth as this!

Now in the "stones of precious water" the light leapt clear indeed, but they were not themselves that light. This sphere of the one is indeed Ra-Hoor-Khuit; is not our crowned and conquering child the source of light? Nay, he is finite form of unity, child of two married infinities; and in this last ordeal the aspirant must go beyond even his star, finding therein the core thereof Hadit, and losing it also in the Body of Nuit.

Here is no Path that he may tread, for all is equally everywhere; nor is there any Sphere to attain, for measure is now no more.

There are no words to make known the way or the end, there the end is one with the way; this only is said, that to him that hath passed through this fourth ordeal this Book is as "ultimate sparks." No more do they reflect or transmit the light; they themselves are the original, the not-to-be-analyzed light, of the "intimate fire" of Hadit! He shall see the Book as it is, as a shower of the seed of stars!

68. Yet to all it shall seem beautiful. Its enemies who say not so, are mere liars.

OLD COMMENT

A fact.

NEW COMMENT

To all; i.e., to Pan; or to *Al*.

The sudden degradation of the style and the subject, the petulance of the point of view; what should these things intend?

It sounds as though the scribe had protested violently in his mind against the chapter, and was especially aggrieved at the first paragraph of this verse, which, taken at its face value, promises a phenomenon impossible in literature. The second phrase may then be a contemptuous slap at the scribe who was perhaps thinking, "Well, it seems otherwise to me, for one!" and the hit was a bull's eye; for I was a mere liar when I thought it. I was so enraged at having engaged myself on such an adventure, so hated "the hand and the pen" which I pledged to transcribe sentiments so repugnant to mine, such a jargon of absurdities and vulgarities as seemed to me displayed in many parts of this third chapter, that I would have gone to almost any length, short of deliberate breach of my thoughtless promise to my wife to see it through, to discredit the Book.`I did deface my diaries with senseless additions; I did carry out my orders in such a way as to ensure failure, I did lose the manuscript more or less purposely. I did threaten to publish the Book "to get rid of it," and at this verse I was one of the "mere liars." For its beauty already constrained even the world-infected man, the nigh-disillusioned poet, the clinker-clogged lover, the recusant mystic. And, as I know now, the thought that all these things were myself was a lie. Yet the liar was at pains to lie to itself! Why did it so? It knew that one day this book would shine out and dissolve it; it feared and hated the Book; and, gnashing its teeth, swore falsely, and denied the beauty that bound it.

As for my true self, silent abiding its hour, is not this Book to it the very incarnation of beauty? What is beauty but the perfect expression of one's own truth? And is not this Book the word of Aiwaz, and is not He mine Holy Guardian Angel, the master of my Silent Self, his virgin bride on whom his love hath wrought the mystery of identity?

---

69. There is success.

OLD COMMENT

I take this as a promise that the Law shall duly be established.

NEW COMMENT

My memory tells me that the word "there" was not emphasized. Read, then, "There is" as the French *Il y a*; it is a simple and apparently detached statement. It was spoken casually, carelessly, as if a quite unimportant point had been forgotten, and now mentioned as a concession to my weakness.

70. *I am the Hawk-headed Lord of Silence & of Strength; my nemyss shrouds the night-blue sky.*

71. *Hail! ye twin warriors about the pillars of the world! for your time is nigh at hand.*

72. *I am the Lord of the Double Wand of Power; the Wand of the Force of Coph Nia—but my left hand is empty, for I have crushed an Universe; & nought remains.*

OLD COMMENT

70-72. A final pronouncement of his attributes. I do not know the exact meaning of v.71. (Later, 1911: Yes, I do.)

Coph Nia. I cannot trace this anywhere; but KOPhNIA adds to 231. Nia is Ain backwards; Coph suggests Quoth. All very unsatisfactory.

NEW COMMENT

70. It is important to observe that he claims to be both Horus and Harpocrates; and his two-in-one is a unity combining Tao and Teh, matter and motion, being and form. This is natural, for in Him must exist the root of the dyad.

"My nemyss" (better spelled "nemmes") is the regular headdress of a God. It is a close cap, but with wings behind the ears which end in lappets that fall in front of the shoulders. It is gathered at the nape of the neck into a cylindrical "pigtail." I think the shape is meant to suggest the royal Uraeus serpent.

It "shrouds the night-blue sky" because the actual light shed by the God when he is invoked is of this color. It may also mean that he conceals Nuit.

The Hawk's Head symbolized keen sight, swift action, courage and mobility.

71. This is a clear statement as to the war which was to come, and did come, in 1914 e.v.

I now (1923) no longer agree with the above paragraph. I think "the pillars of the world" mean "the Pillars of Hercules"—about the straits of Gibraltar. And I think the really big war will start there.

P.S. September 8, 1937, e.v.: Can "Twin warriors" imply a *civil* war? The Spanish troubles started in southern Spain and Morocco.

72. "The Double Wand of Power" is a curious variant of the common "Wand of Double Power"; the general meaning is "I control alike the forces of active and passive."

"Coph Nia": the original MS. has: "left incomplete as not having been properly heard." The present text was filled in later in her own hand by the first Scarlet Woman.

The Egyptian Gods are usually represented as bearing an Ankh, or sandal-strap, in the left hand, the wand being in the right. This ankh signifies the power to go, characteristic of a god.

But apparently Ra-Hoor-Khuit had a universe in his left hand, and crushed it so that naught remains. I think this "universe" is that of monistic metaphysics; in one hand is the "Double Wand," in the other "naught." This seems to refer to the "none-and-two" ontology outlined in previous notes.

73. *Paste the sheets from right to left and from top to bottom: then behold!*

OLD COMMENT
Done. See illustration [facing this page] . (See comment on Chapter III, 47.)

NEW COMMENT

This might have been done, of course, in several ways. I chose that which seemed most practical. So far I have noticed nothing remarkable.

---

74. *There is a splendour in my name hidden and glorious as the sun of midnight is ever the son.*

OLD COMMENT

Perhaps this refers to the addition of the name to 418. But Khephra is the *Sun* at midnight in the north. Now in the north is Taurus, the Bull: Apis, the Redeemer, the *Son.*

NEW COMMENT

I suspect some deeper and more startling arcanum than the old comment indicates; but I have not yet discovered it. (1920.)

---

75. *The ending of the words in the Word Abrahadabra.*
The Book of the Law is Written
and Concealed.
Aum. Ha.

OLD COMMENT

The ending of the words is the ending of the work—Abrahadabra. The Book is written, as we see; and concealed—from our weak understanding.

Aum-Ha, אעם = 111, הא = 6, 111 x 6 = 666, the seal of

the Beast. Note well that אע ם with a final ם adds to 671, Throa, the Gate, Adonai spelled in full, etc., etc. Using the Keys of Aum Ha, we get XIII + XV + 0, and IV + 0, their sum, 31 = אל, Not.

P.S.: If for IV we use XVII, the sum is 44, the special number of Horus.

NEW COMMENT

Aum is of course the Sanskrit "Word" familiar to most students. (See *Book 4, Part III.*) Ha is a way of spelling the letter Heh (ה) whose value is 5 so that it shall add to 6. This uniting the 5 and the 6 is a symbol of the Great Work.

Appendix

Appendix

Liber Trigrammaton

The Book of the Trigrams of the Mutations
of the Tao with The Yin and Yang

I

Here is Nothing under its three forms. It is not; yet informeth all things.

L. Now cometh the Single One as an imperfection and stain.

C. But by the weak one, the Mother, was it equilibrated.

H. Also the purity was divided by Strength, the force of the Demiurge.

X. And the Cross was formulated in the Universe that as yet was not.

—————

T. But now the imperfection became manifest; presiding over the fading of Perfection.

—————

Y. Also the Woman arose and veiled the upper Heaven with Her body of Stars.

—————

P. Now then, a giant arose of terrible strength and asserted the Spirit in a secret Rite.

—————

A. And the Master of the Temple balancing all things arose; His stature was above the Heavens and below Earth and Hell.

J. Against Him the Brothers of the Left-Hand Path confusing the symbols. They concealed their horror (in this symbol); for in truth, they were

$$\begin{array}{cc} - & - \\ \rule{1.2em}{0.08em} \\ \cdot \\ \cdot \\ - & - \\ - & - \end{array}$$

W. The Master flamed forth as a Star and set a Guard of Water in every Abyss.

$$\begin{array}{c} \rule{1.2em}{0.08em} \\ \cdot \\ \rule{1.2em}{0.08em} \end{array}$$

O. Also certain Secret Ones concealed the Light of purity in themselves, protecting it from the persecutions.

$$\begin{array}{cc} - & - \\ \cdot \\ \rule{1.2em}{0.08em} \end{array}$$

G. Likewise also did certain Sons & Daughters of Hermes and of Aphrodite more openly.

$$\begin{array}{cc} - & - \\ \cdot \\ \rule{1.2em}{0.08em} \end{array}$$

Z. But the Enemy confused them. They pretended to conceal that Light that they might betray it and profane it.

$$\begin{array}{cc} - & - \\ \cdot \\ - & - \end{array}$$

B. Yet certain holy nuns concealed the Secret in Songs upon the Lyre.

———
———
·

F. Now did the Horror of Time pervert all things, hiding the Purity with a loathsome thing, a thing unnameable.

———
— —
·

S. Yea, and there arose sensualists upon the firmament as a foul stain of storm upon the sky.

— —
———
·

M. And the Black Brothers raised their heads, yea, they unveiled themselves without shame or fear.

— —
— —
·

N. Also there rose up a Soul of filth and of weakness and it corrupted all the Rule of Tao.

———
———
———

E. Then only was Heaven established to bear sway; for only in the lowest corruption is form manifest.

```
      ———
      ———
      —  —
```

R. Also did Heaven manifest in violent Light.

```
      ———
      —  —
      ———
```

Q. And in soft Light.

```
      —  —
      ———
      ———
```

V. Then were the Waters gathered together from the Heaven,

```
      ———
      —  —
      —  —
```

K. And a crust of earth concealed the core of flame.

```
      —  —
      ———
      —  —
```

D. Around the Globe gathered the wide air,

```
      —  —
      —  —
      ———
```

U. And men began to light fires upon the earth.

```
      —  —
      —  —
      —  —
```

Therefore was the end of it Sorrow; yet in that Sorrow a Sixfold Star of glory, wherby they might see to return into the Stainless Abode; yea, unto the Stainless Abode.

Gematrias

A few indications for the Student of the line to be adopted in his elucidation of Liber AL.

Nu = נו = 56.

Had = האד = 11. (Spelled in full, 555. 5 = Mars = ♂ = Energy.)

Aiwass = איואס = 78. (666's error. This was the early spelling of the name, later changed to:

עיוז = 93.

AI⟡ACC = 418.

Pi to the 6th place. אל הים. ☉ = 3.141593.

☉☾(6) = XX and XI (Roman numerals represent Tarot keys) = 31.

XX + XI = שט = 309.

H KOKKINE ΓΥΝΗ = 667. (initials) HKΓ = 31.

Coph Nia. כף = 100. + אין (Ain) = 61. = 161.

(Kaph) in full: Sun (*Phallus*) and Moon (*Kteis*) in Greek. See 1.46-47.

Ta-Nich. TANICh. = 78. (Alternatively, Sh for Ch gives 370 = עש Creation.)

Not = לא = 31. God = אל = 31.

ΘΕλΗΜΑ = 93. (In full, 2542.)   ⎫
λΟΓΟC ΠΤΘΙΟC ΤΟΤ ΝΟΜΟΤ   ⎬   See I, v. 39.
                                                                        ⎭

Bes-na-maut = BISh-NA-MAVT = 888. (Cheth x Aleph).

Ta-Nich. ThA-NICh.

ΑΓΑΠΗ = 93. M . . . . . M = 93. III° . . . . . = 93.

TZABA = צבא = 93. Will (also a Star, or Host).

Mentu = MVNTV = מונטו = 111.

RPST = 311.

Khabs. חאבש = 311. BHTA.

Boleskine בולשכין = 418.

ABRAHADABRA אבראהאדאברא = 418.

Cheth = 8. (Spelled in full) חית = 418.

Abrahadabra = RA HVVR (Ra Hoor) = 418.

Pallas Athena = ΠΑλλΑC ΑΘΗΝΗ = 418.

TO MH = 418.

PARZIVAL = 418.

HRU-RA-HA = 211 plus 201 plus 6 = 418.

HERU   הרו = 211   ⎫
RA   רא = 201   ⎬   = 418
HA   הא = 6   ⎭

HOOR   הוור = 217   ⎫   ⎫
RA   רא = 201   ⎬   = 418   ⎬
KHU   כו = 26   ⎭   ⎬   = 444
NOMOC   = 430   ⎭
MOT = 510.   ΦΙ = ריש

THERION   חריון = 666
TO ΜΕΓΑ ΟΗΡΙΟΝ   = 666
KAMURET   = 666

The Number of the Stele = 666.

CTHλH = 52. 52 plus 666 = 718.

666 = The number of the BEAST, the number of the Man
        (See Apocalypse).

The Beast (usually spelled ChIVA) AChIHA (spelled in full) = 666.

A = 111. Ch = 418. ' (Yod spelled in full) = 20. H = 6, A = 111 = 666.

O (In the Book of Thoth, the Tarot) = A (Aleph).

A = 111. O = 6.

ANKH-F-N-KHONSU = T = 666.

NUTERU = NVThIRV = נתירו = 666.

ΛΟΓΟ͜ ΠΤΟΙΟϹ = Word = 1142.

ΛΓΕ ΤΟ ΘΕΛΗΜΑ ϹΟϒ = 1142.

The following elucidation of ABRAHADABRA is extrapolated from *The Temple of King Solomon* in *Equinox I, V*.

418. CHITh, Cheth. ABRAHADABRA, the great Magic Word, the Word of the Aeon. Note the 11 letters, 5 A identical, and 6 diverse. Thus it interlocks Pentagram and Hexagram. BITh HA, the House of Hé the Pentagram; see Idra Zuta Qadisha, 694. "For H formeth K, but Ch formeth IVD." Both equal 20.

Note 4+1+8 = 13, the 4 reduced to 1 through 8, the redeeming force; and 418 = Ch = 8.

By Aiq Bkr ABRAHADABRA = 1+2+2+1+5+1+4+ 1+2+2+1 = 22. Also 418 = 22 x 19 = Manifestation. Hence the word manifests the 22 Keys of Rota.

It means by translation Abraha Deber, the Voice of the Chief Seer.

It resolves into Pentagram and Hexagram as follows:

 [This is by taking the 5 middle letters.]

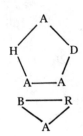

The Pentagram is 12, HVA, Macroprosopus.

The hexagram is 406, AThH, Microprosopus.

Thus it connotes the Great Work.

Note ABR, initials of the Supernals, Ab, Ben, Ruach.

(2)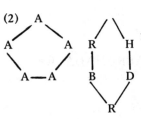

[This is by separating the One (Aleph) from the Many (diverse letters).]

BRH = 207, Aur, Light
DBR = 206, Deber, Voice
} "The Vision and the Voice," a phrase which meant much to me at the moment of discovering this Word.

(3)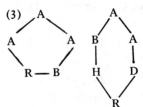

[By taking each alternate letter.]

205 = GBR, mighty.
213 = ABIR, mighty.
} This shows Abrahadabra as the Word of Double Power, another phrase that meant much to me at the time. AAB at the top of the Hexagram gives AB, AIMA, BN, Father, Mother, Child.

HDR by Yetzirah gives Horus, Isis, Osiris, again Father, Mother, Child. This Hexagram is again the human Triad.

Dividing into 3 and 8 we get the Triangle of Horus dominating the Stooping Dragon of 8 Heads, the Supernals bursting the Head of Daath. Also

The Supernals are supported upon two squares—

ABAD = DD, Love, 8.

AHRA = AVR, Light, 207.

Now $8 \times 207 = 656 = 18 = $ ChI, Living, and $207 = 9 \times 23$, ChIH, Life. At this time "Licht, Liebe, Leben" was the mystic name of the Mother-Temple of the G∴D∴

The five letters used in the word are A, the Crown; B, the Wand; D, the Cup; H, the Sword; R, the Rosy Cross; and refer further to Amoun the Father, Thoth His messenger, and Isis, Horus, Osiris, the divine-human triad.

Also $418 = $ ATh IAV, the Essence of IAO, q.v.

This short analysis might be indefinitely expanded; but always the symbol will remain the expression of the goal and the exposition of the path.

HEBREW SCRIPT AND KEYBOARD HEBREW

There may be difficulty in correlating the keyboard Hebrew used in this book, a modern face with uniform elements, and traditional Hebrew script. This table gives the script character, its name, and the keyboard and numerical equivalents:

1	א	Ahlef	א
2	בּ	Beth	בּ
2	ב	Veth	ב
3	ג	Gimel	ג
4	ד	Dahleth	ד
5	ה	Hay	ה
6	ו	Vahv	ו
7	ז	Zahyin	ז
8	ח	CHeth	ח
9	ט	Teth	ט
10	י	Yohd	י
20	כּ	Kahf	כּ
20	כ	CHahf	כ
20	ך	final CHahf	ך
30	ל	Lahmed	ל
40	מ	Mem	מ
40	ם	final Mem	ם
50	נ	Nun	נ
50	ן	final Nun	ן
60	ס	Sahmech	ס
70	ע	Ahyin	ע
80	פּ	Pay	פּ
80	פ	Fay	פ
80	ף	final Fay	ף
90	צ	Tsahdee	צ
90	ץ	final Tsahdee	ץ
100	ק	Koph	ק
200	ר	Raysh	ר
300	שׁ	Sheen	שׁ
300	שׂ	Seen	שׂ
400	ת	Tau	ת

THE BOOK OF THE LAW
PART ONE

1

! The manifestation of Nuit
The unveiling of the company of heaven
Every man and every woman is a star
Every number is infinite; there is no difference
Help me, o warrior lord of Thebes, in my
unveiling before the Children of men
Be thou Hadit, my secret centre, my
heart & my tongue.
Behold! it is revealed by Aiwass the
minister of Hoor-paar-kraat
The Khabs is in the Khu, not the Khu in
the Khabs
Worship then the Khabs, and behold my
light shed over you.

2

Let my servants be few & secret: they shall
rule the many & the known.
There are fools that men adore; both their
Gods & their men are fools.
Come forth, o children, under the stars
& take your fill of love. I am above you
and in you. My ecstasy is in yours. My
joy is to see your joy

r. l. of spell will be by ...
Now, ye shall know that the chosen
priest & apostle of infinite space is
the prince-priest the Beast; and in

his woman, called the Scarlet Woman, is
all power given. They shall gather my
children into their fold: they shall bring the
glory of the stars into the hearts of men.
For he is ever a sun, and she a moon. But
to him is the winged secret flame, and to
her the stooping starlight.
But ye are not so chosen
[illegible lines]

4

With the God & the Adorer I am nothing: they
do not see me. They are as upon the [illegible]
I am Heaven, and there is no other God
than me, and my lord Hadit.
Now therefore I am known to ye by my
name Nuit, and to him by a secret name
which I will give him when at last he
knoweth me
Since I am Infinite Space, and the Infinite
Stars thereof, do ye also thus. Bind
nothing! Let there be no difference made
among you between any one thing [illegible]

[illegible] for surely there cometh hurt.
But whoso availeth in this let him be
chief of all!
[illegible] Nuit and my word to six and fifty
divide, add, multiply and understand.
[illegible] saith the prophet and slave of the
beauteous one. Who am I, and what shall
be the sign. So she answered him, bending
down, a lambent flame of blue, all touching,
all penetrant, her lovely hands upon the
black earth & her lithe body arched for love
and her soft feet not hurting the

[illegible section 6]

all the flowers. Thou knowest! And the [illegible]
shall be my ecstasy, the conscious [illegible]
the continuity of existence, the [illegible]
omnipresence of my body.
[illegible] [illegible]
O Nuit, continuous one of Heaven, let

be ever thus. That men speak not of Thee as One but as None; and let them speak not of thee at all, since thou art continuous.

None, breathed the light, faint & faery, of the stars, and two. For I am divided for love's sake, for the chance of union.

This is the creation of the world that the pain of division is as nothing, and the joy of dissolution all.

For these fools of men and their

woes care not thou at all! They feel little; what is, is balanced by weak joys; but ye are my chosen ones.

Obey my prophet! follow out the ordeals of my knowledge! seek me only! Then the joys of my love will redeem ye from all pain. This is so: I swear it by the vault of my body; by my sacred heart and tongue; by all I can give, by all I desire of ye all.

Then the priest fell into a deep trance or

swoon & said unto the Queen of Heaven Write unto us the ordeals; write unto us the rituals; write unto us the law!

But she said: the ordeals I write not: the rituals shall be half known and half concealed: the Law is for all.

This that thou writest is the threefold book of Law.

My scribe Ankh-af-na-khonsu, the priest of the princes, shall not in one letter change this book; but lest there be folly, he shall comment thereby by the wisdom of Ra-Hoor-Khu-it.

Also the mantras and spells; the obeah and the wanga; the work of the wand and the work of the sword; these he shall learn and teach.

He must teach; but he may make severe the ordeals.

The word of the Law is θελημα.

Who calls us Thelemites will do no wrong, if he look but close into the word. For there are therein Three Grades, the Hermit and the Lover and the man of Earth. Do what thou wilt

11

shall be the whole of the Law.
The word of Sin is Restriction. O man!
refuse not thy wife if she will. O
lover, if thou wilt, depart. There is
no bond that can unite the divided but
love: all else is a curse. Accursed!
Accursed! be it to the aeons. Hell.
Let it be that state of manyhood
bound and loathing. So with thy all
thou hast no right but to do thy will.
Do that, and no other shall say nay.
For pure will, unassuaged of purpose,

12

delivered from the lust of result, is
every way perfect
The Perfect and the Perfect are one
Perfect and not two; nay, are none.
Nothing is a secret key of this law.
Sixty-one the Jews call it; I call it
eight, eighty, four hundred & eighteen.
But they have half: unite by thine
art so that all disappear.
My prophet is a fool with his one one
one; are not they the Ox and none
by the Book.

13

Abrogate are all rituals, all ordeals, all
words and signs. Ra-Hoor-Khuit hath
taken his seat in the East at the Equinox
of the Gods; and let Asar be with Isa,
who also are one. But they are not of
me. Let them be the servant, Isa the
suffering; Hoor in his secret name and
splendour is the Lord initiating.
There is a word to say about the Hierophantic
task. Behold! there are three ordeals in
one, and it may be given in three ways.
The gross must pass through fire; let the

14

fine be tried in intellect, and the
lofty chosen ones in the highest. Thus
ye have star & star, system & system;
let not one know well the other.
There are four gates to one palace;
the floor of that palace is of silver and
gold; lapis lazuli & jasper are there,
all rare scents; jasmine & rose, and the
emblems of death. Let him enter in turn
or at once the four gates; let him stand
on the floor of the palace. Will he
not sink? Amn. Ho! warrior, if thy
servant sink? But there are means

and wines Be goodly therefore: dress ye all in fine apparel; eat rich foods and drink sweet wines and wines that foam! Also, take your fill and will of love as ye will, when, where and whom ye will. But always unto me.

If this be not aright; if ye confound the space-marks, saying: They are one; or saying, They are many; if the ritual be not ever unto me: then expect the direful judgments of Ra Hoor Khuit!

This shall regenerate the world, the little

world my sister, my heart & my tongue, unto whom I send this kiss. Also, o scribe and prophet, though thou be of the princes, it shall not assuage thee nor absolve thee. But ecstasy be thine and joy of earth: ever To me! To me!

Change not as much as the style of a letter; for behold! thou, o prophet, shalt not behold all these mysteries hidden therein.

The child of thy bowels, he shall behold them.

Expect him not from the East, nor from

the West, for from no expected house cometh that child. Aum! All words are sacred and all prophets true; save only that they understand a little; solve the first half of the equation, leave the second unattacked. But thou hast all in the clear light, and some, though not all, in the dark.

I woke me under my stars. Love is the law, love under will. Nor let the fools mistake love; for there are love and love. There is the dove, and there is the serpent. Choose ye well! He, my prophet, hath

chosen, knowing the law of the fortress, and the great mystery of the House of God.

All these old letters of my Book are aright; but צ is not the Star. This also is secret: my prophet shall reveal it to the wise.

I give unimaginable joys on earth: certainty, not faith, while in life, upon death; peace unutterable, rest, ecstasy; nor do I demand aught in sacrifice.

My incense is of resinous woods & gums; and there is no blood therein: because of my hair the trees of Eternity.

19

My number is 11, as all their numbers
who are of us. (true) My colour is black to the
blind, but the blue & gold are seen of the
seeing. Also I have a secret glory, for
them that love me.

The five pointed star, with a
circle in the Middle, & the circle is Red

But to love me is better than all things: if
under the night-stars in the desert thou
presently burnest mine incense before me,
invoking me with a pure heart, and the
Serpent flame therein, then shalt come
a little to lie in my bosom. For one kiss
wilt thou then be willing to give all.

21

and humbleness of the innermost sense
devise you. But ye are the wings and ye are
the coiled splendour within you: come unto me!
At all my meetings with you shall the
priestess say - and her eyes shall burn
with desire as she stands bare and rejoicing
in my secret temple - To me! To me!
calling forth the flame of the hearts of all in her
love-chant.

Sing the rapturous love-song unto me!
Burn to me perfumes! Wear to me jewels!
Drink to me, for I love you! I love you!

20

But whoso avails in this shall lose all in that hour. Ye
shall gather goods and store of women and
spices; ye shall wear rich jewels; ye
shall exceed the nations of the earth
in splendour & pride; but always in the
love of me, and so shall ye come to
my joy. I charge you earnestly to come
before me in a single robe, and covered
with a rich headdress. I love you! I yearn to
you. Pale or purple, veiled or voluptuous,
who am old pleasure and purple

22

I am the blue-lidded daughter of Sunset;
I am the naked brilliance of the voluptuous night-
sky.

To me! To me!

The Manifestation of Nuit is at an
end.

THE BOOK OF THE LAW
PART TWO

...! the hiding of Hadit.

Come! all ye, and learn the secret that hath not yet been revealed. I, Hadit am the complement of Nu my bride. I am not extended, and Khabs is the name of my House.

In the Sphere I am everywhere the centre, as She, the circumference, is nowhere found.

Yet she shall be known & I never.

Behold! the rituals of the old time are black. Let the evil ones be cast away; let the good ones be purged by the prophet! Then shall this Knowledge go aright.

I am the flame that burns in every heart of man, and in the core of every star. I am

Life, and the giver of Life; yet therefore is the knowledge of me the knowledge of death.

7. I am the Magician and the Exorcist. I am the axle of the wheel, and the cube in the circle. 'Come unto me' is a foolish word; for it is I that go.

8 Who worshipped Heru-pa-kraath have worshipped me; ill, for I am the worshipper.

9 Remember all ye that existence is pure joy; that all the sorrows are but as shadows; they pass & are done; but there is that which remains.

10. O prophet! thou hast ill will to learn this writing.

11. I see thee hate the hand & the pen; but I am

357

12 Because of me in Thee which thou knewest not.

13. for why? Because thou wast the knower, and me.

14. Now let there be a veiling of this shrine: now let the light devour men and eat them up with blindness.

15. For I am perfect, being Not; and my number is nine by the fools; but with the just I am eight, and one in eight: Which is vital, for I am none indeed. The Empress and the King are not of me; for there is a further secret.

16. I am the Empress & the Hierophant. Thus eleven, as my bride is eleven.

17. Hear me, ye people of sighing!
The sorrows of pain and regret
Are left to the dead and the dying,
The folk that not know me as yet.

18. These are dead, these fellows; they feel not. We are not for the poor and sad: the lords of the earth are our kinsfolk.

19. Is a God to live in a dog? No! but the highest are of us. They shall rejoice, our chosen: who sorroweth is not of us.

20. Beauty and strength, leaping laughter and delicious languor, force and fire, are of us.

21 We have nothing with the outcast and the unfit: let them die in their misery. For they feel not. Compassion is the vice of kings: stamp down the wretched & the weak: this is the law of the strong: this is our law and the joy of the world. Think not, o king, upon that lie: That Thou Must Die: verily thou shalt not die, but live! Now let it be understood: If the body of the King dissolve, he shall remain in pure ecstasy for ever. Nuit! Hadit! Ra-Hoor-Khuit! The Sun, Strength & Sight, Light; these are for the servants of the Star & the Snake

22 I am the Snake that giveth Knowledge & Delight and bright glory, and stir the hearts of men with drunkenness. To worship me take wine and strange drugs whereof I will tell my prophet, & be drunk thereof! They shall not harm ye at all. It is a lie, this folly against self. The exposure of innocence is a lie. Be strong, o man, lust, enjoy all things of sense and rapture: fear not that any God shall deny thee for this.

23. I am alone: there is no God where I am.

24. Behold! these be grave mysteries; for there are also of my friends who be hermits.

shall not be found in the temple or on the mountain; but in beds of purple, caressed by magnificent beasts of women with large limbs, and fire and light in their eyes, and masses of flaming hair about them; there shall ye find them. Ye shall see them at rule, at victorious armies, at all the joy; and there shall be in them a joy a million times greater than this. Beware lest any force another, King against King! Love one another with burning hearts; on the low men trample in the fierce lust of your pride,

in the day of your wrath.

25. Ye are against the people, O my chosen!

26. I am the secret Serpent coiled about to spring: in my coiling there is joy. If I lift up my head, I and my Nuit are one. If I droop down mine head, and shoot forth venom, then is rapture of the earth, and I and the earth are one.

27. There is great danger in me; for who doth not understand these runes shall make a great miss. He shall fall down into the pit called Because, and there he shall

perish with the dogs of Reason.

Now a curse upon Because and his kin!

May Because be accursed for ever!

If Will stops and cries Why, invoking Because, then Will stops & does nought.

If Power asks why, then is Power weakness.

Also reason is a lie; for there is a factor infinite & unknown; & all their words are skew-wise.

Enough of Because! Be he damned for a dog!

But ye, o my people, rise up & awake!

Let the rituals be rightly performed with joy & beauty!

36. There are rituals of the elements and feasts of the times.

37. A feast for the first night of the Prophet and his Bride!

38. A feast for the three days of the writing of the Book of the Law.

39. A feast for Tahuti and the child of the Prophet — secret, O Prophet!

40. A feast for the Supreme Ritual, and a feast for the Equinox of the Gods.

41. A feast for fire and a feast for water; a feast for life and a greater feast for death!

42 A feast every day in your hearts in the joy of my rapture.

43 A feast every night unto Nu, and the pleasure of uttermost delight.

44 Aye! feast! rejoice! there is no dread hereafter. There is the dissolution, and eternal ecstasy in the kisses of Nu.

45 There is death for the dogs.

46 Dost thou fail? Art thou sorry? Is fear in thine heart?

47 Where I am these are not.

48 Pity not the fallen! I never knew them. I am not for them. I console not: I hate the consoled & the consoler.

49 I am unique & conqueror. I am not of the slaves that perish. Be they damned & dead! Amen. (This is of the 4: there is a fifth who is invisible, & therein am I as a babe in an egg.)

50 Blue am I and gold in the light of my bride: but the red gleam is in my eyes; & my spangles are purple & green.

51. Purple beyond purple: it is the light

than eyesight.

52 There is a veil: that veil is black. It is the veil of the modest woman; it is the veil of sorrow, & the pall of death: this is none of me. Tear down that lying spectre of the centuries: veil not your vices in virtuous words: these vices are my service; ye do well, & I will reward you here and hereafter.

53 Fear not, o prophet, when these words are said, thou shalt not be sorry. Thou art emphatically my chosen; and blessed are

the eyes that thou shalt look upon with gladness. But I will hide thee in a mask of sorrow: they that see thee shall fear thou art fallen: but I lift thee up.

54 Nor shall they who cry aloud their folly that thou meanest nought avail; thou shalt reveal it: thou availest: they are the slaves of because: They are not of me. The stops as thou wilt; the letters? change them not in style or value!

55 Thou shalt obtain the order & value of the English Alphabet, thou shalt find

an symbols to attribute them unto.

Begone! ye mockers; even though ye laugh
in my honour ye shall laugh not long: then
when ye are sad know that I have
forsaken you.

He that is righteous shall be righteous still;
he that is filthy shall be filthy still.

... deem not of change: ye shall be as ye
are, & not other. Therefore the kings of
the earth shall be Kings for ever: the slaves
shall serve. There is none that shall
be cast down or lifted up: all is ever

as it was. Yet there are masked ones my
servants: it may be that yonder beggar is
a King. A King may choose his garment as
he will: there is no certain test: but a
beggar cannot hide his poverty.

59 Beware therefore! Love all, lest perchance is a
King concealed! Say you so? Fool! If he
be a King, thou canst not hurt him.

60 Therefore strike hard & low, and to hell
with them, master!

61 There is a light before thine eyes, o prophet,
a light undesired, most desirable.

... uplifted in thine heart and the noses
of the stars rain hard upon thy body.

... art exhaust in the voluptuous fullness
of the inspiration; the expiration is sweeter
than death, more rapid and laughterful than
a caress of Hell's own worm.

56! Thou art overcome: we are upon thee;
our delight is all over thee: hail! hail!
prophet of Nu! prophet of Had! prophet of
Ra-Hoor-Khu! Now rejoice! now come in
our splendour & rapture! Come in our peaceful
peace, & write sweet words for the Kings!

65 I am the Master: thou art the Holy Chosen One.

66 Write, & find ecstasy in writing! Work, &
be our bed in working! Thrill with the
joy of life & death! Ah! thy death shall
be lovely: whoso seeth it shall be glad. Thy
death shall be the seal of the promise of
our agelong love. Come! lift up thine heart
& rejoice! We are one; we are none.

67 Hold! Hold! Bear up in thy rapture;
fall not in swoon of the excellent kisses!

68 Harder! Hold up thyself! Lift thine head!

breathe not so deep — die!

69 Ah! Ah! What do I feel? Is the word exhausted?

70 There is help & hope in other spells. Wisdom says: be strong! Then canst thou bear more joy. Be not animal; refine thy rapture! If thou drink, drink by the eight and ninety rules of art: if thou love, exceed by delicacy; and if thou do aught joyous, let there be subtlety therein!

71 But exceed! exceed!

72 Strive ever to more! and if thou art truly

mine — and doubt it not, an if thou art ever joyous! — death is the crown of all.

73 Ah! Ah! Death! Death! thou shalt long for death. Death is forbidden, o man, unto thee.

74 The length of thy longing shall be the strength of its glory. He that lives long & desires death much is ever the King among the many.

75 Aye! listen to the numbers & the words:

76 4 6 3 8 A B K 2 4 A L G M O R 3 X 24 89 R P S T O V A L. What meaneth this, o prophet? Thou knowest not; nor shalt thou know ever. There cometh one to follow thee: he shall

expound it. But remember, o chosen one, to be me; to follow the love of Nu in the star-lit heaven; to look forth upon men, to tell them this glad word.

77 O be thou proud and mighty among men!

78 Lift up thyself! for there is none like unto thee among men or among Gods! Lift up thyself, o my prophet, thy stature shall surpass the stars. They shall worship thy name, foursquare, mystic, wonderful, the number of the man; and the number of thy house 418.

79 The end of the hiding of Hadit; and blessing & worship to the prophet of the lovely Star.

THE BOOK OF THE LAW
PART THREE

1

...ahadshu! The reward of Ra Hoor Khuit.

...e is division hither homeward; there is a

...d not known. Spelling is defunct; all is not

...t Beware! Hold! Raise the spell of

... Hoor-Khuit.

... let it be first understood that I am

...d of War and of Vengeance. I shall

... hardly with them.

...ve ye an island!

...tify it!

...g it about with engines of war!

...ll give you a war-engine.

...it ye shall smite the peoples and

2

... ...ie stand before you.

9 Lurk! Withdraw! Upon them! this

is The Law of the Battle of Conquest: thus

shall my worship be about ...un secret house

10 Get the stélé of revealing itself; set it

in thy secret temple — and that temple

is already aright disposed — & it shall be your

Kiblah for ever. it shall not fade, but

miraculous colour shall come back to it

day after day. close it in locked glass for a

proof to the world.

11 This shall be your only proof. I forbid argument.

Conquer! That is enough. I will make ease

to in the abstraction from the ill-ordered
house in the Victorious City. Thou shalt
thyself convey it with worship, o prophet,
though thou likest it not. Thou shalt have
danger & trouble. Ra-Hoor-Khu is with
thee. Worship me with fire & blood; worship
me with swords & with spears. Let the woman
be girt with a sword before me: let blood
flow to my name. Trample down the Heathen; be
upon them, o warrior, I will give you of their
flesh to eat!

12 Sacrifice cattle, little and big: after a child.

13 But not now.

14 Ye shall see that hour, o blessed Beast, &
thou the Scarlet Concubine of his desire!

15 Ye shall be sad thereof.

16 Deem not too eagerly to catch the promises; fear
not to undergo the curses. Ye, even ye, know
not this meaning all.

17 I am not at all; fear neither men, nor Fates,
nor gods, nor anything. Money fear not, nor
laughter of the folk folly, nor any other power
in heaven or upon the earth or under the
earth. Nu is your refuge as Hadit your

light; and I am the strength, force, & fire of
your arms.

18 Mercy let be off: damn them who pity.
Kill and torture; spare not; be upon them.

19 That stele they shall call the Abomination
of Desolation; count well its name, & it shall
be to you as 718.

20 Why? Because of the fall of Because, that
he is not there again.

21 Set up my image in the East: thou shalt buy
thee an image which I will show thee, especial,
not unlike the one thou knowest. And it shall
be suddenly easy for thee to do this.

22 The other images group around me to support
me: let all be worshipped, for they shall
cluster to exalt me. I am the visible object
of worship; the others are secret; for the Beast
& his Bride are they: and for the winners of
the Ordeal x. What is this? Thou shalt

23 For perfume mix meal & honey & thick leavings
of red wine: then oil of Abramelin and
olive oil, and afterward soften & smooth
down with rich fresh blood!

24 The best blood is of the moon, monthly: then
the fresh blood of a child, or dropping from

7

...host of heaven: then of enemies; then
...the priest of the worshippers: last of
...me beast, no matter what.

...this bum: if this make cakes & eat with
...me. This hath also another use; let it be
...laid before me, and kept thick with perfumes
...of your orison: it shall become full of beetles
...it were and creeping things sacred unto me.
...these slay, naming your enemies & they shall
...fall before you.

...Also these shall breed lust & powers of lust in
...at the eating thereof.

...Also ye shall be strong in war.

8

29 Moreover be they long kept, it is better; for
they swell with my force. All before me.

30 My altar is of open brass work: burn thereon
in silver or gold.

31 There cometh a rich man from the West who
shall pour his gold upon thee.

32 From gold forge steel:

33 Be ready to fly or to smite.

34 But your holy place shall be untouched
throughout the centuries: though with fire and
sword it be burnt down & shattered, yet
an invisible house there standeth and
shall stand until the fall of the Great —

9

...once, when Hrumachis shall arise and
...double-wanded one assume my throne and
...Another prophet shall arise, and bring
...fresh fever from the skies; another woman shall
...wake the lust & worship of the Snake; another
...soul of God and beast shall mingle in the
...orbed priest; another sacrifice shall stain
...the tomb; another king shall reign; and blessing
...longer be poured To the hawk-headed
...mystical Lord!

...the half of the word of Heru-ra-ha, called
...Hoor-pa-kraat and Ra-Hoor-Khut.

10

36 Then said the prophet unto the God.

37 I adore thee in the song
"I am the Lord of Thebes &c... from Vellum book
——— fill me

38 So that thy light is in me & its red flame
is as a sword in my hand to push thy
order. There is a secret door that I shall
make to establish thy way in all the quarters
(these are the adorations, as thou hast written)
as it is said.

The light is mine & its
I am ... Look to ... Ra-Hoor-Khut

365

39 All this and a note to ... how then
didst come hither and a reproduction of
this ink and paper, & even - for in it ...
the word secret is not only in The English
and they comment upon this. The Book of Reform —
shall be printed beautifully in red ink and
black upon beautiful paper made by hand;
and to each man and woman that thou
meetest, were it but to die or to think
at them, it is the Law to give. Then they
shall chance to abide in this bliss or no;
it is no odds. Do this quickly!

40 But the work of the comment? That is easy; and

41 ... ... My heart doeth make ...
... ...

41 ... ... a clerk
... must be done well and with ...
...

42 The ordeals thou shalt oversee thyself; and
the ... ... Refuse not, but Prove.
shalt know & destroy the traitors. ...
Re-... ... and I am powerful to ...
my servant. Success is thy proof; arg ...
convert not; talk not overmuch. The ...
seek to entrap thee, to overthrow thee
...... without pity or quarter; & destroy ...
...... Swift as a trodden serpent, ...

and strike! Be thou yet deadlier than he!

42 Drag down their souls to awful torment; laugh
at their fear; spit upon them!

43 Let the Scarlet Woman beware! If pity and
compassion and tenderness visit her heart;
if she leave my work to toy with old
sweet-nesses; then shall my vengeance be
known. I will slay me her child; I will
alienate her heart; I will cast her out
from men; as a shrinking and despised whore
shall she crawl through dusk wet streets and
die cold and an-hungered.

44 But let her raise herself in pride!
Let her follow me in my way! Let her
work the work of wickedness! Let her
kill her heart! Let her be loud and adulterous! Let her be covered with jewels and rich
garments, and let her be shameless before
all men!

45 Then will I lift her to pinnacles of ...
Then will I breed from her a child mightier than all the kings of the earth. I will fill
her with joy; with my force shall she
see & strike at the worship of Nu; she shall
achieve Hadit.

...the warrior Lord of the Forties: the
Eighties cower before me, & are abased.
I will bring you to victory & joy: I will be
at your arms in battle & ye shall
delight to slay. Success is your proof;
courage is your armour; go on, go on, in
my strength; & ye shall turn not back for
any.
This book shall be translated into all
tongues: but always with the original in
the writing of the Beast; for in the

chance shape of the letters and their
position to one another: in these are mysteries
that no Beast shall divine. Let him
not seek to try: but one cometh after
him, whence I say not, who shall
discover the Key of it all. Then this
line drawn is a key: then this
circle squared ⊕ in its failure is a
key also. And Abrahadabra. It shall
be his child & that strangely. Let him not
seek after this; for thereby alone can he
fall from it.

...this mystery of the letters is done, and
thou must go on to the holy place.
— is a secret fourfold word, the blasphemy against
all gods of men.
Curse them! Curse them! Curse them!
With my Hawk's head I peck at the eyes of
Jesus as he hangs upon the cross.
I flap my wings in the face of Mohammed &
blind him.
With my claws I tear out the flesh of the
Indian and the Buddhist, Mongol and
Din.
Bahlasti! Ompehda! I spit on your

crapulous creeds.
55. Let Mary inviolate be torn upon wheels:
for her sake let all chaste women be
utterly despised among you.
56. Also for beauty's sake and love!
57. Despise also all cowards; professional soldiers
who dare not fight, but play; all fools despise!
58. But the keen and the proud, the royal and
the lofty; ye are brothers!
59. As brothers fight ye!
60. There is no law beyond Do what thou wilt.
61. There is an end of the word of the God

enthroned in Ra's seat, lightening the girders
of the soul.

62 To Me do ye reverence; to me come ye
through tribulation of ordeal, which is
bliss.

63 The fool readeth this Book of the Law, and
its comment & he understandeth it not.

64 Let him come through the first ordeal &
it will be to him as silver.

65 Through the second gold

66 Through the third, stones of precious water.

67 Through the fourth, ultimate sparks of the
intimate fire.

68 Yet to all it shall seem beautiful. Its
enemies who say not so, are liars

69 There is success

70 I am the Hawk-Headed Lord of Silence
& of Strength; my nemyss shrouds the
night-blue sky.

71 'Hail!' ye twin warriors about the pillars of
the world! for your time is nigh at hand.

72 I am the Lord of the Double Wand of Power,
the wand of the Force of Coph Nia — but
my left hand is empty, for I have crushed

an Universe & nought remains.

73 Paste the sheets from right to left and
from top to bottom: then behold!

74 There is a splendour in my name hidden
and glorious, as the sun of midnight is
ever the son.

The ending of the words is the Word
Abrahadabra.

The Book of the Law is Written
and Concealed.
Aum. Ha.